D0211209

Jun 2018

A story and song like "Don't Stop Believin'" by Jonathan Cain is a glimpse into the life and motivation, both spiritually and professionally, of a great songwriter, musician, and human being. A music memoir is at its best when it goes beyond the business struggles, difficult relationships, complex collaborations, and often challenging band dynamics that are all part of a successful career in the music business. The title says it all.

JOHN OATES, singer, songwriter, and record producer

Jonathan Cain's amazing "rock star" climb, as you might expect, is also riddled with periods of pain, confusion, and challenge. However, you'll learn that none of it has been without the relentless reach, grace, and love of God in his everyday life. His story will encourage you to hold on and to never stop believing.

DR. TIM CLINTON, president of the American
Association of Christian Counselors

Jonathan Cain is a humble guy who leads us into a journey of hope through every page. We all can walk away encouraged that it's never too late to start over and that there is nothing too broken that can't be restored. What a powerful statement of truth that comes alive throughout *Don't Stop Believin'*! Definitely a must-read.

DARRYL STRAWBERRY, former Major League Baseball great,
author, speaker, minister, and founder of Strawberry Ministries

The words "don't stop believin'" are not hollow and meaningless words to Jon Cain. Everything important in life requires "belief," and this book will inspire you to have that belief in God, in yourself, and in all that you do.

TOM LEHMAN, 2006 Ryder Cup captain

Jonathan Cain has entertained millions of people around the world playing keyboard and writing songs for Journey. *Don't Stop Believin'* is the remarkable story of how he found faith in Jesus.

JENTEZEN FRANKLIN, senior pastor of Free Chapel
Worship Center and *New York Times* bestselling author

Coming of age in the late 1970s and early 1980s gave me plenty of opportunities to enjoy rock and roll love anthems written by bands like Chicago, Boston, or, a favorite of mine, Elton John. But when Journey launched their single "Don't Stop Believin'" in the summer of 1981, nobody knew at the time that music history was being made. It has gone on to become one of the most bought, played, and sung love songs of all time—even now, you're probably humming the opening piano riff. And the man who wrote the song, Jonathan Cain, has now written a book full of the kinds of stories a musician's memoir should have, but it's so much more than that. It is the story of early childhood tragedy, loss of faith, career struggles, and then ultimately a tale of redemption, a coming back around to faith in God. Cain's fascinating memoir reads like a novel and moves you like a well-crafted song.

JERRY FALWELL JR., president of Liberty University

Jonathan Cain is a genuine American icon whose words and rhythms have shaped our culture as significantly as any single person in history. He's a musical genius, a genuine poet, and a profoundly good human being whose art has been shaped by his life experiences. Now you'll know everything you ever wanted to know about someone you've always known. You won't be able to put this one down.

JOHNNIE MOORE, founder of The Kairos Company and recipient of the Simon Wiesenthal Center's 2017 "medal of valor"

Arena rock keeps coming back, and few do it better than Journey. Fans will flock to Jonathan Cain's book for tales of legends like Steve Perry, a thousand near breakups, and confessions that record execs make when they're high. The songwriter candidly reveals what inspired his iconic hits—a winding pursuit of faith and a father's unfailing belief in his son. Much like one of his Journey melodies, these themes will stick with us.

JOSH M. SHEPHERD, culture and religion reporter for *The Stream*

DON'T STOP BELIEVIN'

THE MAN, THE BAND, AND THE SONG
THAT INSPIRED GENERATIONS

JONATHAN CAIN

SONGWRITER AND KEYBOARDIST FOR THE BAND

JOURNEY

ZONDERVAN®

ZONDERVAN

Don't Stop Believin'
Copyright © 2018 by John L. Friga

Requests for information should be addressed to:
Zondervan, *3900 Sparks Dr. SE, Grand Rapids, Michigan 49546*

ISBN 978-0-310-35134-4 (hardcover)

ISBN 978-0-310-35391-1 (international trade paper edition)

ISBN 978-0-310-35197-9 (audio)

ISBN 978-0-310-35195-5 (ebook)

Published in association with Fox Rothschild LLP, California | New York | Washington DC | Nevada | Florida | Pennsylvania | Colorado | New Jersey | Connecticut | Delaware | Texas.

Art direction: Curt Diepenhorst
Cover design and photography: Micah Kandros
Interior and photo insert design: Kait Lamphere
Photo insert: All photos courtesy of Jonathan Cain and family unless otherwise noted

First printing March 2018 / Printed in the United States of America

To my father, Leonard,
who never stopped believin' in me

Go anywhere you can, because a journey is an adventure and adventures are how we learn who we really are.

MICK FLEETWOOD

You know something? Most people's lives get tied up or caught up in making a living, and therefore they never design their life. And they come to the end of their life and they find out they lived one-tenth of it. Not because they weren't intelligent. Not because they didn't care. Simply because they didn't have the energy to follow through.

TONY ROBBINS

This is just a stepping-stone to something greater.

LEONARD FRIGA

CONTENTS

PART THREE:
"The Midnight Train Goin' Anywhere"

PART FOUR:
"Shadows Searching in the Night"

PART FIVE:
"It Goes On and On and On and On"

I'M NOT SURPRISED TO BE STANDING ON THIS STAGE WITH THESE GUYS, BUT I'm grateful. Sometimes hard work can turn into a blessing like tonight. The toughest part is not letting the experience turn into pride. Past and present members of Journey stand front and center at the Barclays Center in Brooklyn. I'm proud to be surrounded by my brothers, my fans, and my family.

We are joining a formidable list of artists. Bands like Led Zeppelin, The Beatles, The Rolling Stones, Aerosmith, and Fleetwood Mac. Icons such as Elvis Presley, Bob Dylan, Aretha Franklin, Bruce Springsteen, and Chuck Berry. They've put all their own talents and tales into songs for generations. A ceremony like this can easily be forgotten, but the music that has been created will inspire listeners decades from now.

Our bandmates give their speeches, with Neal Schon leading the way, followed by Aynsley Dunbar, Gregg Rolie, Steve Smith, and Ross Valory. My turn to say thanks comes second-to-last, with Steve Perry putting the final exclamation on our triumph. It's the first time he's been onstage with us since 1991.

It's good to see my friend.

Raising the award like the Commissioner's Trophy or the Vince Lombardi Trophy as I approach the microphone, I give a shout-out to the Cubs for winning the World Series. Then I begin by acknowledging the reason I'm up here.

"I'd like to begin by thanking my father and mother for believing in me, from the time I was eight years old and after. Dad later said to me, 'Son, don't stop believin',' in a phone call back in the late seventies. He's gone now. I miss you, Dad, and I love you."

For the next three minutes, I give the briefest and palest summary of my own journey, of how in the world I managed to be up here in the first place.

There are dozens of stories for every person mentioned. Hundreds of songs for every section of time. Thousands of miles spent traveling. Yet through all of them, there are two constants who have been in my life from the very beginning: my two fathers. The first, who was my first and greatest hero, and the second, who never gave up on me.

"And thanks to you, Lord, for keeping your guiding hand on us all those years. This honor was truly worth the wait."

I pass the trophy to Steve Perry, smiling as we embrace one another. Finding myself once again standing onstage behind the singer with that one-of-a-kind voice and listening to his genuine words of thanks, I am moved to see how God works in our lives. For a moment, I blink and remember the three-year-old boy entranced by his grandfather's fiddle. Then I hear Steve saying, "Thank you so much, Jon, for all the songs that we've all written together."

It's impossible to fathom the incredible journey between that fiddle and the Hall of Fame. All of those years spent under God's guiding hand. It's a story about patience, persistence, and the pursuit of something majestic. And it's one I'm honored to be able to share.

PART ONE
"JUST A CITY BOY"

ONE

"FOOLISH HEART"

My life can be divided into parts like songs on an album. On February 1, 1987, the first side of the LP summing up mine came to an end in the Sheraton lounge that had miraculously stayed open past two in the morning. As I signed my name on the poster held open by an animated fan, I knew it was over. Not just the tour, but the band. This beast we had worked so hard to feed and build up was suddenly going to be tamed and sent away. Nobody in the band had been told anything specific, and nothing was official. As it turned out, nothing ever would be officially announced about Journey's demise.

We don't always get the chance to choose when a chapter closes on our life, nor do we always have the opportunity to say good-bye. Deep down inside of me, I stayed as long as I could in this lounge to show these fans my appreciation and, in a sense, to say good-bye in my own way. Journey had just finished two sold-out shows in Anchorage, so I wanted to share this sweet moment as a member of the band so many loved. The people encircling me shared stories about how much the songs meant to them. I couldn't tell them the man singing those songs had endured enough.

After concluding three gigs in Honolulu, Steve Perry seemed to be having fun. The folks in Alaska had been cordial and excited to have us visiting their state, with insistent fans inviting us to parties at their homes, two which we actually attended. Since we had only played forty concerts, Herbie Herbert, our manager, took the liberty to book fifteen more shows, only to have Steve immediately pass on them. His response had been simple: "I'm done."

A difficult breakup often can't be summed up with one sentence. Relationships are complex creations, and those found in a rock group are no different. Sometimes a band can create an even more dysfunctional and difficult set of ties, simply because of the conditions surrounding it. The glare of the spotlight contrasting with the dull hue of a hotel room. The roar of the crowd followed by the hum of the bus engine. Always heading somewhere else, Monday after Tuesday after "what day is it today?"

For some bands, losing a lead singer could be problematic, but for Journey, it would prove to be a seemingly insurmountable challenge. It would be a mountain we'd have to climb if we were to carry on. Neil Schon and his soaring guitar and I and my songwriting would be put on hold, standing by as we lost Steve Perry and his one-of-a-kind voice.

"I walked down the aisle to that song," someone said.

"I've been a Journey fan since 1975," another fan told me.

"I cry every time I hear 'Open Arms.'"

Nobody could know that Steve Perry would never sing that song again with Journey. I knew something was over, that this particular season was coming to an end, yet even I couldn't fathom the idea that we had just played the last official concert ever with the front man who had sung his heart out since 1977. I had held similar feelings before, like the time Steve announced he would be following Neal's example and releasing his own solo album. *Street Talk* came out three years earlier and had featured hits like "Oh Sherrie" and "Foolish Heart." But even then, Perry had been committed to Journey.

It would be another few months before Steve shared his intentions with Neal and me, when he would tell us he was toast and he was done.

This would be the start of the dire months that lay ahead for me.

In less than a year, my band would be over, my marriage would dis-integrate, and, worst of all, my father would pass away. The man who never stopped believing in me and who had supported me from the moment I was born had to watch the dream I'd been living evaporate before my eyes. Dad witnessed the highs, yet he would never have a chance to see the fruit of all the years of being my hero and mentor. The man who helped shape my destiny as a musician, songwriter, husband, and father would lose his battle with cancer at the young age of sixty-three.

The year ahead would be one of the toughest I would ever have to endure.

Perhaps I had a premonition of the things to come with the band, and that was why I was still signing autographs at 2:30 a.m. in a hotel. The poster I signed for the *Raised on Radio* album featured five of us posing in shades, with Neal Schon on one side and Steve Perry on the other. I stood in the middle, the only one of the three to look into the camera, while between us stood two strangers to our Journey family. Randy Jackson and Mike Baird were the talented studio musicians we had hired to play the respective bass and drum parts that had been vacated. The decision to move on without Ross Valory and Steve Smith would be one of those mistakes I regretted the most when it came to the band I joined in 1980.

Thankfully, life gives us a chance for redos and makeovers. I've learned through my journey that it's never too late to start over, and there's no division too broken to be restored. We also have to finish what we start.

Even though I was saying good-bye to these fans and to the band I dearly loved, I knew Journey wasn't finished. My time with Neal and Ross and Steve wasn't over either. I also believed there was more on the horizon with Steve Perry. This couldn't be the end. Not like this. Not in this way.

Life is a series of songs that reveal what we're all about. They are unashamed ballads and soaring barnburners. They can be hits and can also be misses we want to forget. We sing to discover who we are, yet in the process we learn who we are ultimately singing for.

I couldn't help but think of the last song on our set list for this tour, the favorite of Steve Perry's mother, Mary. The words I'd written that Steve made everybody remember so well:

"Circus life under the big-top world—we all need the clowns to make us smile."

I looked around the lobby and saw lots of long arms in faded concert tees. The circus was finally over, and we'd be exiting this big-top world. Somewhere along the way, the clowns had stopped making us smile.

TWO

"DON'T LET THE STARS GET IN YOUR EYES"

Music provides an escape for some people, yet for me it's always brought connection. I discovered this for the first time when I was three years old and a long way from my hometown of Chicago.

The country between Illinois and Arkansas fascinated me since I'd never been out of the city before. Dad had left the small town of Paris and the segregated South behind when he left home at sixteen and hopped a train to St. Louis. Years later in the summer of 1953, he decided to take us on a road trip in his shiny new Olds to visit his family eleven hours away.

All I knew of his life growing up around there was he didn't like it much. Especially after his mother died of cholera when he was only four. Since his father worked in a coal mine, his grandmother was the one who would raise him on a farm. Dad took off in seventh grade and wouldn't come back until now.

The long drive ended in the middle of surrounding cattle ranches as we turned down a gravel driveway, long and dusty and seemingly going nowhere until it ended by my uncle's house. The family greeted us with promises of a barbeque and something called a hoedown.

"Do you like frog legs?" Uncle Bernard asked me, at which I only shook my head. "We caught them last night."

Uncle Marcel thought something was funny. "They taste like chicken. Well, actually, they taste better."

Everything in Paris felt different, from the clear, endless sky to the accents slowing down my aunts' and uncles' voices. It took them a while to persuade me to try the bullfrogs, and when I did, they sure didn't taste like chicken. Grandpa John was nowhere to be found, which suited me fine. Everything I'd ever heard about him made me nervous to meet him.

Curious about my surroundings and bored by listening to the adults talk, I left the tables to follow the strings of lights that hung from the trees and led me to the back of the house. The sun was sneaking away from the backyard, an immense meadow lined with a barbed-wired fence. A massive bull stood a hundred yards away, chomping on grass without a care in the world. My three-year-old self decided to sneak up on the Brahma bull to pet him, so I slipped through the sharp barbs and tiptoed up to the creature.

Before I could get close enough to try to pat the large hump right behind his neck, the Brahma turned, and I suddenly froze. He didn't look surprised or annoyed; the bull just stared at me and looked like he was going to gore me to death.

I had made a really terrible mistake.

I sprinted back to the house, to the buzz of conversation and music and life. I could not only hear the hooves behind me, but I felt them shaking my insides. Or maybe that was just my heart racing. Yards away from the barbed-wire fence, I launched myself between its opening, feeling the metal pricks tear into my skin as I managed to escape being trampled. I clutched my left arm and opened my hand to see the blood. A trail of it splattered on my shorts and my new, white Keds.

I began to cry, knowing I was in big trouble. As I turned around to see the silhouette of the creature that had chased me, echoes of a fiddle playing caught my attention. I stood up and rushed back over to the hoedown, knowing it was finally time to meet Grandpa John.

Dad's stories about his father filled my head as I approached Grandpa. There was the one about Grandpa John giving my fourteen-year-old father a sledgehammer and telling him to slaughter a bull and then skin him for dinner. It took Dad a few good whacks before the beast fell to the ground, providing his father with an amazing hide for his chair. I had been told Grandpa John was a mad gypsy fiddler, a coal miner who had lived in Prague, Czechoslovakia, and migrated to Arkansas. His own father had been a fiddler in Russia, and Grandpa John had learned the craft from him.

I could only imagine the mythical figure I was about to meet. Dad and Mom greeted me as I approached the group of musicians, and I blabbered through my tears about the monster in the meadow that really tried to kill me. *I wanted to pet . . . ran away . . . got cut . . .* Out of breath, I started crying again. Soon my aunt, who happened to be a nurse, began to stitch up my arm. I felt dizzy from losing blood and embarrassed for causing a commotion.

When I finally shook hands with Grandpa John and felt his rough and certain grip, I was surprised to see how handsome he was. His eyes and skin color reminded me of my father.

Someone started to dance a jig around me as my grandfather began to play his fiddle. Soon after, I saw a guy scrape his fingernails across a washboard; another guy began to play a bass fiddle; and a third man strummed his old, beat-up guitar. I forgot my encounter with the bull. I was completely entranced. All I could focus on was Grandpa John's fiddle, the one brought over from Russia by my great-grandfather.

The color was a dark reddish brown that gleamed under the lights because of the many years of resin that had accumulated on the finish. The fiddle was an Eastern European knockoff of a famous Italian violin made in Russia around 150 years ago. It had ukulele tuning pegs, since the originals had worn out.

I got lost in the whirling musical conversation as the melody and rhythms were traded back and forth. I forgot about my injured arm but instead began to clap and stomp my feet with the others. When I looked over and saw my father, I was surprised by the expression on his face. It mirrored the joy I saw in the other musicians.

Dad liked to call me Nudini, since every time he brought me to the beach along Lake Michigan, I stripped off my bathing suit and disappeared, wearing only my dime store sunglasses. I was still learning how to swim, so while we were in Arkansas, I could only wade around a little in the rivers or drop into the shallow water from a rope swing. I was taken on a fishing trip on the White River and introduced to alligator gar, an ancient fish that could grow to be eight feet long and weigh three hundred pounds. Dad loved to tell stories about getting knocked out of a boat by these huge creatures.

"They have tough scales that protect their hides," Dad said to me. "You have to hit them between their diamond-shaped scales just to slow them down."

I rode in one of the two motorboats that had been outfitted with bows, arrows, and sharp gaffs to hunt down the elusive alligator gar. Even though I was strapped tight in a life jacket, I was nervous about one of these giant fish capsizing our boat.

Once again, I witnessed my father in a whole new light when we spotted a gar and followed him downstream. Dad took hold of a gaff while we pulled alongside the huge fish; then he hooked it and pulled it into our small boat and sent it rocking.

"Pretty scary, huh?" my father yelled.

"You almost got him," I said.

I got a glimpse of the gar's needle-sharp teeth before it went back into the water, so I knew the sort of damage it could do to someone. I had no idea how they'd even begin to get the creature back to shore if they caught it.

Since there were no swimming pools to visit in Paris, and since it was such a hot day, we headed to a place called Cove Lake, where locals swam. It had a long pier and a raft floating in the middle, where teens could get away from their parents.

The matching bathing suits that Aunt Boops had made for my father and me made me homesick for her and Chicago. It had been five days, and I began thinking I wanted to head back to the city. With Mom feeling very pregnant and staying out of the sun and Dad lounging next to her, I decided to run down to the water near the wooden pier. Just because I couldn't swim well didn't mean I wasn't going to try. The fear of failure, much less the fear of anything, has never been something to stop me in life. I began to wade into the cold water and paddled, feeling the muddy bottom squishing against my feet. Soon I couldn't touch the bottom, and when I began to feel my body slipping under the surface, I panicked.

Suddenly, I forgot how to swim.

I dropped, and as I did, I opened my mouth and gulped in some lake water. Then I felt a strong hand grip my wrist and jerk me out of the water. I coughed and gagged. When my eyes opened, I saw a man with a thick beard and blue eyes hovering above me. Somewhere between my spitting up and nearly blacking out, the big man gave me mouth-to-mouth resuscitation.

"Are you okay?" he asked me when I finally sat up.

I nodded and wiped the tears off my wet cheeks. I looked up and noticed his long hair. He reminded me of a picture of John the Baptist I'd seen in my catechism study guide in school.

For a minute, I wondered if this man was an angel and whether he was suddenly going to disappear right in front of me. But the man walked me back to my parents and told them what had happened, how he saw me slip under the water while he was walking on the pier. My parents looked even more mortified than they had after I showed up bleeding from that bull. They thanked this stranger several times before he told me to be careful and walked away.

Maybe he's my guardian angel.

I wondered if God was watching over me, like they say he does. Did he save me? Did he pull me out of the dark, threatening water?

I should have been frightened, but instead I was grateful. I looked up at the blue Arkansas sky and said a prayer of thanks.

That night, before we left to go back home, Grandpa John's fiddle made one more appearance. This time, as the guys began to jam and seemingly make up the music as they went, I saw my father join in. He found a guitar and began to play a little part that complemented the fiddle's chords. My father's eyes closed as he got lost in the shuffling rhythm of the mountain melody. Even though my father left Grandpa John years ago and had never come back until now, it seemed as though the song suddenly erased all that time. The chords and the melody created this bond that couldn't be broken. At least not for the moment.

I didn't understand what I was seeing or hearing or even feeling, but I did know something:

I suddenly knew what I wanted to do when I got older.

THREE

"ROCK AROUND THE CLOCK"

In the summer of 1955, I would find and lose a best friend, share two different sets of parents, and finally get a prayer answered after many nights of asking. I was only five, but I was already forging memories I would never forget, like attending Mass with my parents.

Every Sunday morning, images of suffering surrounded me. The red brick building on 909 North Avers Avenue seemed harmless enough on the outside, but once we entered Our Lady of the Angels Church, I became submerged in a strange and haunting world. The first time we entered, I had been transfixed by the lifelike statue of the Blessed Virgin and by the image of Jesus hanging on the cross that stood above the altar. The crucifix had left me spellbound, wanting to cry. I had questions and confusion as a little kid. *How could they have done such horrible thing?* Guilt somehow managed to creep into my preschool mind.

Along the walls in the church, the stations of the cross wood-carvings showed the cruelty heaped on Jesus on Good Friday. The sculpted figures only served to confound me more. My five-year-old mind couldn't comprehend the story they depicted. *Why was Jesus crucified? Who did this to him? Why didn't he fight back? Where were all those angels during this?* I tried to convey to my parents the shock I felt.

"Jesus went to the cross; we should be grateful for him," Mom told me, as if it were actually me he died for. This really puzzled me.

27

Staring at the stained glass reflecting the candlelight, listening to the brooding Latin melodies and the mighty organ, and breathing in the frankincense and myrrh, I wondered what sins I had committed.

My father viewed Mass as an intimate exchange of silent prayer and devotion. He always held his tiny prayer book and the rosary he owned as a boy back in Arkansas. Sometimes he would read passages as he knelt in silence. I followed his example, kneeling beside him and watching him pray. When he opened his eyes, my father would wipe away the tears while smiling at me.

"Why are you crying?" I once asked him.

"Those tears are for Jesus," he said.

In the middle of such heavy darkness, this place served as a light for my father. He loved listening to the Latin during the ceremonies, even though he didn't understand a single word. Once after dipping our fingers in the stone urns full of holy water while leaving the church, Dad told me the water had special powers.

I wanted to know how someone as strong as my father could feel that way about this man they called Jesus. It seemed like Dad had a direct communication with him.

"Just call on him," Dad told me. "Ask Christ to come to you."

So at nighttime, I often called out to Jesus, just like my father told me to. For two years I prayed, but all I felt was the carpet below my knees and all I heard was the sound of silence.

The solemn sanctuary of Our Lady of the Angels Church felt a universe away from the similar-colored brick building we walked to only a mile away. We had moved to our three-bedroom apartment on the west side of Chicago in 1953 after my father was promoted at the print shop. Our new flat on 3636 Augusta Boulevard was in a neighborhood of Polish, Irish, Czech, Jewish, and German people, but primarily Italians. In fact, our home was directly above an Italian delicatessen called Venetti's. The owners, Lou and Katie Venetti, along with our landlord, who I called Grandpa Lawrie, soon introduced me to a new world and the Italian way. Every day an adventure awaited in the deli below.

Venetti's was a small, thriving business, a gourmet shop selling all the things Italians had a taste for. They had Chianti in tall, green glass bottles with straw wrapping. Fresh Italian bread was brought in from a local bakery. Huge rounds of Parmesan cheese sat in the window, while long Italian salamis were proudly displayed, along with wooden boxes of dried salted fish called baccalà. On the weekends, they even made their own sausages and cannoli. The deli also happened to be the central meeting place for the Italian elders, who would come into the store in the evenings to buy their lunch meat and bread, chat in their native tongue, and smoke their cigars.

Since the Venettis were in their forties and had no kids, they adopted me as a son. I began to know and respect Lou as a "pastor" to this Italian clan, watching him speak to the elders with a twinkle in his eye and an assuring tone of voice. Because of Katie's heart condition, I began to run little errands for her. I ended up spending much of my childhood behind the counter, watching all the action and taking it all in.

Not only did Venetti's have groceries, but they also had an incredible collection of Italian candy, the kind made with marzipan and coconut. They stocked a variety of miniature bottles of wax candy with sweet, fruity syrup. I could pick from Beemans, Juicy Fruit, and Black Jack chewing gum whenever I wanted.

With my father working late hours and my mother busy taking care of my two-year-old brother, Tom, I found myself spending a lot of my time in the deli. I had a life upstairs as a son and a big brother and another life downstairs as an adopted son in a world full of produce, sweets, and fun.

Years later, I would find myself in a similar situation as a husband and a father who was living two different lives. There was the life I had back home and life on the road with Journey. The difference was my two childhood lives helped me grow up faster and become the man I needed to be, while my separate adult lives broke the man I had become.

In the summer of 1955, as Chuck Berry and Bo Diddley introduced the country to the sound of rock and roll, I met a little boy named Tony Dellagio. An olive-skinned, sturdy-looking boy with dark, shaggy hair and green eyes, Tony lived about a block down the street. He was the youngest of five brothers and two sisters, and he always wore hand-me-downs and faded sneakers. Tony had a cleft palate and had trouble speaking clearly, but I could understand him pretty well—even though most people, including his family, couldn't. He would mumble something, and I would repeat what I thought he said. I'd see his eyes light up and his head nod to let me know I had gotten his meaning. I was happy to have a buddy who knew a lot of kids on our block and introduced me to them in his mangled English.

Tony always made me laugh. He became a close friend, someone with whom I could share anything going on in my head. Someone who seemed to understand. He was always working on some new adventure we could go on down our street. When I introduced him to Mom, she thought he was cute and likable but a little wild. Whenever I ran off with Tony, she always said, "Stay out of trouble with that boy—you hear me?" I never knew what kind of trouble she meant, but having my freedom to go out and get crazy sure felt better than staying cooped up in a warm, muggy apartment with my bossy mother and baby brother.

The summer of 1955 was the fourth consecutive scorcher in a row for Chicago—and the hottest on record. Only 1995 has come close to matching the intense heat that summer brought, when eleven days in a row—from July to August—had a temperature of 90 degrees or higher. The temperature was one thing, but it's impossible to forget the thick blanket of humidity that came with it. It was so bad that Mayor Daley rationed the water supply on the south side, and the police and fire departments gave out tickets to people who tried to water their lawns.

Our neighborhood was blessed with a fire hydrant on the corner in front of Venetti's deli on Monticello Avenue. During those hot summer months, local children were known to steal a plumber's wrench and turn on the hydrant. They lashed a short board against the opening of the hydrant with a rope and turned on the water full blast. This caused a rooster tail that kids could cool off under. Sometimes the rope broke from the water pressure and sent kids flying against the curb. Cars on Monticello had to slow down until the kids moved out of the way, and then they could proceed under the shower.

Lou and Katie understood the fun part, but rooster tails were no good for business, since grown-ups weren't quite as eager as we were to get soaked. But dressed in our shorts, jeans, or bathing suits, we were in heaven playing in this cool, magical shower—that is, until we heard a fire truck coming, at which point someone would hide the wrench and everybody else hightailed it back home. The firemen would show up with sirens wailing, dressed in their helmets and coats, and close the hydrant.

Tony's older brothers had car tools, and that's where we'd get the wrenches. This made Tony the organizer of the Monticello Avenue Rooster Tail Committee. I participated in my first rooster tail that summer. It was exciting to prepare for one of these capers. Tony had the wrench, someone else brought the rope, a third person brought the board, and a fourth was on watch for the fire truck. We swore everyone to secrecy.

The firemen were really angry every time they had to show up. Water rationing was in effect, and we were breaking the law. Mom wanted me to stop being involved. She said we could all go to jail for messing with city property, so I had to sneak out whenever it came time for a rooster tail. Mom blamed my new best friend.

"Jonny, Tony is going to get you in trouble. I said it from the moment I met him."

Up to this point, I had never dreamed of breaking the law. I wondered if this was one of those "sins" they talked about at Mass, the kind you needed to ask forgiveness for. How could something so exciting, something that took timing and courage, something that could shower overheated bodies with cool water on a hot summer day, be so wrong? But one day Mom told me about a visit she had received.

"A fireman, Lieutenant Wojnicki from Engine 85, came knocking on the door today," my mother told me. "He was really upset with you kids. He and his men have got more important things to do than clean up rooster tails all over this neighborhood. He shops at Lou's deli once in a while, and he knows you live upstairs."

I began to have that sinking feeling inside of me once again.

"I know you were in on that, Jonny," Mom said. "You kids have got to stop doing this, or you'll get shipped off to juvenile home."

I had heard about juvenile home, and my mother preached about it whenever my behavior wasn't to her liking. Her warnings made me feel guilty about all the trouble we were causing. I admired the firemen, but at the same time I loved seeing their trucks race to the scene and the way they took charge of a situation with their walkie-talkies and other equipment.

Tony had an older brother named Paul who would come to the deli to buy candy and cigarettes. He befriended me after a few months. Paul was a tall, blue-eyed teen with a crew cut and a large nose. He seemed like a loner and didn't hang out with other kids his age. Paul took an interest in me, since I was able to communicate and be friends with his little brother. One summer afternoon, Paul strolled by the deli and found me sitting with Lou behind the counter.

"Jonny, I was thinking I'd show you my dad's new Buick in our garage. It's mighty special. I got a bag of candy that's too much for me to eat by myself. Let's take a walk over to my place."

I looked at Lou, and he shrugged and said, "Go on. Come back and have lunch with me around two-thirty."

The Dellagios lived about a half block down the street in a brick building with stairs leading up to the front porch. I followed Paul around the pathway to the garage where their stout German shepherd slept. Tony was nowhere to be found. Paul climbed in the front seat of his dad's four-door sedan while I did the same. He turned on the radio, opened the bag of candy, and offered me some. Then Paul exposed himself and asked me to touch him.

That same feeling I had about breaking the rules and opening the fire hydrants flooded through me, except this felt a hundred times worse. I knew something was dead wrong about all of this. Yet for a few moments, I played it cool and did what he asked.

You gotta get outta here, a voice inside me screamed.

I pulled the door handle with my right hand and crashed into the door with my shoulder at the same time. I jumped out of the car, bolted through the garage door, and dashed down the alley behind the houses. I cried as I ran, afraid and confused about what had just happened. I ran up the stairs to where my mother was cooking dinner.

"What in the world happened to you?" she asked.

"Paul tried to put my hand on his thing, Mom," I said. "He wanted me to play with it."

"He did what?" she screamed. "Did he do anything else? Did he chase you when you ran?"

"No, he just stayed there."

When I ran off, Paul was staring at the windshield in some kind of daze.

Mom stormed down the alley with a broom in one hand and me in the other. I wasn't sure what she planned to do with the broom.

When we arrived at the gate to the Dellagios' backyard, she screamed out the mother's name. "Sofia Dellagio! Come out here right now! Your son Paul tried to violate my little boy!"

Mom proceeded to tell Sofia exactly what she planned to do to Paul, using language we were forbidden to use at home. Tony's mother stood at the screen door with a worried look on her face. "I can't believe my son would do such a thing to your boy," she said.

"I'm calling the police when I get home, and I'm going to report this to the proper authorities," my mother announced. "Now where is that sick boy, huh?"

Sofia shook her head as if she didn't know where he'd just run off to.

"You tell him if he ever tries to touch my boy again, I'll break this damn broom over his sick, perverted skull!" my mother roared.

"Nan, I'm sorry. Truly, I don't know what to say," Sofia said, disappearing behind the screen door again.

I had never seen my mother so upset. I could feel my whole body trembling as I followed her back to the apartment, listening to her tell how she had always felt something wasn't right with Paul, about how he gave her the creeps.

"Jonny, you're not to go over there ever again!" my mother declared. "And I don't want you around Tony either. I know you two are friends, but that's ending today. Do we understand each other?"

"But Mom!"

"You're lucky you got away," she told me. "Who knows what else he had in mind for you."

When I asked my mother what I should tell Tony, she gave me a hug and offered some of the best advice I would ever hear.

"Tell him the truth. Tell him what happened so he knows his brother has a problem," she said.

When Tony came to the deli a few days later looking to play with me, I took him outside the store next to the infamous fire hydrant.

"My mom says we can't be friends because of what your brother tried to do."

"Yeah, I know," he said in his broken dialect. "My mom told me he got weird with you in the garage. I'm sorry. I can't believe he messed with you."

Tony gave me a hug and told me he'd miss me and then turned and walked away. It was the last time we ever spoke to each other.

One night, after having spent so many months praying and praying to Jesus, it happened. I felt a sense of security and warmth cover me, the kind that can't fully be explained, the sort that is easier for a child to believe in than an adult. The kind of faithful, tear-filled belief my father held in his silent prayers. I was overcome with the knowledge that I was in God's hands.

I became captivated by Our Lady of the Angels Church and came to know it well. I would end up making my first confession, taking my First Communion, and having my confirmation there. It would be the place I'd sing Latin chants in the choir for my father.

Monsignor Joseph Cussen was a tall, down-to-earth priest in charge of everything at Our Lady of the Angels. When my mother announced that I would be attending the school, he was delighted and genuinely interested. He loved kids and waved to me as I walked home with my parents after service.

My favorite priest was Father Joseph McDonnell. He was a strong, stout-looking Irishman with a ruddy complexion and red hair. He said Mass often and gave great sermons that even a child could understand. My parents and I stayed after church to meet him one Sunday. He was a kind and caring man. I asked him if he knew about Venetti's deli, and he said he'd shopped there a few times. I shared my stories of good fortune with him, and he laughed and said, "Sounds like someone's looking out for you in a special way."

It didn't take long before I announced to my parents that I wanted to be a priest when I grew up. I set up the dresser in my room as an altar and used one of my dad's golf trophies as my chalice. I wrapped a blanket around my shoulders, imitating what I saw on Sundays, and pretended to say Mass in my room. My mother discovered me in my room one morning kneeling and praying, and she wondered about her son. The priests had become my heroes, and this is where my imagination had taken me on Augusta Boulevard. The services in my room went on for months, but my parents believed this desire would pass.

"I'm going make a fine priest 'cause nobody loves Jesus more than I do," I announced.

These were sincere words. I felt close to Jesus during those years and thanked him regularly for my blessed life.

"We'll see, we'll see," my parents would say, rolling their eyes.

I was definitely infatuated with religion and the feeling it gave me at an early age. Our Lady of the Angels was the foundation for my education and spiritual nurturing. It would take something monumental to change my youthful faith.

My heart longed to be a priest, yet my young soul longed to perform music. One of my pastimes was to listen to old 45s on a portable turntable. I learned how to sing Johnnie Ray's song "Cry" and Hank Williams's "Jambalaya," a favorite of my dad's—"jambalaya and a crawfish pie and filé gumbo." Music was thrilling for me, and I got lost in those records for hours. I watched *Your Hit Parade* on television and listened to the radio every chance I could, singing and memorizing songs. Bill Haley and His Comets had released "Rock around the Clock," and their new beat was one of my new faves. My singing talent found its way down to the store. I performed for Lou and Katie and the old Italians, and they loved it. I sang, and they rewarded me with candy and soda. I loved the look on their faces as they listened to me sing.

Maybe if I couldn't sing the Mass as a priest, I could sing my own songs someday.

I CAN HEAR ROSEMARY CLOONEY SINGING "MAMBO ITALIANO" AND PICTURE the man in the white tee with a pack of Chesterfield Kings rolled up in his left shirtsleeve, whistling the tune as he walks along the shoreline of Lake Michigan, carrying his son on his shoulders. His confidence shapes the way I talk and walk and look out at the world. My father's name is Leonard, but everyone calls him Len.

I can listen to "Earth Angel" by the doo-wop group The Penguins and see Nan carrying a blanket and picnic basket as she strolls behind us. She wears a white one-piece bathing suit, a calico scarf in her hair, red lipstick, and Ray Ban sunglasses. My mom is pretty, with a smile that makes me smile too. She tells me I was born in the heat of passion, something I won't understand for quite some time until I compare the date on their wedding photo with the date of my birth.

My parents love to dance, having first met at a USO dance in Chicago, so they either have my aunt or a neighborhood kid watch me while they take a bus to Edgewater Beach Hotel to move to the music of the big bands. Famous celebrities like Clark Gable, Marilyn Monroe, and Frank Sinatra have stayed at this famous Chicago destination. Under the stars, Mom and Dad dance to the sounds of Tommy Dorsey, Glenn Miller, and Xavier Cugat, telling me about their magical nights the next day.

My earliest memories begin with the sounds of yesterday. Sometimes a melody can conjure up a scene more colorful than a snapshot and more moving than a motion picture. Songs can cement the structure of one's life, especially for someone who's built a life around them.

FOUR

"WHOLE LOTTA SHAKIN' GOIN' ON"

In 1957, the country was all shook up with the sound of Elvis Presley and doin' a whole lotta shakin' to Jerry Lee Lewis and walkin' right along with Fats Domino. A generation began discovering heroes emanating from radios and televisions. Yet for me, the heroes resided by my side, whether they were Dad bragging about my musical abilities with strangers at night or our landlord teaching me how to talk to customers during the day.

From the first time I began to memorize tunes from *Your Hit Parade* and also play the old upright piano at Pat's Tavern at the age of four, Len Friga had recognized the love of music I inherited from him. I had figured out how to boogie-woogie with two hands on that piano. My parents had seen me audition for and make the all-boy choir at Our Lady of the Angels School. Even though I was only in second grade at the time, I became first chair alto. Dad was amazed at how much I could do without ever having taken a single lesson.

That year, my father announced to the family that Dr. Deutsch had told him he needed an operation soon. It was called a spinal fusion and would require a specialist at St. Anne's. Dad told us he'd have to wear a steel brace for three and a half years after the surgery.

He'd been living with pain for a long time already, so we all knew Dad was tough enough to deal with all of this.

The spinal fusion my father needed was a result of his time spent in the Aleutian Islands carrying heavy equipment while serving in the army during World War II. He slipped on ice while unloading supplies from a cargo truck and injured his back and was discharged. Len tried to get the army to pay for the operation, but they had lost his records, so no checks came from Uncle Sam. Thankfully, the printers' union had good medical benefits, so he was covered for this exorbitant expense.

Dad didn't mind talking about his time serving in the war. I once asked him what his time overseas was like.

"Cold and monotonous," he said.

"What does monotonous mean?" I asked him.

"Uninteresting. It got boring being on a frozen island for months on end. It drove some of the guys at the base a little crazy."

"Did you go crazy?"

"No," my father told me. "We played music to keep sane. I played the rhythm guitar, and some of the other guys knew fiddle and bass. We got pretty tight after a while. You've seen that picture Mom has of me with the boys."

"What'd you do?"

"I gave information to the American pilots who were flying to the islands around Japan."

"Did you ever get shot at?"

Dad only smiled at my question. "No, son, no one ever got that close to our base."

"Did you ever carry a gun?"

"We all learned to handle weapons during basic training."

I had studied his uniform carefully in the picture.

"I love all the patches they gave you," I told my father.

"They all mean something—the division; the company."

"Did you win the war?"

"The United States won, and Japan surrendered."

"I wanna put all of your patches on a jacket," I said.

"Your mom or Boops can help you with that."

Aunt Boops would end up doing exactly that: helping me out once again and sewing those patches onto my leather jacket. Boops was a nickname my mother's older sister, Louise, had acquired when the two of them had gone to a Saturday matinee of "Betty Boop." Mom thought Louise resembled the main character, and ever since then, the name had stuck. Left to support my mom and her parents after their three brothers went off to World War II, Aunt Boops worked two jobs a week. She had grown used to helping others out since she had done that her whole life as the oldest of five siblings. Now, many years later, Aunt Boops's baby sister was helping to take care of her.

It started when Aunt Boops suddenly began having seizures and her memory began to slip. One doctor said she was becoming an epileptic, but blood tests proved negative. After being examined at the Illinois State Mental Hospital, Aunt Boops was diagnosed with Wilson's disease. Since this was a rare disease, it took her a while to receive proper treatment. She was even put in a straitjacket a few times. After two years of treatment and a diet change, her condition improved, so Mom convinced my father to help get her released from the nuthouse, as my aunt called it, and live with us. I was only two when she moved in.

Aunt Boops was a kind, thoughtful, and loving person. She spoiled me rotten during the holidays and brought me with her to watch her beloved Cubs from the bleachers. I loved having her live with us in the apartment. It really felt like I had a second mom, a sentiment that brought its own share of problems with it. My mother became a bit jealous of her sister's close relationship with me, so she began playing games with my head about not being a good boy and not deserving her love. As a young kid, I couldn't fully comprehend my mother's mercurial behavior.

The distance between me and my mother grew as she answered

my questions tersely and stopped singing songs we used to share. An accident in the kitchen produced a spanking on my bare bottom with a plastic hairbrush so severe that Mom broke it. Dad would always take Mom's side. I learned she was his queen, no matter what. I had to obey her and be careful to stay out of the doghouse.

Years before the book and movie would become a permanent part of pop culture, I witnessed *The Godfather* firsthand whenever I accompanied Lou Venetti to South Water Market to buy produce. We rode in the older Cadillac with the backseat removed so he could haul groceries. Lou had not just one Cadillac but two. He got a new car every other year, leasing it and writing it off as a business expense. His newest vehicle would be his prized possession, a symbol of success others in the neighborhood surely recognized. Lou had earned that success the old-fashioned way: through guts, grit, and hard work.

The South Water Market where Lou took me bustled with a hundred aromas and a thousand items to choose from. Everyone seemed to know Lou and spoke to him with respect, some in English and others in Italian. Lou was a people person, but he was also a great haggler who tried to buy the best produce he could find for the least amount of money. He wasn't cheap but clever, as well as charming. Carrying his grocery list with him, Lou only bought what he needed, never going overboard.

I took everything in, from his conversations with vendors to all the items he showed me. It boggled my mind how much he could stack in his tiny store to make a profit, so I asked him to show me on Sunday nights how he managed his inventory. It was beyond my third-grade math capabilities, but I began to see Lou's system. Watching Lou stamp canned goods with blue ink, I started to memorize the prices of things in the store. I loved everything about being there.

"Why do you have to go back to work?" I asked my father when the time came for him to go back.

"All of us have to work. It's good for you."

"Does your back hurt?"

"I'm wearing my brace, and it helps," Dad said.

The way Dad moved slowly and sometimes grimaced after coming home from his job showed that he still felt lots of pain. He didn't complain. Hard work, it seemed, was just part of life. So I decided I wanted to work too, just like Dad and Aunt Boops and Lou.

"I want to work in your store," I told Lou one day.

"You will have lots of responsibilities if you work at Venetti's," he said with one eyebrow raised. "Do you think you can handle it?"

"Yes, sir."

"Maybe one day. But you need to pay close attention to everything. That's the only way you'll ever learn a business."

FIVE

"GREAT BALLS OF FIRE"

Carol and Cathy Shabel were twins, and they were the prettiest girls, besides my mother, I had ever laid my eyes on. From the moment I saw them on my first day of first grade at Our Lady of the Angels School, I was transfixed. The shy one, Carol, had long, dark brown curly hair and blue eyes. I still can see the OLA patch on her navy-blue jumper. Her sister, Cathy, was as cute as Shirley Temple, with light-colored hair and perfect, glowing skin. They smiled the first time they saw me. It was as if they knew one day I'd be writing love songs, and that in some small way, their beauty and friendship would influence those compositions of mine.

The girls weren't just cute; they were also smart. They lived three blocks from our building. We became close friends over the years as we shared the sweet-smelling and pretty Sister Mary Remi as our first-grade teacher. We were also in the same class the following year, when we had a rude awakening with Sister Mary Faustina, an older, slender, and gruffer nun not unlike the witch in *The Wizard of Oz*. Looking like she was eighty years old, Sister Faustina disciplined the class like a young drill sergeant.

From making the boy's choir to participating in my First Communion, second grade was a momentous time for me. After a full summer of Little League baseball and a two-week vacation in Twin Lakes, Wisconsin, I started third grade at OLA in the fall of 1958. This was an exciting era, with new things introduced weekly, like Cocoa Puffs, Rice-A-Roni, the Chevy Impala, and stereophonic recordings. My new classroom, Room 101, was on the first floor in the south wing of the school, with ten-foot windows looking out on Iowa Street. Our tough but fair Irish teacher, Sister Mary Edgar, had a sense of humor and loved to laugh. *Thank God,* I had thought after having endured Sister Faustina's scowl for the entire second-grade year. I knew it would be a good year when Sister Mary Edgar made silly jokes before class and constantly sang Irish folks songs to herself during the day, sometimes even having us join in.

I sat right behind Carol Shabel in class, so I got to look at her brown, curly hair in front of me all year long. I enjoyed being so close to her. We often ate lunch together. She had become my best friend, and we shared some secrets. Even though I was closest to Carol, I still enjoyed talking to Cathy on our two-mile journey back to our apartments after school. After a summer of not seeing them much, I was struck at how much different they looked. Cathy's features had darkened, making her even prettier with those big baby blues, while Carol looked taller and skinnier.

Our little brother, Hal, would be born that October. Taking care of him and also dealing with my five-year-old brother, Tom, proved to be hard work for my mother. Tom refused to eat what my mother cooked for dinner, and Mom refused to let him off the hook. The battle went on for months. When things got exceptionally bad for our mother, Dad would have to "get the belt." We hated the belt, and there were more than a few times our dad let us have it. Dad was a stern disciplinarian who grabbed and squeezed our wrists with his powerful hands.

The first day of December seemed like any other cold and crisp morning in the Chicago area. I wore my favorite jacket to school, the brown leather bomber jacket with Dad's army patches sewn on the shoulders and chest. As I walked to school with the twins, we talked about how the local ice rink would soon be flooded and provide a place to hang out. Sister Mary Edgar was out sick that day with a bad cold, so our substitute was Sister Mary Florence Casey, an older nun who was wise and patient and whose energy was contagious.

The day progressed like any other. We returned from religion class around 2:20 in the afternoon. All of us in Room 101 smelled the smoke at the same time. No fire alarm was ringing, but Sister Casey promptly marched us out of the building and onto the street, not even stopping for our coats. Soon the classes from the entire first floor were lined up single file along Avers Avenue, just as we had done during countless fire drills. But this wasn't a drill. After a few minutes, Sister Casey disappeared with her black robes trailing into the building, leaving our class on our own.

The fire alarm finally sounded, piercing the eerie silence.

I grabbed Carol's hand, not saying a word. We waited on the street, wondering where the rest of our schoolmates were. None of the classes were coming down from the second floor. Avers Avenue felt abandoned as we stood there waiting. Just waiting. Waiting and wondering why our friends weren't coming out the front door or down the fire escape.

When we finally started to breathe in the toxic smoke, our suspicions were confirmed.

"The school's on fire," I said, even though we could not see it from where we stood.

"Where is Cathy?" Carol shouted. "I need to find her!"

I felt her hand break free and watched as she ran to the end of the street to look for her sister. I should have broken line and gone after Carol, following her and making sure both of the Shabel sisters were safe, yet I froze.

I looked at my Mickey Mouse watch and saw that it was quarter till three.

School was almost done. We had been so close to leaving.

Soon the silent street became an auditorium for terror. We began to see students stick their heads out of half-opened windows on the

46

second floor and scream for help. No one in my class moved. A girl climbed out of a window to the ledge of the second floor, her hair in flames, her body suddenly dropping to the pavement below. Landing so suddenly, so lifelessly. More students followed her example as the intense, stinging smoke continued to wrap itself around them.

Jesus, help us. Don't let this happen. Please, God, please help them!

When the first fire truck finally arrived, I saw Lieutenant Wojnicki of Engine 85 rushing out. Running over to Avers Avenue and seeing students jumping out of second-story windows, he called for more units and got to work. Soon more firemen arrived, as well as parents who rushed from their homes with ladders. With a ten-foot ceiling and half of the basement above ground, the second story of the school was actually two and a half stories tall, so ladders wouldn't reach.

As the first firefighter's ladder went up against the building on Iowa Street, my mouth opened wide as I saw Sister Mary Florence, our substitute teacher that day, rushing up it with a fireman to help the students. The petite nun managed to grab a girl from a fireman above her and proceed down the ladder with her on her shoulders. None of my classmates except Carol had moved a step from our line, but that changed when we heard an explosion. The roof of the building began to crumble. All of us scrambled.

I found Carol standing on Iowa Street, in the middle of panic-stricken parents searching for their children. She looked abandoned without her sister right next to her.

"We have to find Cathy and get home," I told her. "Don't move from that spot. I'll be right back!"

I ran and saw Avers Avenue and Iowa Street covered in a maze of fire hoses while deathly orange and red flames seemed to laugh their way up to the heavens. The hoses looked like wild serpents under my feet as I tried to move out of the firefighters' way. *This is what it must've looked like for soldiers fighting in World War II.*

The fire started in a thirty-gallon cardboard barrel at the foot of a stairwell in the northeast wing of the school, right under a vent pipe leading up to the roof space above the second floor. The heat and smoke found their way up the vent to the roof, igniting the tarpaper. The fire spread to the floor, walls, and staircase in the basement.

Sister Mary Davidis had opened her class door in Room 209 and saw the corridor full of black, acrid smoke, so she immediately shut it and told the boys to cover the cracks of the doors with books and pile desks against the doors, while she ordered the girls to stand by the window.

Sister Mary Geraldita in Room 207 had seen the thick smoke in the hallway and had decided to lead her students out the rear door of the classroom that led to the fire escape, but she found it locked and had forgotten the key at the convent. As their room filled with oily smoke, Sister Geraldita asked the students to form a semicircle and began to lead the class in the rosary. Soon she instructed the students to cover their noses with clean rags she kept in the closet.

As students were grabbed by firefighters and brought to safety, others leaped down to a canopy over a stairway covering the entrance to the first floor. Sister Davidis helped all but one of her students escape the fire.

James Raymond, the school's janitor and the father of four OLA students, burst into Sister Geraldita's class, along with Father Hund, one of the parish priests. Both of them were covered in black soot. The sister and her class were rescued because of them.

Other classes in other rooms weren't as fortunate. Smoke poured under the door of the fourth-grade classroom in Room 210. The students panicked and began jumping to try to save their lives before they would be burned to death. Twenty-eight fourth graders and their teacher died, while fifteen students were injured. In Room 211, twenty-four students died.

Perhaps the saddest outcome was Room 212. During geography class, the students became warm as the fire worked its way into walls and the ceiling. Someone opened a door to the deadly corridor, and the thick, black mist of death enveloped their classroom. Trying to get air to breathe, another student opened a window, which added oxygen to the fast-moving flames. The students who stayed at their desks praying were asphyxiated. Twenty-six pupils and their teacher died in this room.

Out of the approximately sixteen hundred kids in grades kindergarten through eighth grade at Our Lady of the Angels School, ninety-two children and three nuns died. I couldn't begin to fathom this as I watched the carnage firsthand on the street. I held my breath, knowing the hot air was too thick to breathe in.

All I wanted to know was whether the twins were still alive.

CATHY IS MISSING, AND NOW CAROL IS NO LONGER IN THE SPOT I LEFT HER.
I assume she must have gone into the church next door, so I sprint and rush through the doors in a daze. Once inside, I see my fellow classmates kneeling on pews, praying. Their faces are shadowed with soot and desperation, while white lines follow the trails of their tears. The low murmur of weeping can be heard. A sister is up front at the altar saying the rosary.

The twins are nowhere to be found in the dimly lit church.

I ignore the kids around me as I walk up and down the aisles. Carol and Cathy aren't here.

My shock has turned to frustration. I hate this feeling of panic and dread. The sister's voice drones underneath my anger.

I look up at the stained-glass window and see Virgin Mary lit up. Behind her, the flames rage and wreak havoc on the school so many have seen as a sanctuary, looked after and protected by God the Father. The fire is so close, too close.

This isn't a safe place. I'm in danger.

I run away from the nun's rosary and past the pews and out the church door, racing back to my apartment and my family. I think about my favorite leather jacket, the one with all Dad's army patches, being torched in the fire. I think about all my friends in other grades, about their parents and families. Then I think of the twins. All the while, I run faster and harder than I've ever run, running away from Our Lady of the Angels School, which no longer stands.

SIX

"SMOKE GETS IN YOUR EYES"

Three black Cadillac hearses pulled up in front of the convent across the street from Our Lady of the Angels Church. I maneuvered through the grown-ups in the crowd to see men in black suits begin to unload the contents of each vehicle, gently lifting three bronze coffins out of the hearses. Each coffin was adorned with a silver crucifix and nameplate and was accompanied by a large basket of white carnations. The crowd parted to let pallbearers place the coffins on the sidewalk of the convent, and then one by one, nuns approached and knelt down beside them, holding hands and praying for their fallen sisters.

For a moment, I thought of Carol and Cathy, how I had run home and waited to hear if they were okay. How my brother, Tom, had clutched me the moment I stepped foot in the house, and how my mother thanked God I was alive. How I told them what had happened and how the news showed the fire on television. The scenes were straight out of a horror movie, with children being taken away on stretchers and nurses comforting broken parents. I couldn't watch the screen.

All the questions—*How did it start and how many died and where are we going to go to school and are the Shabel sisters okay?*

I was finally able to call their house the next morning, and Carol answered the phone. She told me she had found Cathy and they'd gone

53

inside the church and then had run back out to find me. Eventually they made their way home and found their mom, who walked back with them. I felt relief, not only that they had survived, but that they understood the shock we were all going through.

Two days later, nearly two thousand mourners lined the street to pay their respects to the sisters who had died. I listened to Bishop Raymond Hillinger lead the prayers and the rosary just before the coffins were moved to the chapel for the wake.

The following day on December 4, more than one thousand people packed into the church for the Mass, including my mother and me. A color guard from the police and fire departments was present. Every person in attendance looked bewildered and exhausted from the tragic events of the past week. There were many questions that needed to be answered. The parishioners wanted the truth. The heartbroken parish needed an explanation.

I wanted and needed an explanation.

It was the first time I had been back to the church after the fire, and I couldn't shake the memories of the chaos and disaster. As I looked up at the sun shining through the stained-glass windows, familiar thoughts tugged at me.

Jesus spared my life, one voice inside me said.

Jesus allowed so many to die, another voice whispered.

My idyllic life full of friends and Italians and music and love had suddenly been interrupted by this silence. A silence that carried no answers. I wanted the darkness to go away, but I knew the stain of soot would forever be marked on my soul.

Another Mass was held at the Illinois National Guard Northwest Armory for twenty-seven victims the following day, but Mom and I decided to simply watch it on television instead. Stories of tragedy and bravery began to show up in the Chicago papers. On December 8, an artificial kidney failed a burn victim, bringing the death toll to ninety-two. Fifty-seven children still lay in hospitals, ten of them in critical condition.

The week after the fire, my mother got a call for me to come get anything I might have left at school. I was anxious to look for my bomber jacket, so I took the familiar walk to school. I was directed to the convent, where clothes hung on portable racks that had been brought in.

I found my books and lunch box and stopped to look across the street at the remains of OLA. It looked like it had been bombed, just like I'd seen in war movies. Rooms were missing walls and ceilings, and the interior was charred and damp. All of the second-floor windows were broken. Scores of burned shoes, clothes, and desks were piled in the middle of Iowa Street, waiting to be taken away. I hoped they would be gone before Sunday when we would come back for the service.

After searching for twenty minutes, I finally came across my beloved jacket with my father's patches stitched onto it. It was slightly damp, but in pretty decent shape. As I put it on, I recognized the smoky smell all too well. It felt too heavy, too dirty. I couldn't help hearing the screams from the kids on the second floor. I pictured their bodies cracking on the hard street below them as they jumped.

Some people had said the phrase "God's will" during the last week, and while standing in the skeletal remains of our school, I thought about this again.

How can this be God's will? How could he let so many die? So many children. And nuns too.

An anger began to build inside, a slow-rising tide that would continue to grow with time. I was angry with the church and with the authorities. My mother had started to question the fire investigation, and I was starting to think she was right. The church hadn't said anything, and the police had said very little. None of us who had been there that day were given the real truth about what happened. Why was it taking so long?

I looked at the bomber jacket I was wearing, slipped it off, and put it on the pile of tainted belongings. I didn't hesitate as I left it there, taking a familiar walk home that now felt different somehow. When I entered the apartment, my mother asked if I had found my prized leather jacket.

"Yeah," I said to her, "it smells like smoke and death."

"Where is it?" she asked.

"I'm not bringing that into our home."

The jacket, just like my school, would be left behind—along with the childhood dreams I'd carried with them.

PART TWO

"BORN TO SING THE BLUES"

THE ROAR OF THE ENGINE SHAKES ME IN THE BIG LEATHER SEAT OF THE CAR.
I clutch the armrest, my seat belt nowhere to be found, the buildings
on both sides passing by like the walls outside a subway. We're racing
down an alley somewhere in Chicago, somewhere off a main road.
Shadows cover the back road.

I glance out the front window and see the brick wall a hundred
yards in front of us, standing like a towering barricade blocking any
intruders.

The car actually speeds up. I yell out at the driver but don't look
his way. Instead, I just keep staring at the oncoming barrier, a thousand red bricks standing in our way. I scream as they keep getting
closer and closer. Then I think of sitting in the front seat of the car
with Tony's creepy older brother, Paul. I do the same thing I did
then—clutch the door handle and jerk it open.

The brick wall is only a dozen yards away. We're going to crash
into the center of it.

I propel my body out of the car, bracing for impact against the hard
concrete surface, waiting for the pain to come. But I never feel the crash.
I don't feel anything. I don't hear the car engine anymore or the violent
bashing of the front of the vehicle. I'm in limbo, waiting for the hurt and
pain to come, wincing and worrying and then suddenly waking up.

I find myself disoriented on the floor, feeling pain from hitting
the hardwood floor. Mom is by my side, helping me up and guiding
me back to bed. It's not the first time this has happened. The dreams
had started before the fire, but they seemed to have been inflamed
ever since the tragedy.

"We're going to take you to see Dr. Deutsch," Mom tells me as she slips the blanket under my chin.

He will just say the obvious: that he believes I'm processing the trauma I experienced from the fire. Carol tells me she has bad dreams too, but hers are about being burned.

The dreams aren't the only thing. There are the nosebleeds that appear out of nowhere in the middle of class. The kids showing up with unrecognizable faces and grisly burns on their arms and legs. The investigators coming in and asking us questions, reminding us about this thing we all want to forget. The rumors about the investigation. The complaints about the conditions of the school before the fire.

There's Mom. Blaming and demanding and questioning and ultimately condemning the church for the fire.

And there's me, wanting to move on. Wanting to forget this all happened. Wanting to climb into the front seat of a car and be driven away. Yet every time I'm in that seat, I find myself charging toward another brick wall, unable to do a single thing.

SEVEN

"JOHNNY B. GOODE"

The dying glow from the Our Lady of the Angels fire would never be fully put out. Years later, while writing "Ask the Lonely" with Steve Perry, these lyrics would emerge: "As you search the embers, think what you've had, remember, hang on, don't you let go now."

Perhaps in a way, I was writing to the young boy scarred from that afternoon. Visible signs couldn't be seen, like in some of my classmates, but they marred my insides. Life, however, couldn't pause and try to cope; like a river, it kept moving.

Without the benefit of grief counseling, the surviving students met in front of the church the following Monday after the fire to be bused. It was a cold and bitter morning, and my mother walked me to our meeting place in front of the church. The sight of survivors showing up in bandages and crutches felt awkward; I tried not to stare at the bewildered students lining up in classes that had been devastated by the fire.

Before a new school was built on West Iowa Street, the OLA student body was bused to four different parochial schools. Monsignor McManus also found extra classrooms in nearby public schools— Cameron, Orr, and Hay. New nuns and lay teachers joined the BVM sisters in the borrowed classrooms so we could resume our education. All of us students had already learned a brutal lesson about life: how it can change in an instant, and how we should always be grateful for every moment God gives us.

Along with everyone else, I heard information as it leaked out from the media. It seemed like the church didn't want to talk about anything, but rumors swirled around the neighborhood and gossip spread in the deli. The more my mother discovered about the fire, the angrier she became with the Catholic Church. The National Fire Protection Association had investigated the conditions of the school before the fire and determined the building was a recipe for disaster. The school had been grandfathered in to the old Chicago building code, so it was excused from adhering to the current fire prevention standards. The fire alarm wasn't wired to the fire department. There was no alarm in the north wing. The fire extinguishers were placed seven feet off the ground, out of the reach of many of the teachers. There was only one fire escape, and the door to it was locked.

Once Mom made up her mind about something, it was pretty much set in stone, and she laid the blame squarely on the wealthy Catholic Church for not bringing the school up to modern-day fire code safety standards. Schools in other states had been retrofitted, she said, so why hadn't OLA? Mom felt the church could have afforded, at the very least, to install a sprinkler system and wire the alarm to a fire station.

"All that death could've been avoided," Mom said. "I'm going to write a letter to the pope."

I saw her point, yet I knew that blaming others wasn't going to bring those students back.

My mother wasn't the only disgusted parent who demanded answers. Parents of victims were filing lawsuits against the church and lining up high-powered Chicago lawyers. Some parents came into the deli and vented their anger and frustration to anyone who would listen. Accusations and finger-pointing flew freely, with one victim's parent even threatening Father Joe Ognibene with a gun. I heard people say how much they hated Monsignor Cussen. Lou Venetti would always try to end the discussion if I was nearby, whispering that I was a survivor of the blaze. I knew people wanted closure and someone to blame. I simply wanted closure.

No amount of encouragement coming from adults or the church seemed to help the hurt deep inside me. Something else brought me peace—something that would open a door I could walk through and lose myself inside.

My healing began with music.

"Hi, Mr. Friga. Can you stay for a few moments? I'd like you to see how well Jonny is doing."

The cool young man in the dark-framed glasses was Vince Geraci, the music teacher I had started working with in the spring of 1959. He was a local musician who taught music during the day and played professionally downtown at a supper club at night. Vince invited my father into the soundproof studio I practiced in.

"Show your father how you can name the notes," Vince told me.

I loved this game we played. He had me sit in the corner with my back to him as he played notes on the piano and asked me their names. My answers were right most of the time. As he showed my father this particular talent of mine, I guessed all the right notes.

"He has a nearly perfect pitch," Vince explained to my father. "He can identify the names of the notes without an instrument for reference. He has a better ear than I do."

My father looked proud but not surprised. He had been the one to recognize my love for music at an early age, noticing my ability to sing tunes from *Your Hit Parade* and play the old upright piano at Pat's Tavern from the time I was four. I had figured out how to boogie-woogie with two hands on that piano. My parents had seen me audition for and make the boys' choir at Our Lady of the Angels School. Even though I was only in second grade at the time, I had made first chair alto.

Dad was amazed at how much I could do without ever having taken a single lesson. After seeing ads for a local music school, he surprised me with private music lessons at the American School of Music on Armitage Avenue. It didn't matter that my father had to sacrifice ten dollars a week of his hard-earned paycheck; he knew it was time to start me on my musical journey.

When I first arrived at the music school, they asked if I wanted to take guitar or accordion lessons. Since my hands weren't quite big enough to master the neck of the guitar, the choice was made for me. Accordions were light and easy to manage compared to pianos, not to mention that they didn't need to be tuned regularly. My accordion—a Galanti—cost my parents four hundred dollars. Since that was more than they could afford, my father bought the red Italian-made squeezebox on a payment plan. Even though it wasn't a full-sized accordion but a trainer, I was so small I still needed a booster strap to play, which harnessed me to an instrument half my size.

I listened to Vince brag about my musical abilities to my father. I admired his cool and patient demeanor. He had his union card and was able to make a decent wage playing at night. His example was almost enough to change my desire to become a priest. Almost.

"Jonny can hear a song a few times and sing it perfectly," Vince said. "This is both a good thing and a bad thing. It's great that he can play a song almost immediately, but the bad thing is he doesn't read all the notes printed on the page, and he puts in extra ones that sound good to him."

As someone who dearly loved music himself, I could tell this only lit my father's fervor for dreaming about my future. He would be my first fan and end up becoming my biggest.

I was Vince's last lesson of the day, so Mom took me on the bus at six o'clock on Wednesday nights, and Dad picked me up in the Oldsmobile. Eventually, I learned to ride my bike to the music school two miles away, and Dad stashed the bike in the trunk for the trip home. Since Hal was only a year old, Mom watched him and Tom while Dad and I stopped at Pat's Tavern, his favorite watering hole, on the way home.

Some nights as I followed my father into the tavern, I'd notice the stiffness in his step. I knew he was wearing his back brace and was probably sorer than usual from the intense work at the print shop. The Scotch and water my father always ordered at Pat's seemed to loosen him up.

My father would give me quarters to put into the jukebox. There were so many great tunes to choose from, like "Great Balls of Fire" by Jerry Lee Lewis and Bobby Day's "Rockin' Robin," or "La Bamba" by Ritchie Valens and The Coasters' "Yakety Yak." The tunes always brought a little joy and cheer, like The Coasters' "Charlie Brown," which made me laugh when the low voice would say, "Why's everybody always pickin' on me?" Or the upbeat "At the Hop" by Danny & the Juniors, which made you want to move.

As the tunes played, I strolled over to the piano in the corner of Pat's and tried to see if I could pick out the melodies I heard. One night, a man at the bar saw me playing, and after a few minutes, he and my father were talking about my accordion lessons.

"What is he gonna do with all those lessons, Len?" I heard the man ask.

My father took a drag on a Chesterfield and answered, "He's gonna be a famous musician and play in front of thousands someday."

I felt embarrassed. "Dad, don't say that . . . I don't . . ."

He gave me his confident glance while sitting on the barstool. "Son, you've got special music in you. You're gonna write and play it, and the world will know about you when you've grown up."

As I sipped my ginger ale, I knew Dad had a vision for me and music.

Determined to master my weekly lessons, I practiced for an hour or two every day. My repertoire grew quickly as I learned familiar peasant songs that were popular for beginning accordion students—polkas from the Slovak states, jigs from the Irish songbook, and bouncy Italian dance numbers like the tarantella and "Funiculì, Funiculà."

The Italian songs I brought home were a hit at the deli. Lou could hear me upstairs in our apartment studying classic melodies he knew and cherished as a child. After I'd been playing for about six months, Lou reckoned I was ready for my first public performance. He had several of his patrons over for a glass of homemade wine. I had to have Lou drag the accordion case down the stairs into the store. The men from the old country were sitting in wooden folding chairs that Katie had set up especially for the night's festivities.

"You boys all know this is Jonny from upstairs, huh? He's gonna play some songs from the old country, just for us tonight, so put your hands together and make him feel welcome!" announced Lou.

"I've only been playing for six months, so I don't know that much yet," I explained.

"That's okay, Jonny. The only thing these guys can play is the radio!" said Lou. He repeated what he had said to his cronies in Italian, and the room exploded in laughter.

I started my recital with "Santa Lucia," went into "'O sole mio," and then the lively folk dance called the tarantella. Lou and the others had tears in their eyes as they watched my fingers work their way across the buttons and keys. The Italians began singing along in their native tongue, and I got to hear the lyrics that went with the melodies I had learned. I felt magic happen as their voices soared along with my instrument. *I'm taking them back to Italy on a little musical trip,* I thought. Mom stood behind the counter with Lou sipping a glass of Chianti, beaming like a proud parent. When my recital ended, Laurie took me to a glass of wine he had poured on the counter and handed me the bread.

"Dip the bread and soaka in da wine, Jonny" came the familiar phrase I had heard many times.

"You make a me so proud, Jonny, so proud!" Laurie said, and he hugged me.

"Hey, everybody, 'Muscadine Jonny'—he's a good accordion player, huh?"

The Italians all nodded their heads in approval and clapped and cheered again. I hugged my mom, ate the wine-soaked bread, and shook hands with all of Lou's cronies.

"Nan, your son is incredible! Thank you, Jonny. You made me so happy with your music," said Lou.

The applause and affection I received would be reported to my father later when he came home from work. "He played those songs without a mistake and had them all singing and clapping right down in the deli!" Mom told him.

"I'll bet you weren't even nervous, were you, son?"

"It was really fun watching them go crazy for those old songs," I answered.

"Well, it's just the beginning for you," Dad said as he gave me a hug.

The river of time kept flowing as the school was rebuilt; I became a stock boy for Venetti's deli; and Mom caught the measles that caused her to go temporarily blind. The latter circumstance had caused me to momentarily become reacquainted with the Jesus I had been trying to forget since the fire—as I prayed to the Lord to heal my mother. Thankfully, Mom did eventually have her eyesight restored, yet this was also the beginning of her painful odyssey with multiple sclerosis, something the doctors knew little about in 1960.

Before going back to the newly built Our Lady of the Angels School in September 1960, I couldn't help feeling dread, like so many other kids felt. Mom was among those observers who didn't like the new, modern look of the building.

"It's cold and ugly," she said. "The old building was classic and sophisticated. This building doesn't look anything like the church it's next to."

I didn't mind, however. "I'm just glad to be going to my school again." Most of the returning students felt the same way.

On that first day back, I felt nervous. Carol Shabel was in another class, but at least I had her sister, Cathy, who was still a good friend. Echoes of the past followed me down the hallways and through the doorways. I ended up telling my parents that if I couldn't focus on homework, I wanted to transfer.

As my confirmation in the Catholic Church approached, I tried my best to forget about those screaming kids with their hair on fire who called out from second-floor windows and jumped to their deaths and the hysterical parents who wailed as they wandered the streets trying to find their children—or their children's bodies. I tried to focus on other things and move on with my life, but every once in a while, the anger and disappointment popped up.

If the church can't handle the truth about the fire, how can they tell me what I'm supposed to believe in?

I'd never had any doubt about my faith until now, and it worried me. I carried it around like a book in my backpack, one I never took out and shared with others. I simply became as busy as I could be to keep my mind off any depressing feelings.

Dad eventually announced that he and Mom had been looking for a new house to buy, noting that the fire had caused our neighborhood to change and that there was increasing violence in nearby neighborhoods. We ended up moving to a place in the suburbs near O'Hare Airport called Schiller Park.

After hearing the news, I knew what I needed to do, so I said to my father one evening, "Dad, if we move, I want to go to Cameron with Tommy next year."

My dad raised his eyebrows, folded his arms, and paused for a second. "Sounds like you've made up your mind, son."

"Yeah. I don't like remembering everything at our school. Sometimes it makes me really sad."

My father nodded his head. "Well, even though OLA is a better school, it'll do you some good to be around different kids for a change. Tommy is happy, and you can walk your brother to school every day. That might be fun for the two of you."

"Yeah, that *would* be fun," I said.

"They've got a playground where we can play baseball," Tommy added.

"Then it's settled," Mom said. "You'll go to Cameron next year with your brother."

"What about my job at the deli?" I asked.

"Son, you'll have to say good-bye to Katie and Lou when the time comes," Dad said. "Maybe you can get a paper route or something after we move."

I said my good-byes to my school and neighborhood in the summer of 1962. That same year, the papers finally printed a story about a thirteen-year-old boy who confessed to setting the Our Lady of the Angels School on fire. He had previously started other fires around Cicero, a nearby town. Despite the boy's testimony to the city's reputable fire investigators, the presiding judge threw the case out of court on the grounds that the testimony was obtained illegally. Cardinal Albert Gregory Meyer, who was rumored to be friends with the Catholic judge, was unofficially quoted as saying he couldn't live with "one of their own" being pinned with the crime.

Many blamed the city for their antiquated fire laws, while some blamed the Catholic Church for the fire. Regardless of who was to blame, the surrounding neighborhood and parish died a slow death, along with the faith of some of those who lived there.

EIGHT

"HOUSE OF THE RISING SUN"

In the summer of 1964, Cheryl Forrest and a Cordovox captured my attention, though if I had to be honest, I dreamed more of the new electric accordion than I did of the pretty girl I took to the eighth-grade prom. Both, however, were uncertain bets in my life at the time. With high school approaching, I spent a lot of time with Cheryl and assumed she was my girlfriend, though it turned out someone much older had eyes for her. As far as the Cordovox went, Vince Geraci, my accordion teacher, had bought one and was raving about all the amazing sounds it could make.

"Look—it's basically an organ," Vince showed me. "The accordion is used as a controller."

The Cordovox had forty vacuum tubes in one cabinet and an amp and speakers in another. The accordion could be played at the same time, or it could be buttoned up and used strictly as an organ. The buttons on the left-hand side triggered an upright bass sound. It even had a volume pedal that could do bends like a Hawaiian guitar.

"For a thousand bucks you can be a one-man band," Vince told me.

I knew I had to have it.

After attending Cameron Elementary in sixth grade, I went to Lincoln Elementary for seventh and eighth grades. It was there I met a fiery, twentysomething Jewish redhead who directed the school choir. Rosana Klich meant business and also played a mean piano.

Since I had one of the better voices in the group, Rosana paid more attention to me from the start, so I asked her if she would come to our house to give me piano lessons. She knew I had close to perfect pitch and had an understanding of music notation, so she not only worked with me on technique but also taught me music theory—the nuts and bolts of harmony and songwriting.

I had been a part of a musical group before, having sung with a special boys' choir at OLA that sang Gregorian hymns at Mass for special occasions. There had been eight of us, and we sang *a cappella* entirely in Latin with no time signature, following our director and flowing as she led us through the ancient music from Pope Gregory's reign. It was an elite group, so to have been chosen was an honor. All the boys had nearly perfect pitch.

That changed over the summer between fourth grade and fifth grade when my voice dropped as I began puberty. When I returned to sing that fall, the director said I could no longer sing with the group, since my higher register had vanished. Devastated, I would have to learn how to sing all over again with my changed voice.

Convincing my dad to rent a piano took some doing, so I agreed to give up my lessons with my hip musical mentor, Vince Geraci. I started with Rosana as soon as the old Knabe baby grand was moved into our living room. My left hand had grown used to being turned around like a claw from playing the buttons on the accordion, so we first worked on drills to strengthen and coordinate it with my right hand. Being used to playing horizontally on the accordion, my hands had to adjust to a more vertical position and learn to move together. I remember the way they would ache, even when I played a simple scale. I was determined to get past these setbacks and master the positions on this new instrument. I knew there were many more possibilities of tonal expression on the piano than the accordion could achieve.

My determination and refusal to accept my limitations wasn't true just for music. I also found myself trying out for sports for the first time. Unlike OLA, my new school had a nice gym and a strong PE department. Since I didn't have a job after school anymore, I decided to try out for basketball and track. I was good at playing accordion and singing songs, but physically I was out of shape compared to the rest of the boys in my class. I had some catching up to do.

I made the basketball team but sat on the bench most of the time. Coach Belza was a hard-nosed teacher who had little patience for my timid nature on the court and my lack of skills and knowledge about the game. Still, I was determined to learn and adapt to his system and become one of the B team reserves. I will always remember how Coach Belza kicked my butt after practice. In one-on-one sessions, he pushed me to be aggressive and taught me how to guard in the paint, how to set screens, and how to do the pick-and-roll. By the end of the season, I was in shape and learning a game I came to love.

In the same way, Rosana pushed me in my lessons, teaching me theory—the basics of how chords, scales, and notation worked in tandem. I learned quickly and was hungry to study every song I played. I identified the tonic, wrote out the positions of chord inversions, and learned the notation symbols. Rosana also sensed my love for improvisation, so at the end of every lesson, she let me make something up out of the blue and expand on it. She had me write down the basic chart of my compositions after she left and checked it the next week.

Three years later, in eighth grade, I was asked to perform one of my compositions for a school play. The song was about a girl I had a crush on—Madalyn. Since the piano was off to one side of the stage, Rosana convinced me to go to the center of the stage to play the accordion and sing into the microphone. Despite my nerves, the song came off perfectly and eventually got me a kiss from Madalyn. A few parties and dances later, I realized I wasn't going to end up with her. Ironically, at one of those same teen parties, I met Cheryl Forrest, a cute eighth-grader with whom I ended up playing a kissing game called Seven Minutes in Heaven.

By this time, I was in my first band, The Futuras. I had become friends with a Ferris Bueller–type guy—the kind of guy who seemed to have had everyone and everything in the neighborhood wired, the one who always knew what was happening and where. I'd been to Randy Turner's house in Franklin Park and watched him play his Gibson Melody Maker. He'd been taking lessons and seemed quite confident we could put a band together.

"I know this drummer—Pete Bruno," Randy said. "We can rehearse in his basement."

Pete was a solid drummer who played in the school band and had a feel for the music of the day. The three of us, along with Larry Ostberg, who played a guitar and owned a new Magnatone amp, headed over to Pete's house after school.

"Listen to this," Pete said one day as he blasted The Ventures on the huge hi-fi stereo turntable in his living room, a German-made Grundig console. He loved surf bands like The Ventures, while I loved the English bands The Animals and The Zombies and their songs "House of the Rising Sun" and "Time of the Season."

We played our favorite songs over and over and then tried to copy them in Pete Bruno's basement. I used my accordion like an organ. It was electrified with a pickup and plugged into an Airline amplifier from Montgomery Ward, and we were rockin'—well, sort of. I laugh now when I think about me on that little red accordion trying to pull off rock songs. We practiced three times a week and quickly learned eight songs.

The Futuras made their debut at the opening of a new chicken rotisserie restaurant in Franklin Park. I was excited to be performing in my first-ever gig, one where I even sang lead on a few of the songs. With the scent of roasted chicken surrounding us, my fellow bandmates and I jammed on the flatbed truck sitting next to the restaurant,

While I played, I carefully watched the old Turner mic connected to Larry's amp, one that had two channels and reverb that sounded decent. I'd already been shocked on the lips a few times from touching the microphone when it wasn't grounded properly, and I had static on my shoes. Randy played lead and Larry played rhythm guitar. Pete Bruno played the drum solo, note for note, on The Ventures' "Caravan." People seemed to find us interesting enough to hang around a while and eat some chicken. Performing on the truck felt almost as good as the concerts I used to give for the Italians at Lou's deli.

After a couple of years of living on Sterling Lane in our subdivision in Schiller Park, my brothers and I had gotten over the culture shock of moving from the colorful Italian village in downtown Chicago to a tract home in the suburbs with lots of room to run wild. I was relieved to be away from memories and reminders of the fire, yet I missed my job at the deli—as well as Lou and Katie and the twins. The transition from city to suburb in the winter of 1962 felt like flipping a channel on the television. It wasn't like I was purposely trying to forget, but the totally new environment, complete with new friends and surroundings, provided the perfect way out from living in the shadows of the OLA tragedy.

Every now and then, a memory jumped out of the shadows, like the one night at a PTA meeting my mother and I attended at Lincoln Elementary. The group decided to show a fire safety movie, and halfway into the film were clips of my old school in flames, complete with kids crying and parents running and screaming. I felt like I could smell the smoke all over again. My tears fell so fast I almost didn't notice them. Without saying a word, Mom grabbed my hand and quickly yanked me out of the dark room and headed for the exit before I even knew what was happening. When we got out into the street, she wept and cursed my new school for showing such a terrible thing. OLA had become the model for what not to build when it came to schools and fire safety.

Even though I had subconsciously let go of my life on Augusta Boulevard, I still had chances to reconnect, like the times Lou and Katie came to our house in Schiller Park for dinner and for our birthdays. Or the few times I asked Dad to take us to church at OLA so I could see Carol and her parents. Those trips seemed less frequent the longer we spent in the suburbs.

With The Futuras' first gig under our belt, our newly formed band signed up for the local Battle of The Bands contest held at the VFW hall. Mom said we needed to look different so the judges would remember us and decided to make us matching gold pullover shirts for the gig. Aunt Boops even got into the act and monogrammed the front pocket with a black "F." Looking like a band of gypsies, we played our two songs well but finished in third place—and we took home a small trophy for our troubles. Encouraged by our newfound success, we planned to take our band into high school as freshmen. We planned to play in the East Leyden gym on Friday nights, and Randy Turner's older sister, Sue, offered to book us.

By the time The Futuras were scheduled to play a sock hop the second week of October in my first semester at East Leyden High School, I had already been dumped by my summer sweetheart, Cheryl Forrest, and had gotten punched in the face by Fuzzy Bogden, the jealous boyfriend of the freshman girl whose locker was next to mine. My high school consisted of a fairly large campus that encompassed two city blocks in Franklin Park, and like so many other schools in Chicago during the 1960s, it was the scene of a major social class conflict. On one side were the "greasers," who dressed in Italian knit shirts, wore baggy gray pants and combat boots or pointy-toed Italian dress shoes. Greasers usually loved Motown and rock, bands like The Chessmen and The Kinks. Since they didn't study much and were inevitably headed for Vietnam, they were out to prove how tough they were. The other class was the "soces" or "doopers," which stood for "Dear Old Oak Parkers." They usually wore jeans with madras shirts and penny loafers. They liked folk music and folk rock, artists like Dylan and The Mamas & the Papas. Since they usually got good grades, they were college bound.

I dressed like a greaser most of the time, minus the baggy grays and the T-shirt. For the upcoming sock hop we were going to play at, Randy would be wearing a letterman jacket with real leather sleeves, so I wanted one too. The problem was Mom and Dad wouldn't give me cash for it, so I needed a job to earn my own money. As a thirteen-year-old, I didn't have many choices, so I settled on a local paper route. I delivered the *Tribune* and the *Sun-Times* to about one hundred households in a three-mile radius of Sterling Lane. I bought a second-hand Schwinn Panther, the kind that had a shock absorber on the front fork, and attached a huge basket on the handlebars—and I was in business.

On a Friday night that October, The Futuras played their first dance in the gym. Decked out in wine-colored sharkskin jackets, white shirts, and cross ties, we took the stage and rocked our school to a few sets of classics. The song of the night was "Louie Louie," just like we thought it would be. We played it three times that evening and got a great response. The ambient sound of the wood floor made the drums sound thunderous and gave the guitars a low, echoing sound. I think they paid us forty dollars for the evening. Randy's sister waived her commission, so we each got ten bucks. My first time playing music in front of my classmates felt empowering and well worth all the work I was doing at home with Rosana, my piano teacher. It felt natural to be performing music, and the applause after each song made me wish the gigs would never end.

After the gym concert, we were asked to play at several parties around town that next summer, so between the money I made from the gigs, my paper route, and birthday money, I eventually saved up more than one thousand dollars—enough to get the Cordovox. Randy Turner knew a guy who sold musical instruments out of his basement. His name was Al Hagenburger, an old Jewish hustler who had lost his music store on the west side. Al said he could get me the Cordovox I wanted for two hundred dollars cheaper than the local music store sold it for.

On a Saturday morning in the fall of 1965, my Dad took me over to Al Hagenburger's house to pick up the Cordovox. We took the stairs leading to a basement apartment, and when we walked in, we saw boxes of musical instruments lining the walls and piled up to the ceiling. No one knew where Al got his goods, and no one asked. He had the Cordovox set up and plugged in so I could play it as soon as I got there. It smelled new—the leather straps, the Naugahyde covering on the amps. I took it through some new numbers I had been working on. It sounded huge. The buttons that triggered the bass were solid, and the keyboard sounded similar to a Lowry organ. The accordion was average-sounding, but with the electronics playing alongside, immediately the accordion was cool again. I knew I could make the instrument sing from the time I played the first song. We settled up with Al and quickly loaded the unit into my father's Oldsmobile.

On the way home, I worked on my father to get Tom some drums and told him how cool it would be for both of us to jam in the basement. "We could be like The Everly Brothers and harmonize," I said. My father nodded as I went on and on. My mother had heard about Tom's interest in the drums and was worried about the noise.

Mastering my new instrument came quickly as I learned to mix the various organ patches into the popular songs of the day. Excited to try it with The Futuras, I found it had just the right volume to be heard above the drums and guitars. Although it was an accordion, it added a distinctive sound by using the organ sounds and the bass with the bellows shut.

Eventually, at my brother's request, I took fifty bucks he had saved and went to Al Hagenburger to buy him a snare drum, drumsticks, brushes, and a cymbal. It wasn't a brand-name drum set like Ludwig or Slingerland—it was a Japanese copy—but it was good enough to practice and learn on. Despite my mother's earlier protests, she realized how much this meant to her son.

Pete, our drummer in The Futuras, gave my brother a few lessons, and he was off and running. Tommy quickly learned to play rhythms and different grooves and perfected his technique in the basement after school. It was only a few months before we were playing songs together—rock, pop, and swing. Jamming with him, I realized he had great tempo and feel. As a drummer, Tommy was a natural. He eventually put his own band together with a neighbor kid, Jimmy Spadero. They played at a few of his grade-school dances, and Tommy got a reputation as a wonder-boy drummer.

In the summer of 1966, while working hard on my paper route, along with a new summer job in a steel mill that made silo parts, I continued to long to one day play music for money. I dreamed of being like my accordion teacher, Vince Geraci, of being able to teach music and also to play it night after night. That summer, my first step at achieving that dream came true.

Someone from the VFW hall down the street had heard about me and The Futuras, but since they had a small stage, they only wanted a solo act to play on Friday and Saturday nights. I told them my brother could play the drums pretty well, so we could do it as a duo. For two weeks, my brother and I rehearsed standards and Top 40 songs for the weekend. Singing lead was new for me, but Rosana gave me some tips about the keys I sounded best in. Determined to make music my full-time job, I was off and running as a young crooner. We made thirty dollars the first week and were asked back for four more weeks. Thrilled with our payday, Tommy and I headed downtown to buy matching blazers.

The second week my brother and I played, a middle-aged Italian gentleman came up to me during our break. Dressed in a sport coat, with his gray curly hair slicked back and a thick cigar clinched between his teeth, the man pulled a business card out of his wallet and introduced himself.

"I'm Jimmy DelGuidice. I play the sax around town and lead a band."

Jimmy told me he liked my style and wanted me and my voice for some weekend gigs. He had a drummer, and they played private parties such as weddings and bar mitzvahs.

"Do you have wheels?" he asked.

"Not yet, sir, but I'm sure my mom would let me borrow her car on the weekends."

"All right then, son. Call me sometime this week. I'll get you a fake book so you can learn the songs we usually play. The standards and wedding stuff."

He asked if I read music, which I did, and I told him I was studying theory and harmony.

"How long you here for?" he asked. "Do you belong to the union?"

"Four weekends is all. I haven't joined yet."

I tried to sound all professional, just like Vince Geraci might sound.

"You'll need to go downtown and get your card next week," Jimmy told me. "We are strictly a union outfit."

"Got it."

He turned and waved, put on his hat, and left the hall.

My brother wanted to know if they needed a drummer, but I told him they had one already. I could tell Tommy was hurt that I had accepted Jimmy's offer, but I told him it was only a four-week gig. Besides, I had been the one to get him into the VFW gig. And I did need the money for a car and for college. But as that day came to an end, I could tell something had changed between my brother and me. It wouldn't be the first time we would be pulled in different directions.

Jimmy delivered the fake book as promised, more than three

hundred pages of bootlegged sheet-music lead sheets bound in a plastic spiral binder. I'd seen one before, but nothing like this. Jimmy circled the songs he wanted me to learn. I spent hours playing, starting with Hoagy Carmichael's "Stardust." In a few weeks, I had memorized twenty songs and was ready to head out to my first performance. Jimmy turned out to be a solidly average sax player, and his drummer was the old fogy I had suspected.

These weren't the most exciting shows, with the only "rock" song being "Hang On Sloopy" by The McCoys, but Jimmy paid me in cash and I worked almost every weekend. Sometimes they were cocktail parties downtown; sometimes they were elaborate weddings. My mother agreed to let me borrow her Oldsmobile and eventually let me buy it from her. While my weekends were booked solid, my friends at high school were asking me to join them in drinking parties at the bowling alley. When I'd pass, they'd roll their eyes and tease me about becoming a wedding singer. I didn't care what they thought. I was making enough bank to quit my paper route. Because of all the bookings, Jimmy said I really needed to head downtown to the musicians' union. Reps would come periodically to shows and check everyone. I needed to get my union card.

Having been a paperboy for four years, I relished the fact that I could sleep in on weekends, something I hadn't done since eighth grade. It didn't last long, however. Saint Maria Goretti Catholic Church asked me to play the pipe organ at their Sunday services. That meant more music to learn and a new instrument to try to tame. I was thankful to Rosana for giving me the skill to read music and thrilled to finally be a professional, card-carrying musician.

The dream of becoming a priest had gone up in flames on that fateful day in third grade. The dream of becoming a musician, however, had come to life, and by the time I was a junior in high school, I realized I could make a living doing what I loved.

THE DOOR TO ROG'S INN OPENS, AND I FOLLOW MY FATHER TO A FAMILIAR barstool. The place smells like smoke, French fries, and stale bourbon. I immediately see him—a small man at the piano bar, a Cordovox strapped to his shoulders as he plays the bass line with his left hand, a bass drum with his right foot, and a burning jazz solo on the piano with his left.

The notes are different. Creative. Playful. All over the place, but somehow fitting in beautifully. "Pennies from Heaven" has never sounded so magical and unique.

Dad and I meet the jazz musician with a hunchback and a slight limp. Vic Scaccia's voice is slightly slurred as he says lots of words like *cats* and *joint* and *cool* while we talk about the Cordovox. Soon I'm playing and discussing and studying music with Vic every Saturday afternoon in his basement, with my dad by my side.

Another door opens, this one to a local piano bar in the city that Vic connects me with. With my union card in my pocket, dressed in a bow tie and dinner jacket, I play and sing four sets of standards and Top 40 hits. Dad is in the audience, pacing himself on Johnnie Walker Red whisky and water and trying not to chain-smoke. He never complains as he sits through long evenings and even helps me pack up my gear on Saturday mornings.

The door to the VFW hall also opens, with Tommy accompanying me for the set. My brother is thirteen and is playing the drums like a pro. During a break, a heavyset man with an unlit cigar approaches us, telling us he knows a lot of people in town and can book us in lots of cool joints.

Soon Tommy and I are wearing matching tuxedos, walking through the door at the Pheasant Run playhouse in St. Charles as the Johnny Lee Duo, performing nightly at the Baker's Lounge. Two kids knocking down three hundred dollars a week for three nights. The big man with the cigar knows what he's doing. During two summers, we meet celebrities like Larry Hagman, Stefanie Powers, Dyan Cannon, and Hermione Gingold, who are all starring in various plays held at the theatre.

The door to our house opens, and we find Dad looking tired from work and having little to show for it. With a twinge of guilt at our sudden good fortune, Tommy and I decide to pay Dad three hundred dollars a month to help with household bills.

I blink and see the door to the Drake Hotel in Chicago opening for the night of our junior prom in the springtime. During the dance, I join the orchestra to croon a few songs in the grand ballroom, and all the while, a certain someone watches from the back.

I'm already playing to the ladies, and I haven't even graduated from high school yet.

NINE

"BEGINNINGS"

The moment I stepped foot into the small church, I felt something different. It was like standing on a mountaintop and feeling the wind whipping around me, except the stirring was happening inside my soul. I would never have been at that church on a Wednesday evening for a Bible study if it weren't for the tall, pretty blonde by my side.

Virginia Olson was a senior from East Leyden. I had noticed her in history class my junior year. She was the younger sister of an alum who had attended our high school on crutches, suffering from chronic polio. From the first day of class, I knew we would have a thing for each other. She seemed so comfortable to be with, so familiar. She was smart and funny and a member of the swim team. I was captivated by her and smitten in a matter of weeks.

Ginny, as everyone called her, knew me from the gym dances and loved the fact that I was in a band. We felt safe in each other's arms and shared all of our secrets with each other. Besides making out with me in the forest preserves, she invited me over to her house, where I met her parents and her brother. I had dinner with them frequently and later found myself in her room with the door closed, where she played Johnny Mathis records. It wasn't long before we were kissing to songs like "Chances Are." It would get so late that by the time I got home, my parents were wondering what exactly was going on between Virginia and their oldest son.

By the time Ginny told me about this Bible church she had stumbled across, I trusted her and would have followed her anywhere. I didn't know exactly what this Bible study/prayer thing was all about, but the moment I walked into the modest sanctuary without the ornate architecture and stained-glass windows I was accustomed to, I knew the Spirit of God was present. It was exactly what Ginny had told me I'd feel too.

"There's a feeling of grace there," she explained before we had gone. "The pastor is anointed."

I can't for the life of me remember the name of this small church, but it wasn't a traditional Catholic service at all. It was my first experience stepping foot into an evangelical church. There was a lot of praying and people falling down in the aisles going on there. The word of God was preached, and at the end of the sermon, there was a massive altar call.

Even before the music played and everybody sang "I Surrender All" and I felt compelled to step out into the aisle to walk toward the preacher, something was happening to me. I didn't fear going up to the front of the church. I needed to go. I wanted to be completely open and free, knowing I needed the love the pastor spoke about. It was a love I had left behind ten years ago.

That third-grade kid had been waiting for a long time. I was a senior now, months before graduation, yet in some way the only things that seemed to have truly grown in me were the scars I carried. I stepped into the aisle and walked to the Reverend, with Ginny by my side.

As the Reverend came up to me and placed his hand on my back, I began to cry. It didn't matter that I was in front of strangers, that people were watching me, that I was eighteen and still anxious and immature. I didn't care that I was crying in front of my girlfriend. If I could have seen her, I would have noticed Ginny was crying too.

I tried to explain to the man embracing me why I was weeping, but it was difficult to tell my full story, to share with him everything that had happened, to fully show the weight of the load I had been carrying for so long. He simply listened to me, telling me things were okay, telling me I was loved.

"I haven't thought about God in so long," my choked-up voice muttered.

Somehow the Reverend understood.

"You've been running away for a long time," he told me. "You don't need to run anymore."

I felt God's Spirit again and prayed to him for the first time in a long time.

It's been so long. I'm so sorry. I'm sorry I've ignored you all this time.

The tears didn't come from shame, however, or from the hurt and pain I had muzzled and made numb all these years. I wept because I realized that God was still inside me. My Lord and Savior had never left me. Just as Jesus had been there for me at the fire, he was there in this small church too.

"Come to me, all you who are weary and burdened, and I will give you rest."

I held the pastor's hand and continued to weep as I prayed with him. Ginny stood by me and prayed for me too.

God hadn't abandoned me, even though I had abandoned him. All this time, he was still there. Still watching over me and loving me and waiting for me to come back to him.

Thank you, Jesus. Thank you for being there. For inviting me to come to you once again.

Like an album I once listened to over and over again, I had slid God back into a sleeve and then forgotten where I placed the record. It had been too long since hearing his voice. I didn't want to neglect it ever again. I couldn't.

Virginia and I attended senior prom together, dancing the night away and staying out all night and then driving to the sand dunes in Indiana the next day with a buddy and his date. I was grounded for two weeks for not telling my parents where I was, and by then, Mom had grown hostile about my relationship with Ginny. One day I found her in my room, where she had rifled through my drawers to find the many love letters Ginny had written to me on perfumed stationary.

"You and this girl have become way too involved as far as I'm concerned," Mom yelled. "She's even wearing the class ring we bought you around her neck. I told you not to give that to her. I want things to be over between the two of you. You're no longer welcome in this house with our family as long as you're involved with this girl. Do you understand?"

How dare you, I thought, knowing I needed to get out of there. My mother had invaded my personal space. She'd read everything Virginia had written, which was intended for my eyes only. Things between us quickly spun out of control. Because of her ultimatum, my mother refused to attend my graduation, leaving my dad alone in the audience with my brothers. As the ceremony came to an end, tossing my cap into the air in the gym seemed like a euphoric release.

I know now that my mother's actions were in part due to the multiple sclerosis she was battling, a fight she didn't even fully know she was in the midst of. The disease prompted much of her irrational behavior. Still, when I went to ask my pastor at Saint Maria Goretti for advice and laid out the options my mother had given me, he told me that I could get a room for forty dollars a month at the Irving Park YMCA. My father would have to sign for me, but at least I'd be away.

I'm a man now, and it's time to move on with my life.

Dad sympathized with me, feeling Mom had no right to give me an ultimatum like that, especially since my relationship with Virginia seemed healthy and genuine.

The next morning, I called Aunt Boops, who cleared out her guest room for me up in Glenview and came to pick me up. Saddened to hear about my mother's behavior, she listened to my side of the story and cooked a beautiful dinner. Boops convinced my father it was best for me to leave home.

When Dad and I stood at the front desk of the YMCA, he appeared a bit lost.

"You can sign right there, sir," the manager behind the desk told him.

For a moment, Dad resisted and turned to me with a rare look of defeat.

"You don't have to do this," he said.

"Yeah, I do."

"We can make things right. I can help smooth things over with your mother."

"I'm eighteen."

"I know, but that still doesn't mean you have to move out," my father said.

"What I do with my life and who I date is my business," I said. "Mom can't tell me who I can and can't date. She can't just go into my room and pry into my life like that."

He nodded, looking down at the sheet of paper he needed to sign.

"She shouldn't have done that," Dad admitted. "It was wrong."

When he looked at me again, he could tell I had made my decision. He took the pen, took a deep breath, and scribbled his name—signing me up for my new home.

Even though I'd been accepted to Northwestern University's school of journalism, I knew my father didn't have that kind of money, so I decided on the Chicago Music College at Roosevelt University. I took the northwest train from the YMCA and got off at a stop at Wabash, only a block away from school. One morning right after starting school, I saw a line of soldiers standing at attention along Wabash Avenue with bayonets mounted on their rifles. All of a sudden, the scenes I had seen on television of military forces and protestors had appeared in the city I had grown up in.

It was the end of August 1968, and the Democratic Convention was held in downtown Chicago. A group known as the Yippies, led by Abbie Hoffman, had come from different cities in the United States and descended on the Windy City in droves. Some people feared that they intended to disrupt the proceedings and intentionally cause chaos and wreak havoc. Police officers were being taunted and beginning to retaliate, not to mention getting bad press daily. The National Guard had finally been called in.

Mayor Richard Daley struggled with the proper protocol and was criticized for the actions the police force took during the riots. It seemed he was not going to let this radical group have their way. Many of my classmates disappeared from class during these years. I never knew if they were drafted or had lost interest, yet I knew I was going to study hard in my little room at the YMCA and stay in school.

The college of music at Roosevelt University was located at the corner of Congress and Wabash Avenue. The school was a good fit for what I wanted to study: piano, theory, composition, and voice. The conservatory on the ninth floor seemed like an oasis at Roosevelt, which was peppered with students who were Black Panthers, Marxists, atheists, and even neo-Nazis. Posters for their various meetings were stapled onto the walls at the entrance of the school.

My new piano teacher, Mr. Frederick Schauwecker, a retired accompanist for famous opera performers, introduced me to a whole new technique. For my first few lessons, he had me spring my hands and fingers from my lap and let them fall on the piano, surrendering my elbows and arms as my hands and fingers stayed curved like a ballerina doing a plié. Weeks of lessons went by until I perfected his method of color and tone. With my fingers having the weight of my arms and shoulders, I could go from a whisper to a roar and make the piano behave like a symphony orchestra. Mr. Schauwecker always said I had the energy of a wild horse, and if he could harness and refine it, I could have virtuoso possibilities. But my sight reading didn't reach the level of most students there, so I struggled.

Another remarkable man of discipline and passion who was instrumental in my musical education was Mr. Ralph Dodds, our theory and ear training teacher. During dictation, he made me write out Bach chorales in three different clefs, while the rest of the class wrote in two. On the hottest spring days, he would be in a suit and tie, never even breaking a sweat while the rest of us sat in our seats wringing wet and fanning ourselves. Soon he had me tutoring others in ear training. He gave me extra credit for it, but I would have done it just for the experience. I was amazed that virtuoso players could not discern the difference between a fourth and a fifth, which, for example, is being able to distinguish between a note going from a C to an F and a C going up to a G.

As I began college that fall, the military started enforcing the draft with a heavy hand. Students enrolled in college had to maintain a B average, or they'd be eligible for boot camp and eventually Vietnam. Most of the greasers from my senior class who had no plans for college were shipped off the following fall. Lottery numbers were pulled according to birthdays. As I watched the lottery selection live on TV, my number was announced as 345, so I was exempt from service as long as I maintained good grades in school.

While playing a New Year's Eve gig with my brother and Nick DeBrown, I can recall someone at the dance reporting an ambush in Nam, where the Viet Cong had attacked one hundred soldiers. Several of those young men were our former classmates. The reality was sobering. Here I was, doing this thing I dearly loved—entertaining a festive crowd celebrating the coming year—while guys my age were cut down by gunfire and shredded by enemy explosives.

I devised a plan for myself in case I was drafted.

I'll apply to play in the USO band. I know all the standards and can carry a tune.

Thank God, they never called me. God had another plan for me.

The trio I was a part of with my brother and Nick DeBrown, known as The Brotherhood, had disbanded, so Tommy and I performed as a duo and pocketed more money, dollars I needed to stay in school. Virginia and I dated for those first few college years, yet as she became more interested in smoking pot, I became less interested in her. I kept asking her why she was always getting high, but she enjoyed it and was going to a different school with different friends. I could see the impact it was having on her. She showed up on our dates stoned and acting strange. I was dead set against using drugs, and I refused to smoke with her. Eventually, the distance between us became the reason we would go our separate ways.

While at Roosevelt University, I attended my first real rock concert with Tommy. A group of guys who had attended DePaul University had begun playing Top 40 hits, calling themselves The Big Thing. I had seen them on Rush Street. They had a great sound with a tight brass section. They went on to change their name to Chicago Transit Authority. Their self-titled debut album released by CBS in April 1969 turned out to be a smash record. Their return to their hometown saw them playing their new songs at the Auditorium Theatre at Roosevelt University, a beautiful hall designed by Louis Sullivan.

An early song in the set list was their hit "Beginnings." As the acoustic guitar began to play, soon to be joined by the drums and the keyboard and then the trumpet and sax and finally the trombone, my skin felt electric and my soul unhinged. The six guys played brilliantly. It was remarkable to have seen their transformation from a club band to recording artists. They were simple kids from Chicago with a dream to make it in the music business.

That could be me up there.

The song continued to build as if it was a plane taking off. These guys were truly at the beginning of something magical and legendary. Eventually, they'd be forced, by threat of legal action, to change their band name from Chicago Transit Authority and shorten it to Chicago. Their band would go on to sell millions of albums worldwide, and it continues to make music and tour still today.

It wasn't hard to imagine myself in their shoes. Singing and playing and performing and rocking.

I am *in their shoes.*

I knew this was what I was meant to do. God had shut the door and allowed me to stay out of Vietnam. For what? To end up finishing music school and eventually teaching others? I knew my heart wasn't set on being a teacher, and I wasn't cut out to be a virtuoso.

I needed to focus on songwriting and music. It was time to return home and mend things with my mother and reunite with my brothers, Tommy and Hal.

As Chicago Transit Authority kept telling me over and over, this was "only the beginning."

TEN

"HOLD WHAT YOU'VE GOT"

With the responsibilities of school and a serious girlfriend no longer occupying my time, I focused on music in 1969. Soon life consisted of loading our van and setting out on our musical adventures. We had quite the stash: a Shure Vocal Master PA, a cut down B-3 organ, a Leslie speaker, a Wurlitzer piano, drums, and guitar amps. We also had the perfect vehicle to transport all of it in. Our manager, Everett Slade, knew someone working for the phone company who suggested we buy a used phone truck that was due to be sold at an upcoming auction. Jimmy, Tommy, and I, along with Everett, wanted to get a good deal, so we ended up buying the step van for six hundred dollars—money we had saved from gigs.

Moments after driving it home from the auction that Saturday, we discovered it would only go up to forty-five miles per hour, top speed. The exhaust pipe made a loud and obnoxious sound when we drove it down our quiet street. It was too big to park in our driveway, so Everett arranged for it to be parked at the nearby Holiday Inn on Mannheim Road. Undaunted, we painted our band name on the side and depreciated the truck as a band asset—Everett had the spirit of an accountant in him as well as being a comedian.

Jimmy Benso had joined Tommy and me for the band. I remembered seeing him play at East Leyden when I was a freshman and he was a senior. He had impressed me with his phrasing and chords and was easily the best musician to ever play at the gym on Friday nights. I found out from Randy Turner that Jimmy had done a tour in Vietnam as a platoon sergeant and had returned to his parents' home in Des Plaines. Knowing he would be a perfect addition to play with me and my brother, I went to his house to recruit him. It wasn't easy; Benso hadn't picked up his Gibson L-5 in five years, and when I pulled it out of his closet and handed it to him, tears fell down his cheeks. Memories of his time in Vietnam haunted him. I couldn't imagine serving in the military overseas, but I could empathize with seeing death and carnage firsthand.

Jimmy proved to be a great addition. He knew hip musical chord forms and had a great right hand for rhythm as well. Everett Slade listened and approved of our new member, and in a few weeks we had our first gig at a club called the Easy Street Lounge. We played around the Chicagoland area. Not only could Jimmy play guitar, but he could sing backgrounds and play valve trombone as well. We began doing harmonies, adding songs by The Lettermen and The Vogues, bands that had hit records on the radio. Everett took us clothes shopping and groomed us into a show band like The Swingin' Lads, his buddies—complete with matching outfits, comedy skits, and razor-cut hairdos.

On this particular afternoon, we pulled the truck into our driveway to load our gear for a gig on Mannheim Road. When we were ready to go, I slipped behind the steering wheel, still fairly new at driving a stick, not to mention a huge step van. The loud grumble of the exhaust began as I maneuvered onto our street, bouncing over the curb as I turned. I heard another rumbling noise accompanying us, and it was so loud in the cab I didn't hear anybody outside yelling at me to stop.

After a few moments, I grew concerned at the sound and stopped. When I climbed out of the huge step van, I saw the neighbor's car bumper a few yards behind us. I had accidentally hooked it to the truck and dragged it two houses down on Sterling Lane.

Everett cursed at me in disbelief. "You're gonna kill someone in that thing!"

We all stared at the detached bumper on the street and laughed in amazement.

"Watch out for the beast!" Everett cried out. "It's coming to get you!"

The neighbors joined in our hilarity as we hoisted the bumper off the towing hook on the back of our band truck.

When winter arrived after we'd done a few road trips in the old step van, we discovered the heater didn't work and would cost a fortune to repair. Undaunted again, we bought an oil heater and kept it with us in the front cab. The fumes nearly made my brother and me sick. By the time we got to Cleveland one night, we knew we had to get something else to haul our gear. We sold our beloved van and decided on more practical vehicles.

Jimmy had his station wagon, but he suggested that Tommy and I buy Chevy vans. He saw another musician who had the same van finished off in carpet and reckoned our gear could fit snugly in two of these vehicles. We bought vans and set about screwing hardboard and gluing green shag carpeting on the walls and ceilings. We laid plywood on the floor and got matching green indoor/outdoor carpet to roll the heavy equipment on. Jimmy went a step further and built a closet behind the driver's seat for our clothes and suitcases. There was a door that sealed off the back area so gear couldn't come sliding forward. The vans were incredible. In the end, we were safely and comfortably mobile, ready to take on the USA in our Chevrolets.

While touring Ohio, Missouri, Indiana, and Georgia, our trio made pretty nice money playing a mix of rock and pop. The gigs were great, yet I still considered this to be a starting point and not the final destination. Along with all of our equipment, I was carrying something even more valuable with me.

They were songs I had written. Like me, they had every intention of going somewhere special.

Sometimes you don't have to wait for a door to open. Sometimes you simply let yourself in. That's what I did with Bill Traut, a record producer who had started a Chicago-based garage band record label called Dunwich Records. He had produced hits in the sixties for local bands like The Shadows of Knight ("Gloria") and The American Breed ("Bend Me, Shape Me"). A former jazz musician who played saxophone with pianist Bill Higgins, he knew music and the business.

Feeling good about my songwriting, yet knowing I had a lot to learn, I needed to find someone who knew how to critique my songs. Without an appointment, I walked into the Dunwich Records office downtown and asked for Bill Traut. The receptionist asked for my name and said Bill was in a meeting. Since it was late in the afternoon, toward the end of the workday, I told her I'd wait. Surprisingly, he appeared in the lobby and asked me to come back to his office. I had a tape reel with my song demos we had recorded, and I asked if he'd listen. At the end of each song, he paused the tape deck and commented on the things he liked and didn't. He'd say the intro was too long; the hook in the chorus wasn't strong enough; the lyrics were trite—all were comments I needed to hear to be able to move forward and improve as a songwriter. After he had heard my music, Bill Traut said I was welcome in his office to play my music, as long as I came at the end of the day.

At the same time, I booked time at Golden Voice Recording, which was nestled in the cornfields in Pekin, Illinois. A session had run over by a day or two, and we had to wait to set up our stuff. Dan Fogelberg, a local singer/songwriter, was finishing up his new album. After two days of rehearsal with my brother and Jimmy in a barn Everett had found for us, we were ready to roll tape.

Hard work, talent, and timing can all work together in this business. In this case, the owner of Golden Voice, Jerry Milam, was also the engineer and acoustic designer. He told us he liked our energy and commitment, as well as one of the first songs I'd written, "God Made Woman." He said he wanted to make copies of all the sessions we recorded to see if any of his friends in Nashville and Chicago were interested. I was thrilled about the idea and quickly agreed after I got my copyrights back in the mail.

When I returned home to Schiller Park, I realized I had come a long way from The Futuras. I began to start dreaming about the possibility of my song being heard by some record company. *What if?* and *How cool would it be?* and other questions filled my heart for several months until Jerry Milam called.

"I sent your tape to a guy in Nashville, who loved 'God Made Woman.' His name is Buddy Killen. He wants to sign you to a singles deal."

Buddy was a co-owner of Tree International Publishing, one of the largest music publishers in Nashville, and he had a small label called Dial Records he created to distribute funk records he produced for a soul singer named Joe Tex. Buddy and Joe had their first hit with "Hold What You've Got," which went on to sell more than a million copies by 1966. More hits followed, like the song "Skinny Legs and All," which got tons of airplay back in the late sixties.

"So this is a good thing, right?" I asked him.

"A good thing?" Jerry said with a chuckle. "It's a big deal for Buddy to like your song. He's a force in the business."

Jerry Milam was one of those angels God put in my life, someone who took an interest in me and gave me a chance. Shortly after my nineteenth birthday, I got on a plane for the first time and flew with my dad to Nashville to sign a deal with Buddy Killen. During the flight to Music City, my father bragged to the flight attendants about his son signing his first record deal and how I was only nineteen. It was a Delta flight, and they gave me my first pair of wings. I was so nervous about flying for the first time that I hardly said a word. I simply smiled and nodded as Dad went on about me, hoping the plane wouldn't take a nosedive and end my career before it ever really began.

After Dad and I took a cab to Buddy's office, we met country legend Dottie West in his office that afternoon. Buddy had a twinkle in his eyes as he played my demo, which he cued up on his reel-to-reel for Dottie. The singer who crooned "Here Comes My Baby" looked captivated as she heard young Jon Friga singing his heart out on "God Made Woman."

"Don't you just love that lyric in the chorus?" Buddy asked Dottie. "It really pays off, doesn't it?"

"Sure does," Dottie said in her smooth Southern drawl. "And I love your vibrato. You got a nice sound there, Jonny."

"Really?" I stammered. "Thanks."

I couldn't help blushing. I think my heart was racing the entire time I was in Buddy's office, talking with him and Dottie and signing my first official record and publishing contract with an acclaimed producer and music man out of Nashville. I felt I was another step closer to my father's dream.

Buddy Killen was a maverick, someone who did things his own way and didn't care what others thought. He loved funk music and was instrumental in the careers of artists like Joe Tex. Not everybody was fond of such a thing, not back in the late sixties and early seventies when the racial divide in the country was so evident. As much as people admired Buddy, people in the music industry would talk behind his back about how they couldn't believe he was working with black musicians. It didn't bother Buddy.

As I flew home to Chicago with my father, I wasn't a bundle of nerves like I had been on the way there. Once again, I knew I was at another turning point in my career. Those long nights of performing for a few dollars and for even fewer people were paying off. Those hours of practicing, traveling, and playing were finally being validated.

I STAND IN THE ISOLATION BOOTH STARING THROUGH THE GLASS WINDOW, looking at the band sitting behind their instruments, ready to get to work. Waiting to start playing so I can sing along with them. Live and in person. I feel naked without the piano in front of me, but I know the piano player I'm looking at has it all covered. And then some.

The Swampers have had lots of superstars covered.

That's their nickname, but they're officially known as the Muscle Shoals Rhythm Section. They're not just any band playing for singers in the recording studio; they're the house band. These guys have played with Percy Sledge on hits like "When a Man Loves a Woman" and Etta James on "Tell Mama." And now they're playing with nineteen-year-old Jonathan Cain—aka Johnny Lee.

These guys jammed on Aretha Franklin's "Think" and "Respect."

Think about it, I tell myself.

"Ain't gonna do you wrong," I vow to these guys in the room.

They've backed up rhythm and blues artists like Wilson Pickett, Solomon Burke, Don Covay, and King Curtis. Did someone make a mistake and think good ole Johnny Lee is a black singer from Chicago?

Then again, these guys are just four ordinary-looking white cats.

Roger Hawkins sits behind the drums, and Jimmy Johnson adjusts his guitar. The bass rests in David Hood's hands, while Barry Beckett mans the piano. Dad and I had no idea the Muscle Shoals Rhythm Section would show up to play in my session at Soundshop Studios. It's the second time Buddy Killen has flown us to Nashville. He'd released my single, "God Made Woman (for Man to Love)," to radio, but he felt something was missing behind the music. So I'm back here, but this time I'm doing the session with *his* players.

Buddy only wants my songs and my vocals.

Tommy isn't happy being left behind, but we both know this is an opportunity I couldn't pass up.

The first member of the Swampers I spotted was Barry Beckett, looking like a pirate with a patch over one eye from a recent injury. He listened as I played my two songs for him while the rest of the band sat around the old Steinway and quietly wrote odd-looking charts consisting of numbers and symbols. The band uses words like *diamond* and *channel* and make me wonder what they mean when it comes to recording.

I sing the scratch vocal—one that serves as a guide to help with cues. Then I can feel my knees shaking a bit as I hear the mix in the headphones.

Man, these guys can groove.

It's like being up front with an engineer on a freight train barreling down the tracks. Hawkins and Hood are solid on the drums and bass. Beckett dazzles on the keys. The Memphis Horns with Wayne Jackson and Andrew Love sound tight and more in tune than anything my brother and I could have ever played.

We record my two songs in a few takes. "Song of the City" and "Travelin' Rock 'n' Roll Band" are finished within an hour. I can't believe the end result. I've never sung with players of this caliber, so I have to sit back and sing in a driving groove I've never done before.

This was easy, at least compared to singing on the tracks we did down in Pekin.

Before the guys from the Muscle Shoals Rhythm Section leave, they all tell Buddy and me how much they enjoyed the session.

ELEVEN

"YOU BETTER THINK TWICE"

The Rolling Stones blared over the crackling speakers of the bar at the local bowling alley in Kankakee, Illinois. Hearing "Brown Sugar" made me think of the trip to Nashville to play with the Muscle Shoals guys two years earlier in 1969. Months after I recorded my two tracks, the Rolling Stones would cut their smash hit with the guys at the Muscle Shoals Sound Studio in Sheffield, Alabama. "Brown Sugar" was the first single off *Sticky Fingers*, arriving in April 1971.

Needless to say, "Song of the City" didn't turn out to be any "Brown Sugar." I received the 45-inch vinyl in a white jacket in the mail two months after recording it in the spring of 1969. The single featured the Dial logo, the song title, and the name "Johnny Lee" on the cover, along with "produced by Buddy Killen." The B-side was the other song we'd recorded, "Travelin' Rock 'n' Roll Band." I had chosen the last name of Lee because Dad's name was Leonard—and it was the middle name they'd given me.

Recording my first single wasn't the only thrill during my second trip to Nashville to see Buddy Killen. He asked if I had any musical heroes, so I mentioned Chet Atkins. Dad and I were crazy about his guitar playing and his take on popular songs of the day. Before one of the sessions began, Buddy surprised me and set up a lunch on Music Row with none other than the man himself. Atkins was warm and friendly and seemed genuinely interested in what Buddy and I were doing in Nashville together. Buddy also introduced me to Ray Stevens and Bobby Goldsboro, who owned Soundshop Studios, where we had recorded with Buddy.

After a steak dinner in Printer's Alley with Dad, we returned to the studio to get a mixed version of our two songs the next morning. I can still see Buddy's eyes twinkling and my father smiling as he closed his eyes during the playback of my songs on the big speakers. I couldn't believe they sounded just like the records I had as a kid growing up.

Months after holding my first 45 in my hands, I searched for any signs of airplay in *Billboard* magazine. I had called Buddy and been told it was a slow process of getting added to an already crowded playlist. As days and weeks passed, we had to face the reality that "Song of the City" would not be the hit all of us had hoped for. There were a handful of spins in the Midwest and South, but no buzz on the radio.

Having a record deal and a single released on the radio didn't change your gig status. The places we played didn't seem to get any better. Unless you got to the Top 40 in high rotation on the radio, you really weren't in demand for TV show appearances or openings for popular artists of the day. Realizing it was a process, I still enjoyed the studio—creating a sound for an original composition and trying to make it come alive.

The list of gigs at forgettable lounges turned out to be long. During the summer of 1971, after playing at the bowling alley in Kankakee, I met a young couple at the bar. Sydney was a tan, buxom, brown-eyed twenty-two year-old, while Pete was a tall, athletic older man who wore glasses and was madly in love with her. They were regulars at the club and invited us to try waterskiing on their boat that weekend. I don't remember why, but I was the only one in the band to show up the next morning. I took to waterskiing fairly quickly and was up on one ski after a few hours. Sydney seemed very talkative and spent the day chatting and flirting.

That night, Sydney showed up alone at the club, the carefree and smiling expression I'd seen on the water that day absent for some reason.

"Pete is jealous of you," she said before our set started. "He's beaten down the front doors of guys who've tried to date me."

I didn't know why she was telling me this, but it suddenly made me extremely anxious to get our gigs done and move on to our next destination—St. Louis.

The next morning, Sydney found me at the motel, saying Pete had been furious with her about coming to the club to see me. She explained she had no other male she could talk to about her situation, so I was a safe person, since I was a traveling musician passing through. I said I understood but also told her it was probably dangerous for her to be there talking with me, since her car was parked in front of my motel room. Especially since everyone in town seemed to know her.

On Sunday evening, Pete was the one to show up at our gig alone—looking unhinged. He asked me to come out into the bowling alley, so we sat in the plastic seats, staring at the bowlers competing in the Sunday evening leagues.

"I know what you did," Pete said with eyes that refused to blink. "I know you had relations with my Sydney. My best friend saw her car parked in front of your motel early this morning. I have a gun outside, and I'm thinking about using it on you."

The blood rushed to my forehead as I swallowed hard. I could barely talk.

"Listen, Pete, there's no way. I wouldn't dream of pulling something like that. You guys have been nothing but kind, inviting me on the river and showing me how to waterski. Why on earth would I do something like that?"

"'Cause she's the hottest thing in this town, and you know it and I know it," he said. "And I'm the guy who's head over heels in love with her. Look, I don't wanna do anything I'm gonna regret. Look me square in the eyes and swear you didn't sleep with her!"

I shook my head in disbelief and full confession. "Man, I swear to you on my father's grave—nothing happened. I have too much respect for both of you. I'm leaving here tomorrow, and I'm not coming back, I assure you."

Sweat dotted his forehead right above eyes that looked like those of a man possessed. I could see a thick vein popping up around his temple.

"I don't believe you. Not a bit. But I guess shooting you is no answer. Just don't ever come back here, or I'll use that gun on you. I promise."

With that warning, he got up and stormed out into the night, driving away in his black pickup truck. I felt stuck to my seat, my body soaked with sweat. Thankfully, Jimmy and Tommy had been watching the two of us, and the bartender had called the police, who were waiting outside next to his car. Just in case.

The next morning dawned, and I was eager to get out of town. I heard a knock on my motel room door.

There's no way . . .

But sure enough, as I tried to focus my eyes in the bright, sunlit morning, I saw Sydney's figure in the doorway. I let out a curse.

"What are you doing back here?" I said.

"Oh, Jonny, I'm so sorry for what Pete did last night. He had no right. I told you he was crazy. Are you okay?"

Something told me that if I told Sydney I wasn't, she would try to help me become okay. In whatever way she could.

"I'm fine," I told her. "We just talked, and he left. That's about the extent of it. Something tells me you have a real problem if you stay with that guy."

Sydney moved closer to me, nodding. "I know. I just feel something special between us, that's all. You know you're attracted to me."

She suddenly leaned in and kissed me on the lips. I didn't fight it. It lasted a long time and was frankly intoxicating. I finally opened my eyes and thought of the waiting gun and came to my senses. She needed to leave, and so did we.

"Good-bye" was the last word she whispered as I watched her walk away. In a cloud of smoke from the gravel driveway, her white Mustang raced away and disappeared down the highway.

Waking the others, I skipped my shower, got dressed in a hurry, paid our bill, and headed out on the highway. Looking in the rearview mirror of my Chevy van for a Dodge pickup truck following me, I decided to skip breakfast until we got far out of town. I had no appetite, feeling like I'd literally just dodged a bullet.

Maybe it's the angel again, looking out for me.

It felt good to be alive.

I never ventured back to Kankakee, nor did I ever find out what was up with Sydney and Pete—nor did I care. I was just glad to be down the road without a bullet in my head.

It turns out it was a good thing I had met Pete and Sydney. A year after the dangerous encounter at the Kankakee bowling alley, a stranger who had happened to see me there called out of the blue.

"Hey, Jonny, I'm Nick Papas. A friend of Everett's. I'm the PR guy for Wolfman Jack."

Of course I knew about the legendary DJ personality in Hollywood. Nick had heard me play at the same bowling alley where I nearly met my demise. Nick learned about my songwriting and my love for the studio from Everett, who knew I had to move on to the next level musically and creatively.

With no word from Nashville and Buddy after two years of working with him and recording "Song of the City," I asked him if I could be released from the publishing and record deal, since we weren't planning on recording anything in the future. He agreed, so I continued playing clubs around the Chicagoland area, with Everett Slade as our manager. Our band name changed to Chapter III since this was our third incarnation after Tommy and I were a duo and Johnny

Lee and The Brotherhood came to an end. We played hotel bars in St. Louis and Cleveland with Tommy and Jimmy. But no Kankakee. Everett was getting pretty good money for our trio, and rooms were comped, so we always came home with cash in our band accounts.

Being so close to O'Hare Airport, the clubs around Schiller Park were filled with stewardesses, pilots, and booking agents. Apartments sprouted up along the main highways that led to O'Hare, so much so that the town was being called "Stew Zoo," a reference to the flight attendants. Tommy and I seemed to meet our share of these women who traveled the "friendly skies" for a living. They worked hard and partied hard, and their promiscuous behavior was well-known—even all the way downtown. Men looking for adventure traveled miles on the expressway to these bars just to take a shot at getting lucky for the evening. The Thirsty Whale was an establishment where well-known local bands headlined, and wild stories were told in our once sleepy little bedroom town about the "meat market" the scene had turned into.

Chapter III became Chapter VI when Jimmy Benso got tired of playing pop music and wanted to play rock. Tommy and I had listened to what Jimmy wanted and decided to add a bass player and a two-piece horn section. We agreed to move in a more rock-oriented direction and decided to go after different clubs in the city. I wrote charts for the horns, and we worked up songs by the rock-horn bands of the day: Chicago Transit Authority; Blood, Sweat & Tears; The Electric Flag; and Spiral Starecase. Everett warned us that the group would be harder to book, but we moved forward with Jimmy's vision.

After a year of playing as a six-piece, however, the new band members were disillusioned with the gigs and direction, talking behind our backs about leaving and starting their own band. Jimmy had been smoking a lot of pot with the new guys and was drifting away from Tommy and me as a partner and a friend. It became clear he wanted out, so we disbanded.

Our replacement ended up being Jimmy Arnold, a serious student of the guitar who was eager to get on the road and make some money.

A true rock aficionado, Arnold had a great collection of rock LPs and shared his knowledge of the genre with my brother and me. We wanted to move in a rock direction as a trio, so we began to play numbers that Jimmy suggested. Buffalo Springfield, the Allman Brothers Band, and Poco were some of the bands we emulated. We had cut the four legs and built-in stool off my Hammond B-3 organ, lightening the four-hundred-pound instrument so we could transport it easier.

It was during this time that I got the call from a high-energy, fast-talking Midwesterner, Nick Papas. Nick had been helping Wolfman Jack with his career since the late sixties. They had a production company on Kings Road in Hollywood and had signed several acts, including Redbone, whose big hit was "Come and Get Your Love."

I officially met Nick during a break at a gig one night. He sat at a table and welcomed Tommy and me with a generous smile and handshake as if he'd known us for years.

"I loved what I heard the other night," Nick said. "Love the songs and your voice. You guys gotta come out to Hollywood."

I glanced at Tommy and wasn't sure exactly what to say.

Is this guy for real?

"Look, I'm getting married, and she doesn't like the house I have in Laurel Canyon. Says it's too small. So you guys can stay there, since we're moving out."

Nick said the rent would be minimal, only three hundred dollars a month, and we could live there as a band. For a few moments, we talked about the new songs I'd written.

"I'll get you guys back into the studio to cut some more songs. I've been in the music business for a while now. I know people and can hook you guys up."

This wasn't some slick salesman, but rather an upbeat, confident guy who saw something in us.

"You can still play the clubs out there to make some money, but you can also write," Nick said. "We have our own in-house producer— J. C. Phillips, great guy."

Phillips was working for the production company and could help me with my songs and get them recorded in a professional fashion.

Nick didn't have any reservations about Tommy and me. "I got it all lined up out in LA. You gotta come out. You're gonna make it. No doubt. You have what it takes."

It didn't take long to make up my mind. As much as I loved Everett Slade and my family, I knew it was time to move on. Besides being tired of the club scene, I'd found that Chicago had lost its excitement, with local record companies fading and acts breaking up. I didn't want to end up playing the bars for the rest of my life. This offer was what I had been waiting for. With Everett standing in the shadows, I knew this decision broke his heart, but this was an opportunity I couldn't turn down.

Led Zeppelin had released its fourth album at the end of the last year, and it featured the ballad "Going to California." This was exactly what Tommy, Jimmy, and I decided to do, accepting Nick's offer and moving to Hollywood in the summer of 1972.

I can still remember our twelve-year-old brother, Hal, standing out in the middle of Sterling Lane, waving good-bye with tears in his eyes as we drove away to chase down our dreams.

PART THREE

"THE MIDNIGHT TRAIN GOIN' ANYWHERE"

"THE WOLFMAN IS EVERYWHERE."

I remember well this line in *American Graffiti*. In some ways, the DJ does happen to be everywhere. Right now, he's at the cast party for the new film being released. I know, because I'm standing next to him.

More than a year ago, I was playing dim and musky bars, singing pop songs to uninterested patrons. Suddenly I'm waking up to sunshine in the beating heart of today's music scene and rubbing shoulders with the up-and-coming Hollywood stars of the day.

Wolfman Jack's PR guy, Nick Papas, is showing me around the town and taking me places like this one. I'm already known as his protégé, and he's got a swagger that's contagious to everyone around him. Nick's a dreamer from the Midwest, just like me. He's always telling me the same thing over and over: "You snooze, you lose, Jon."

There's no losing with Nick.

After watching the premiere of *American Graffiti* at Grauman's Chinese Theatre on Hollywood Boulevard, we go straight to the cast party at Ernie's Steakhouse in Century Center. It has a great view of the city, so for a moment, I glance over Los Angeles and think about how lucky I am to be here.

Things are happening. It's all beginning to really happen.

The movie I just watched seems to be a reminder from God. It's a portrait of my youth, the time I left behind in Chicago. The only difference is that I never shared that innocence portrayed on the screen. My innocence was stolen when I was eight years old and saw it set ablaze.

I see the director, George Lucas. I hear he's a graduate of the

University of Southern California and quite the up-and-coming film-maker. I recognize Opie Taylor from *The Andy Griffith Show*, though Ron Howard is now a young man. Other actors from the film are unknowns.

The beautiful actress playing the elusive blonde sitting in the white Thunderbird walks past. Her name is Suzanne Somers. Not long after that, I sit down next to someone who introduces himself as Harrison.

I'm in a room full of people like me. Artists hoping to make it big. Creatives trying to break out. Young people perhaps on the cusp of something great.

I'm only twenty-three years old. George Lucas is twenty-nine. Richard Dreyfus is twenty-six. Harrison Ford is thirty-one.

God is surrounding me with so many talented people who seem to be going somewhere. I can almost hear him asking me the question time and time again: "Are you on the cusp of something great too?"

I feel like I am. I know I might be. Nick has no doubt that greatness awaits us right around the corner.

I think of another line from the film: "It doesn't make sense to leave home to look for home, to give up a life to find a new life, to say good-bye to friends you love just to find new friends."

But that's what you have to do. To leave and to let go.

I've already done that here in LA. Perhaps just like so many of these people surrounding me.

We're all just young dreamers wondering what the future might hold.

TWELVE

"ROCK IT DOWN"

"I'm not dressing like that."

That was the first thing Tommy said after we exited the Whisky a Go Go with a ringing in our ears. The club at 8901 Sunset Boulevard on the Sunset Strip had been around since 1964, and by the time my brother and I attended our first concert there in the summer of 1973, it was already legendary. Led Zeppelin, The Velvet Underground, the Jimi Hendrix Experience, The Who, The Animals, Janis Joplin—everybody who was anybody had played at the Whisky. The Doors even served as a house band for the venue.

Tommy and I had ventured into the club to see David Johansen and the New York Dolls perform. The formidable rock band had just released their self-titled debut album, featuring the guys dressed in drag with caked-on makeup and high heels. They looked the same on stage, as they teased and taunted the crowd with not-so-subtle songs like "Trash" and "Personality Crisis." The glam rock era was in full swing, with personas like David Bowie's flamboyant Ziggy Stardust having emerged on the scene. Concerts hadn't really taken off yet—one of the biggest at the time was Bowie at the Hollywood Palladium in March 1973. Tommy and I wanted to check out the musical scene. The New York Dolls were elevating their music to introduce glam metal to the world. They would play a huge role in igniting the upcoming punk scene.

Tommy didn't know what to think after the show. Both of us had watched the show with a sense of awe. Afterward, Tommy expressed his concern and questioned if we'd come to the right place to pursue our careers. I just laughed and told him our new manager, Don Kelley, wasn't going to have us wearing dresses and heels anytime soon.

"Not everybody's into glam," I reminded my brother. "Look at Elton John and *Honky Château*. We can do *that*."

Elton John's 1972 album had reached number one in the US charts and featured the funk of the title track and the piano ballad that shot to the stars in "Rocket Man." It felt closer to the music I wanted to make. And we were in the right place to make it too, since Sunset Boulevard was the epicenter of the music scene in LA. The record labels and management firms all had bungalow-style headquarters right on the street. Neal Bogart had started Casablanca Records; David Geffen had Geffen Records; Terry Ellis and Chris Wright had Chrysalis Records at the end of the boulevard next to the chic restaurant Nick's Fishmarket.

Tommy, Jimmy, and I arrived in Laurel Canyon with everything all set up for us. It was unbelievable. Our new house was exactly as Nick had described it—a charming house above a garage on a little side street called Elrita. It had a cottage feel, with small rooms and windows with a view of a fantastic stone patio, along with huge eucalyptus trees flanking the walls of the garden. Our Midwest senses welcomed the strong, exotic aroma they gave off.

Don Kelley was in charge of Wolfman Jack's career. They had met in New York City just as the maverick DJ's star was taking off. Don and Nick already had lots of ideas mapped out for us, and all we had to do was say yes or no. We were able to attend the Tuesday night tapings of Wolfman Jack's new TV show, *The Midnight Special*, and had been invited to events like the cast party for *American Graffiti*, where I met the likes of George Lucas and Harrison Ford. Don liked my previous records and felt he'd be able to develop my sound over time with the help of producer J. C. Phillips. He also had access to a studio in Torrance, Quantum Recording Studio, where he'd get us free time with his buddy, Donnie Sciarrotta, who was the owner.

I had been surprised so much was in place for us already. Nick had meant business when he'd asked us to come out to LA. Our producer, J. C., shared his concepts of writing and recording songs. He got straight to the point, telling me my songs needed sharper lyrics and I needed to ditch the brass and go with a more guitar-driven sound. As soon as I got new songs up and running with the band, J. C. told me he'd love to help.

Tommy, Jimmy, and I were like fish out of water when we tried to jump into the Sunset Strip club scene. We were invited to a few parties and found all the girls spacey and hard to talk to. They probably felt the same about our Midwest ways, but we couldn't relate to the wild rock lifestyle permeating the culture in Hollywood. We would see singers like Jackson Browne, Joni Mitchell, and Olivia Newton-John while shopping at the local Canyon Country Store that specialized in health foods.

J. C. Phillips proved to be the mentor I needed, and in the months to come, I wrote five pretty solid songs. He had been peeking over my shoulder for the lyrics and the arrangements and suggested some strong ideas that lifted them to a different level. One ballad called "'Til It's Time to Say Goodbye" would be our first studio venture together. It was about leaving a girl back in Chicago, and everyone thought it had single potential. We carefully crafted a dramatic arrangement that used Jimmy's wall of guitars in a driving intro that melted into a lonely, solo piano motif.

One day, Don Kelley told me he wasn't crazy about my professional name.

"There's already a country singer named Johnny Lee," he said. "Your real last name is Friga, right? No one's ever going to remember that name, much less be able to pronounce it correctly. I want you to think about choosing a new name. One that has star potential. Like Elton John. Did you know his real name is Reggie Dwight?"

Don wanted me to come back the following day with a few ideas. The trip east down Sunset Boulevard to Laurel Canyon was congested with rush-hour traffic. As I sat at a stoplight, I saw a clothier's sign on the corner that read "Michael Bain."

"Michael Bain—Michael Bain—Jonathan Cain," I said out loud.

That's a good name.

The next afternoon, I tried out my new name on Don.

"I like it—very strong—but how should we spell it now? With a 'c' or a 'k?' With an 'a-i' or an 'a-n'?"

After studying the spellings, Kelly said, "There's Cain from the Bible—the one who slew his brother, Abel. But I don't think that matters in this day and age, especially for a name being used in the business."

"I like it," I said.

Kelly's face lit up with his idea. "If we add all the letters together, they equal twelve—a powerful number. I believe in that stuff. I think it's fascinating, don't you? So let's see: 'The Jonathan Cain Band with their new hit single, "'Til It's Time to Say Goodbye.' It has a ring to it, by God. I think you nailed it! Your brother has to be Tommy Cain as well. He shouldn't mind."

"I sure hope not," I said sheepishly.

Tommy and Jimmy were fine with the idea, and so was my father.

"People won't bother me for free tickets when you become a big star," Dad said.

There he was, always dreaming big, always confident it was going to happen one day.

After recording my songs at Quantum Recording Studio with J. C. Phillips, an independent record company named October Records released my single, "'Til It's Time to Say Goodbye." Not long after that, Don Kelley called me in to tell me that Dick Clark Productions had called about our band being on *American Bandstand*. Wolfman knew Dick well and had dropped off our single at his office. He liked it and wanted us on the show with Natalie Cole.

"American Bandstand?" I asked, stunned by the good news. "Really, Don? Are you kidding me?"

"We booked you. You and your band will play in two weeks on his show. They're not equipped for a live performance, so you better start practicing your lip-synching technique in front of a mirror at home with the tape."

It felt like I floated back home on the drive that afternoon down Sunset Boulevard and then turning up Crescent Heights toward our house on Elrita. When I arrived at the house, I announced that we'd gotten booked on *American Bandstand*. Jimmy and Tommy grabbed me and started jumping up and down.

With Wolfman Jack's blessing behind us, we went on the show on a Saturday afternoon and did quite well. Reading my bio and knowing I had studied music in a conservatory, Dick Clark scripted an interview with me as we discussed classical music. He wanted me to make fun of it on the show, something I wasn't quite comfortable with. I told him it was like going to a museum and looking at fine old paintings you wouldn't necessarily want hanging in your house. Later on, Wolfman would tell me how he loved that bit. While in the makeup room, I met Natalie Cole, who was making her debut performance of her smash hit "This Will Be."

Our record went up the charts a few places after the airing of *American Bandstand*, but nothing else changed much in our careers. The record stalled in the high thirties and then dropped; because it was a hit only locally, it didn't have enough spins to sustain life in other areas. We found ourselves playing a pizza joint in Santa Ana the same night our record peaked on the charts.

+ + +

Along with helping me learn how to write interesting lyrics and original songs, J. C. Phillips knew a lot of great guys in the industry. He'd get me brief interviews with them. One time, I got to meet Gabriel Mekler, a musician and record producer who had worked with Janis Joplin, Etta James, and Three Dog Night. I was especially interested to meet him, since he had helped Steppenwolf craft their sound on their first self-titled album.

I visited Gabriel at his house, where we sat on luxurious Persian carpets on his floor and spent an hour talking about his classical training in music and his work with Steppenwolf. I wanted to know what it was like to work with the group and get the sound they had come up with.

I had always been curious and eager for instruction, so the more time I spent in the studio or around engineers, the more questions I'd ask. I asked producers and engineers what they had changed and what frequency they were using. I knew it drove them nuts after a while and forced me to shut up and simply watch. But I really wanted to learn how everything worked. My goal was that someday I'd be able to make all those decisions myself.

The opportunity to talk with someone like Gabriel Mekler was incredible. He didn't just talk about the technical side of things, but he also educated me on the personal side of being in a band. When I asked him why Steppenwolf sounded so rockin', his answer was quick and to the point.

"They don't like each other so much," Mekler said, "but they're stuck with each other, so they try to outplay each other. There's a good sort of tension there."

"Is that really a good thing?" I asked.

"It can be a *very* good thing," Mekler said. "Especially with a band like Steppenwolf."

At the time, I thought, *That's crazy.* And yet over the years, I discovered how true it could be. Conflict in a band can indeed help the creative process and propel the sound. When I finally joined The

Babys, I saw a bit of that chemistry between John Waite and the rest of the guys, and then later on with Steve Perry and the rest of his bandmates in Journey. It was the sort of tension—one that most of the time went unspoken—that was indeed good.

At least it was good when recording the albums and touring.

I realize now how just how rare those opportunities are to meet talented people like Gabriel Mekler and to dive deep into the musical process. I soaked up every bit of wisdom I could.

Recording my first official album turned out to be as memorable as boot camp might be to a marine. After a record company executive saw our band play one night at a bar called the Mineshaft, he loved what he heard and wanted us to make a record at his studio in Woodstock, New York. The exec was Albert Grossman, a legend in the business during the sixties and seventies. Manager of Bob Dylan, Janis Joplin, and The Band, and president of Bearsville Records, Grossman had an ominous presence, with his long gray hair pulled back in a ponytail. Although he talked in a gruff, loud voice and had eccentric mannerisms, he seemed to have the Midas touch for artists he worked with, successful artists like Gordon Lightfoot; Peter, Paul and Mary; John Lee Hooker; and Richie Havens.

Although Grossman was known in all the New York music circles, I found out after chatting with him that he had grown up in Chicago and attended the same college I'd gone to—Roosevelt University.

Signed by a music mogul and fellow alum from Chicago, my hometown. *How cool*, I thought.

With J. C. Phillips poised to produce the album to be released by Bearsville Records, we made our way to Woodstock in upstate New York. When we arrived, we found Bearsville Studios to be in a state of disrepair. The air conditioner had quit running, and the old Quad Eight console had noise problems. It had rained on and off for five straight days, the temperature had climbed into the high eighties, and the humidity in the woods around the compound was stifling. We decided to rehearse while things were getting fixed, but it was so hot in the cutting room that we ended up overheated and dripping with sweat. We stayed at a lodge down the hill, the Turtle Creek Barn, which was part of Albert's complex. Jimmy Arnold recognized the rooms and said it was where The Band had filmed songs from its *Music from Big Pink* album.

The stream behind the lodge was quite loud, and it had the potential to either help or hinder one's sleep. During the night, I started to hear things scratching on my door and voices coming up the stairs. It wasn't long before I realized the place was haunted. Tommy and Jimmy heard it and felt it too. We started to wonder if we had come to the wrong place to record our music. If that wasn't bad enough, a singer/songwriter signed to Grossman's label who would eventually make a name for himself had a house close by, so he'd come and steal things like a two-inch splicing block and microphones. He even used the echo chamber for his yoga and chanting one afternoon, leaving the place in disarray.

Someone should have known it was a mistake to put a bunch of city boys in the back of the woods. Nothing worked, and it was too hot to rehearse, After feeling stuck in a wilderness for days, we all began to go a little nuts. It felt like everything that could have gone wrong was going wrong. Especially when I got back to LA and learned what Albert Grossman *really* felt about the new album we had just made.

It turned out Albert didn't like the work we had done in Bearsville and planned to shelve the album. I was furious. *He had been there every step of the way*, I thought. I had no idea what prompted his change of heart. To find out why he was so against releasing it, Nick and I arranged a meeting with him at the Chateau Marmont on Sunset Boulevard.

The hotel was on the north side of the Sunset Strip and was more legendary than the rock exec we'd be meeting with. Howard Hughes had lived there for several years. James Dean was rumored to have jumped through a window to audition for *Rebel Without a Cause*. Led Zeppelin's John Bonham drove a motorcycle through its lobby. A long list of stars had flocked to and crossed paths in this famous hotel. It was where *Saturday Night Live* star John Belushi was found dead in his room after a drug overdose in 1982.

When Nick and I arrived that night, we saw Grossman in the hotel room sitting on a couch. He was toking pot out of a French's mustard bottle. He asked us if we wanted to partake in his little buzz session, and while I didn't usually smoke pot, I thought it might break the ice. As he emptied the smoke from inside the mustard bottle, I thought of Jimmy Benso's rock band, Just Mustard.

By now I knew Grossman well enough to know he could be either a genius or a critic who said the worst possible things to you. His behavior seemed very bipolar, so you never knew if he'd be "Good Albert" or "Nasty Albert." For a while, I was talking to Good Albert. I didn't realize his plan had been to offer me an olive branch and then kick me in the tail after helping me get high.

After some time passed, I asked Grossman why he wasn't releasing *Windy City Breakdown*. Suddenly, his mild-mannered character changed. His face became serious and his tone of voice grew ominous. I thought it might have been the pot. He stood up, leaned into my stoned face, and told me I'd made a crappy record, though his language was a bit more explicit.

"It lacks the urgency and passion I saw when I first signed you," he said, adding several more colorful adjectives.

I reminded Albert that he had been there every day, nodding his head in approval. Then I also jogged his memory about how guys had been stealing equipment from us, how so much of what we needed didn't work. But he wasn't the least bit sympathetic.

"I'll write it off—don't worry," he said in a slow, couldn't-care-less tone. "No one will buy your wretched album, I promise you!"

I laid into Grossman, telling him it was going to come out one way or another. I was too high to talk, but I could still tell him off, warning him I was getting my lawyer. I couldn't believe his gall.

You don't get people high to insult them!

None of this took me by surprise. By this time, I'd already seen the underbelly of the music business because of my mentor and friend, Nick Papas. While my own professional career had started to falter in Hollywood, I had been watching Nick's personal life unravel. The happy-go-lucky guy who had invited us to LA had disappeared.

Everyone needs an angel in their life, and Nick was one of mine. He was supposed to be someone who was always there for me. From the moment we began living in the house he had moved out of, Nick believed good things were about to happen. Yet only a month after moving to LA, a tragedy occurred that would jeopardize Nick's own happy story.

While driving a speedboat on a lake with his fiancée, Nick recklessly took a turn too fast. The love of his life flew into the water and drowned. Her family ended up accusing him of second-degree murder, a charge he had to battle in court. Nick was devastated to lose his fiancée and then to be charged with her death. The judge eventually threw out the case, yet Nick still felt guilty and was unable to move on. Meanwhile, as all this was happening, Tommy and I were living in the house Nick owned.

The tale that followed is one told too often in our business, yet I had to witness it unfold with a brother I respected. Nick's career continued to blossom, and he suddenly found himself earning a good paycheck. He rented a big house in Redondo Beach and started having massive parties on the weekend. When I visited, I found a house full of women and drugs, and in the center of it all was Nick. The epidemic of cocaine was everywhere during those days, and it had seized Nick's life. All I could do was watch his life quickly slide down into the dark, whitecapped ocean waters. I remember watching him cut an 8 ball of cocaine with baby laxative, and I could only think how I loved this man. He was like a big brother who just wanted to take care of me.

Nick battled to keep my album alive. We ended up going to the president of Bearsville Records, Paul Fishkin, and made our case. Nick was relentless and eventually worked it out with the guys in New York, ponying up the last bit of money to get my album mastered and released—all five thousand copies. The album title was based on the opening track, the first of many song titles I wrote that foreshadowed my future—"Windy City Breakdown." Even though one song—"Go Now"—got a little airplay, I knew the album wasn't going anywhere. Hardly anyone noticed, except a music journalist from San Francisco who gave it positive reviews. She even got us a gig at The Warfield to play for a KSAN radio party with R&B artist Sylvester.

As Nick's downward spiral continued, I witnessed the way the business and drugs could absolutely destroy someone. He had always believed he could outsmart the industry he was in, and for a while, he was able to stay on top of things. Nick told me about the attitudes of many of the music executives and other people in the business, and I met many of them at his parties. Many of the big players were simply getting their highs at Nick's expense, and I saw firsthand how the only thing that drove them was the money. The love of music and desire to create great art took a backseat.

"You snooze, you lose," Nick said once again, his belief in me still not blinded by his own addictions. "Look, Jon, I know an engineer working with Richard Perry at Studio 55. His name is Howard Steele. I'll get him to produce some songs."

So at the same place where The Pointer Sisters and Leo Sayer recorded their albums, I recorded four more songs, thanks to Nick. He had assembled an all-star band that included Steve Lukather, who played guitar on Boz Scaggs's albums; Mike Baird on drums; and Lee Sklar, a bassist who played on James Taylor's and Linda Ronstadt's records. It was similar to the feeling I'd had in Nashville when I was surrounded by an amazing group of talent. We laid down the tracks in a couple of hours.

Nick had a tour booked for us, and I felt good about the demos when I submitted them to Warner Brothers. Yet when I visited their offices to talk with Lenny Waronker, the head of A&R at the time, I realized my solo career was basically over.

"We're not interested in doing anything with you," Lenny said.

As we talked, I began to feel as though I was being dismissed from my duties as a singer/songwriter. I felt floored.

These songs are full of soul. Who wouldn't like them?

I couldn't keep up with the conversation.

"So what are your plans for the rest of the summer?" he asked me.

I assumed I would be touring and continuing to perform music.

I made up some story about building houses in the San Fernando Valley with an uncle who had a construction business, yet the truth was I had no job plans.

The reality really stung.

It was April 1977. I had been in LA for almost five years, recording music, playing in clubs, and connecting with artists and people in the music industry. Wolfman Jack loved me, and *American Bandstand* had welcomed me. I'd released my first album, *Windy City Breakdown*. But all of that would be like a warm ocean wave washing over my feet on the beach.

The wave always heads back out to sea.

In just a couple of months, the crest of my music career had crumbled, and I could feel the pulling tides. I realized that things had to change. I had to stop forcing my musical dreams on other people. I needed to stop and take a step back to evaluate my strengths and weaknesses before moving forward.

I thought of my childhood dreams of becoming a priest and the years I spent feeling bitter toward God. I didn't want to do the same thing with music—something I was still so passionate about. I would continue to write songs, but I had to get a day job to pay the bills. So I eventually told Jimmy and Tommy the news.

"I can't play the clubs anymore."

"Why not?" Tommy asked.

"How am I going to be original when I have 'Play That Funky Music' echoing in my head?" I said.

"Yeah, but how am I gonna pay rent?" Tommy responded.

"I need to write my own songs," I explained. "I can't be killing myself playing other people's music. I'll never have an original thought in my head ever again."

Appropriately enough, the last show Tommy and I did took us two hours to drive to. The next Monday morning, the check they gave us bounced. So did I, getting away from the constant repetition of performing cover songs. Tommy eventually moved on too, marrying his girlfriend that summer and taking the Laurel Canyon house for themselves. I moved into a little studio apartment in North Hollywood.

I knew songs would be written in my new little home. But if I was meant to stay in this business, then God would have to open a few more doors to let me actually play them to somebody.

THE RAILROAD TIES RESEMBLE THE SAME NOTE IN A SONG REPEATING THE same motif. Hour after hour and day after day. I walk over them at dusk, staring at the straight lines that seem to go on forever. The ache in my arms and shoulders and back and thighs and knees is still there. Yet it's my heart that hurts the most.

I dread calling my father later tonight. I hate asking him for more money, but I have to. I need to pay rent. And I need food to give me some fuel for my part-time job.

I'm spending all day with beer without having a sip of it while working for Manpower, stacking boxes of Budweiser on a loading dock. It's a long way from recording with the Muscle Shoals Rhythm Section or singing on *American Bandstand*. Yet the throbbing all over my body never prevents me from writing music at night, nor does it stop me from checking in with my father.

When I call Dad later that night, I don't waste any time.

"I gotta borrow a little more money," I tell him. "I don't get paid until next Friday."

"How much do you need?" he asks without a hint of hesitation.

"Maybe a thousand."

"I'll loan you two. You just stay the course. Okay?"

"Yeah, sure. Thanks."

The days when Tommy and I gave Dad some of the profits from our shows also feel like a lifetime ago.

"Good things are gonna happen, Jon," Dad tells me. "Stick to your guns."

After I hang up the phone, I scribble down those four last words and put them on the fridge as a reminder of why I came to LA in the first place, why I didn't run back home to Chicago like my mother had suggested after I was kicked down. Sure I'm down, but at least I'm writing songs.

They're getting better too.

A week later, after seeing Dad's four words for seven straight days, I write "Stick to Your Guns" alone in my apartment on the secondhand Kawai baby grand Nick bought me.

"Not knowing which highway to choose . . . I was ambushed by runaway blues . . .

'Hear my Daddy say, 'Son, when there's no place to run . . . stick to your guns.'"

With my TEAC reel-to-reel, some microphones, and a turntable, I record everything I write, including this song. It's a bluesy, Bad Company kind of tune, a smoky number with a Robin Trower thing going on. When I send the tape to Dad, he tells me he loves it.

"That's a great song," he says. "Keep 'em coming."

Grandpa John with his fiddle, my father, and my uncle.

Leonard Friga, my father, playing the guitar in the army.

Dad and his bomber jacket.

Brothers.

Swimming with
Mom and Tom.

Tom and me.
Born to perform.

Dressed up for church.

Mom and Dad.

The Shabel twins.

Our Lady of the Angels
ROOM 1 MARION HALL
1956

PHOTOGRAPHY BY
THE PALOMAR STUDIOS CHICAGO

My class two years before the fire. That's me in the front!

Our Lady of the Angels Elementary School in flames.

A day of mourning.

Paying respects to the fallen sisters and children.

An accordion half as big as me.

Tom and me performing for Hal.

All we needed was a set of drums and a Cordovox.

Our first
publicity shot.

Trying out a
different name.

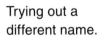

Johnny Lee and The Brotherhood

A proud papa.

Mr. Tambourine Man.

My first single
in 1975.

Evel Knievel behind the keyboard.

Performing next to Jimmy Benso.

JONATHAN CAIN BAND

L to R: GARY RICHWINE, TOMMY CAIN, JIMMY ARNOLD & JONATHAN CAIN.

WARNER/REPRISE

The Jonathan Cain Band.

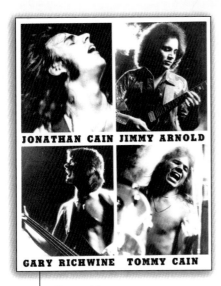

JONATHAN CAIN   JIMMY ARNOLD

GARY RICHWINE   TOMMY CAIN

Scorching.

1977's Windy City Breakdown.

The Babys.

"Back on My Feet Again."

MANAGEMENT: HERBIE HERBERT
NIGHTMARE, INC.
SAN FRANCISCO, CA.

8107

My new band.

Onstage with Neal.

On the road with an incredible crew.

Laughing with the boys.

My proud father at his first Journey concert.

Hanging out
backstage.

Janet Macoska

Performing
with Neal
and Steve.

Janet Macoska

Hold on to
that feelin'.

June 14, 1981,
at Calaveras
County
Fairgrounds
in California.

"Keep On
Runnin'".

"Only the
Young
Can Say."

The team celebrates the release of our *Escape* album.

Brothers.

THIRTEEN

"ISN'T IT TIME"

A few months later, I was still sticking to my guns, but the outlook looked even bleaker for me. Nick had disappeared, and nobody knew where he had gone. The never-ending parties and the endless supply of coke were over. I knew he had begun to have his own financial problems, owing the people who supplied his drug habit. That was why I had eventually refused to take money from him. There was no way for me to know the mess he was in. After he vanished, I knew the bad guys had finally showed up to demand their money.

As for me, I spent my days smiling at customers in an audio shop as I wore the ugliest jean vest I'd ever seen. The beer-loading job was in the distant past, but my job selling home audio equipment for Cal Stereo felt worse. Since they knew I was a musician when I applied, they assumed I wouldn't last long as a salesperson at the store. So as a form of hazing, the boss had me clean toilets every night before I left the store.

He wasn't going to stop me, and neither was the detestable vest I hated putting on every morning. I knew the cheap Cal Stereo bookshelf speakers were made in Mexico and marked up five times what they were worth, so I deliberately tried to get customers to steer clear of them. Whenever irate patrons came back into the store with blown speakers and decided to blow up the manager, I hid in the back of the store in my ridiculous vest and laughed.

There were little unexpected luxuries I discovered at the shop—like playing around and learning about frequencies on the speakers when nobody was there. I heard what sounded good and bad as I fiddled around with the knobs. I could study the curves on the equalizer, always asking what something might do and then discovering it for myself.

I was inspired by and jealous of all the amazing music suddenly emerging. Eric Clapton's *Slowhand* and Stevie Wonder's *Songs in the Key of Life*. Bob Seger was working on his *Night Moves*, and ABBA announced its *Arrival*. Foreigner released its first self-titled album, while Lynyrd Skynyrd released its final album, *Street Survivors*, when the music world was still stunned by the plane crash that killed three band members. Steve Miller kept reminding me day after day in my detestable denim vest that time kept slipping away.

Every evening, I would get back to my apartment and the baby grand. Music was my therapy, just as it had always been. I could create and record songs, keeping them for the future that time kept slipping into.

I'm sticking to my guns, Dad.

As 1978 rolled around, I continued to play on my own and listen to melodies others were making. I bought a new album released in January and found myself struck by the voice on the opening track.

"When the lights go down in the city . . ."

Journey's going in a new direction, I thought as I held *Infinity* in my hands.

Boston had recently enjoyed multi-platinum success with a high tenor. It seemed CBS had the same plans for Journey. The album was melodic and soon kept me company. I played it often.

Journey's new high tenor was something else. Never in my life had I heard a voice like Steve Perry's.

The wheel in the sky kept turning, and I kept imagining where I would be tomorrow, working as hard as I could to get there.

The door to the spacious house in Coldwater Canyon opened, and Robbie Patton stood there in a smoking jacket, pajamas, and slippers. As the Englishman with a slight accent greeted me, I couldn't help studying his red hair that looked like Bowie's Ziggy Stardust gone awry. Later, in the early eighties, the lead singer of A Flock of Seagulls would have a similar hairdo.

The musician and songwriter seemed at ease and confident as he invited me into his impressive house to have a cup of tea. It didn't take long before I explained my situation—that I'd had a band and had lost my record deal with Bearsville a year ago, that I was now working part-time at Cal Stereo. I told him I was still a writer for Albert Grossman's publishing company, but only by default.

In March 1978, I got a phone call from a woman at Grossman's publishing company, wondering if I was interested in cowriting with Robbie Patton. I was surprised to hear from Albert's camp, but I accepted the offer. I talked to Robbie on the phone, and he told me about his recent cowrite with Christine McVie from Fleetwood Mac and other successes he'd had with cowrites. Robbie loved *Windy City Breakdown* and was anxious to get together.

So maybe working with Albert Grossman was a blessing after all.

When I saw the place Robbie was renting, the crib in Coldwater with a spectacular view, I was pleasantly surprised.

All you do is write songs, I thought when I saw his lifestyle. *So it's possible to make a living doing this thing I love to do.*

"So what have you written lately?" he asked me.

"I've got a song called 'Stick to Your Guns,'" I said, knowing it was the best thing I'd written since quitting the club scene. I believed my father when he said I was finding my voice.

I knew Robbie liked it after he started listening to it. When it was finished, he only shook his head.

"Wicked song, just wicked," he said, his British accent heightened by his enthusiasm. "You're a rocker."

The optimism inside me momentarily had a heartbeat—until he went on.

"Love the song, but I need a ballad," Robbie said.

After a few sessions, it turned out Robbie and I hit it off well. We cowrote several songs, one for his solo album and one for a French singer, Sylvie Vartan, called *Distant Shores*. After going to his house one morning, I was surprised when he mentioned that an English band called The Babys was auditioning keyboard players. He wanted me to go.

"Look, check out this out," Robbie said as he brought me to a coffee table and showed me a compact mirror with The Babys' picture on it from their album *Broken Heart*. Mirrors were infamous for their use around Hollywood to chop up cocaine, he explained. Right away I felt a sinking feeling as I saw the foursome in the picture, long-haired and glammed up.

One thing I love about music is its power to break down people's preconceived notions. This happened when Robbie put on their latest album and played a track called "Give Me Your Love." It reminded me a lot of Paul Rogers and Bad Company. I instantly loved their ballad "Isn't It Time." I liked the pipes of the singer, John Waite; the playing was soulful, and the sound of the record was sonically great. The Babys' production and performances were solid and passionate. But I still wasn't sold.

"Robbie, man, I don't fit in with these guys. They wear makeup and earrings. I'm a Midwest guy who writes songs."

"Don't be silly, darling. You're rock 'n' roll—your playing, your voice, your look. They'll love you. You *have* to go to the audition."

"I don't know," I said.

"Remember that song you played me when we met—'Stick to Your Guns'? Sing that for them if they ask you for a song you wrote. The audition is next Tuesday at SIR's rehearsal studios on Santa Monica. Say you'll do it. Trust me, you're perfect. You're going to get the gig. It's going to be beautiful. Come on, darling."

I figured I had nothing to lose, so I went to Tower Records that afternoon and bought The Babys' albums to study. Michael Corby was the member I would be replacing, a founding member who played guitar and doubled on keyboards. I noticed that session guys were playing the piano on the new album and wondered why.

Heading to the popular rehearsal space on Santa Monica Boulevard, I arrived at SIR with my complete live setup—a Yamaha CP70, an ARP Omni synth, a Hohner clavinet, and a cutdown B3. Two English roadies were eager to help me get my stuff ready, something I'd never had the privilege of experiencing during my days of live performing. The Babys were set up in a large room with a stage. There was a drum set in the center, and I noticed that the bass and guitar rig seemed miles from the center, which made it look like they didn't like each other much.

The band was rehearsing "Give Me Your Love" with the PA speakers cranked up very loud. Wally Stocker played a Gibson Les Paul through a Marshall bass amp that produced a rich, thick tone. The lead singer, John Waite, played bass, and I noticed immediately that his voice was rawer and more bluesy than it sounded on the albums. They took a break to chat with me and seemed cordial enough. One of the roadies mentioned there were almost forty keyboard players they planned on playing with before they'd make a final decision. I thought of the long and awkward process of playing their music with strangers and wondered why so many.

We played five of their songs, including their hit song "Isn't It Time." I had learned the string and horn parts and played them with my left hand, something I had been practicing diligently at my apartment. A woman had sung with John on the chorus on the record, so I sang her part in a fluid falsetto. They were impressed. I wondered what they were planning to do when they performed it in concert. Tony Brock played a solid, soulful drumbeat that was easy to follow, so my audition started out strong.

After taking a break, Waite asked me if I could play something I had written.

"Yeah, I have one," I said, thinking of Robbie's favorite song of mine.

I closed my eyes and sang "Stick to Your Guns" as if my life depended on it. And in a way, it did.

It's time to shine, Jon.

By the time I got to the second chorus, John Waite began singing a harmony part that gave me chills. When the last note rang out on the old upright piano in the corner, I waited for their reaction.

"Strong tune," Waite told me. "Reminds me of Bad Company. You can really sing. Interesting voice. Is that song on a solo album?"

"No. I wrote it not long ago. It's something my father said to me."

"Well, I love it. Very memorable. Listen, we need to carry on here. Do you know any more of our tunes? We need to run over them, and I'd love to hear your take on the rest of our material."

I had done my homework and stuck around for the rest of the rehearsal. There were smiles all around the room as we ran through a dozen more of their songs. It felt exhilarating to finally play again, and it reminded me of the times I played with the session kings at Studio 55 who helped me cut my demos. I'd come to find out that John, who was from Birmingham, England, liked soul music and wanted to jam on a few songs like Wilson Pickett's "Mustang Sally" and "Midnight Hour." I knew and loved this music and was amazed that someone who had grown up on the other side of the ocean could like the same songs.

John Waite and I had a lot in common. He had grown up in a tough middle-class community and had to fight his way into the business, similar to the way I had. The only difference was that he was in his early twenties. He was obviously talented and prolific beyond his years. His voice was vulnerable and raw at the same time. John had range and tone and sang the way I only dreamed I could sing. As I watched and listened to him, I knew I wanted to hear him sing something we would write together.

The band's name was spelled out in boldface letters under the Whisky a Go Go header. I glanced at the sign and couldn't believe The Babys were headlining the sold-out New Year's Eve show in 1978.

And I'm playing the keyboard for them.

The last few months had been a blur, so busy that I hadn't had time to stop and realize everything that had happened. One moment I was scrubbing a commode in my Cal Stereo vest, and the next I was getting a passport and heading to Holland and Germany to play with the band. I was paid $250 a week, more than I got paid trying to convince people not to buy bad stereos.

There had been a lot of turmoil and change within The Babys in the year that led up to their invitation to join them. Chip Ranklin, their new manager, had come to rehearsal to meet me and was the first to give me the real bottom line. While the band was putting the final touches on its next album, *Union Jacks*, the founding member, Michael Corby, had left due to differences in musical direction and a personality clash among the band members. A guitarist who dabbled at keyboards, Corby was described as "the pretty boy" in the band, the one who envisioned them in makeup and wanted the band to go in a teen-glam direction. The rest of the guys wanted to be a rock band with a tougher edge. They also told me Corby was known as "difficult."

Not only had Corby left the group, but so had their previous manager, Adrian Miller—the guy who gave them their name at a café one night. The name was supposed to be a joke, but somehow it stayed with them. John Waite said it was the only way the record companies paid them any attention. It was a departure from the obvious rock band moniker and got them their deal at Chrysalis Records. After landing from the UK in Hollywood, Adrian set up the band, their wives, and their roadies in their own apartments on Kings Road, along with a couple of rental cars. Since they were getting a lot of airplay, he booked a 99-cent tour, packing the venues so it looked like they were selling out. Somehow, Adrian got the record company to fund this, and then he left after a dispute with Chrysalis and the band. The Babys ended up with a debt to the tune of a million dollars. Chip Ranklin was eventually brought in as its new manager.

At first glance, the band seemed to be on its way to really making it. They had two hit singles and had toured the United States as headliners. Yet Ranklin was the one to inform me that The Babys were $750,000 in debt as I joined the band. So while I was excited to tell my father the great news that I had been hired, I also had to be honest when it came to the financial situation.

"How much are they going to pay you?" Dad asked.

"I get $250 per week—more than I got at Cal Stereo!"

I explained to my father how they were in debt for a variety of reasons. I knew no dream could soar with financial restraints and baggage weighing it down. An artist didn't just have to be smart with music and performances; he or she needed to be shrewd at business. Of course, my father was already part of the adoring audience, applauding me onward.

"It's just a stepping-stone," he told me, always encouraging me, even in those times I didn't need encouraging.

Playing at the Whisky a Go Go on New Year's Eve sure felt like more than just a stepping-stone. I remembered seeing The New York Dolls here with Tommy after we'd just arrived in Hollywood. The memory seemed like it happened yesterday but also like a lifetime ago.

I had some butterflies inside, but after the first few chords, we were all totally in sync as we roared through a ninety-minute set. The bar felt alive and electric, and I noticed an array of flashbulbs from the press that had shown up. John was in great voice, and we gave Hollywood something to talk about for the next few weeks.

In February 1979, my first official rock interview was conducted at our hotel by a Dutch journalist armed with a tape recorder. After landing in Germany to do a couple of variety shows, we had gone to Amsterdam to tape two TV shows, since The Babys were quite popular there. It was strange that he wanted to talk just to me, alone. With his thick accent, he went through the usual questions, such as where I was from and how long I had been playing. One question caught me off guard.

"Jonathan, how does it feel to be *somebody* after being *nobody* for so long?"

"What do you mean?" I snapped back. "I've always been somebody. I had my own record deal and have been playing professionally for over twelve years."

"Well, no one in Holland has ever heard of you. We wondered why they replaced Michael Corby, a founding member, with an unknown musician."

I stared at the interviewer as he puffed away on a clove cigarette as we sat in the empty lounge. He could clearly see I was irritated with him, while I could see the earnest expression on his face. I took a deep breath, remembering he was translating Dutch into English. I realized that despite his clumsy language skills, he sincerely wanted to know how my newfound success felt.

"It's certainly gratifying to be acknowledged for my work after so many years," I answered. "I am grateful the lads in The Babys gave me this opportunity."

"I see. Thanks very much. That is all I have for you."

He smiled and shook my hand, and mercifully the interview ended.

After returning from Europe that winter, we were whisked off to another frozen tundra, North Dakota, to start a tour with Alice Cooper. Fresh out of rehab, he was supporting a new album release, *Welcome to My Nightmare*. Alice rented a private turboprop plane that had room for our band and our roadies. As we climbed the stairs to the aircraft, I noticed his logo from the album painted on the side.

Greeting the pilot and the stewardess, we filed to the back of the plane and waited for Alice to board. When he finally showed up, he seemed to be in good health and spirits, ready to sit in on a card game with his manager, Shep Gordon.

"Babys! Nice to have you on our tour! Any of you got any Lynyrd Skynyrd tapes?" he roared.

The irreverent remark seemed funny at the time, but I cringed as I thought of the fiery plane crash that had taken the lives of six people, including their lead singer and manager. The plane we were on seemed safe enough, and the pilot assured us that the Bombardier, a four-engine Canadian plane, could glide with no engines and make a perfect emergency landing.

Opening up in Grand Forks, North Dakota, The Babys played for a sold-out crowd of ten thousand people. It was the first big rock show for me with full production lights and sound. The arena reverberated as the sound of Tony Brock's Ludwig snare drums cracked against the back wall and Wally Stocker's Gibson Les Paul wailed and soared. John Waite wore a blue tartan plaid suit that Glenn, an English tailor on Melrose Avenue had made for him. Waite had never sounded better.

As we roared through our forty-five-minute set, I thought of what my father had said at Pat's Tavern when I was eight years old: "He's gonna be a famous musician and play in front of thousands someday." His prophecy had come to pass. I hadn't written any hits yet, but it felt exhilarating to finally be acknowledged.

Life for me had shifted and turned upside down in less than a year. The depressed guy wearing an ugly jean vest and walking the railroad tracks talking to himself had managed to perform in front of ten thousand people. I knew God had done this. It felt in one sense like it had been overnight, that I had experienced an "altered state." God had given me a sudden break that I could barely wrap my head around. I heard him talking to me in an accent sounding like Robbie's.

Jon, you're a rock star. How does it feel?

I felt proud and vindicated. I felt I had endured and persisted through all the work and all the moments of failure and all the reasons to give up to finally be on that stage. Did I deserve to be up there? Absolutely.

I belong on this stage. It's where I always should have been.

I hadn't been wrong. Dad hadn't been wrong. And as for God . . .

God is never wrong.

Right at the lowest point of my career, I had become a full-fledged member of a traveling rock band. It made me think of Bob Seger's lyrics on his album *Night Moves*: "Come back baby, rock and roll never forgets." Truth was, I didn't know much about the rock 'n' roll lifestyle or how to walk the swagger—or, for that matter, even how to write the song. But I was about to learn.

FOURTEEN

"TURN AND WALK AWAY"

The sound of my roller skates echoed throughout the empty concourse in the Oakland Coliseum. I wasn't just killing time before the show; I was getting rid of my nerves. The crew had started right after we arrived at the venue early in the morning on buses. They needed all the time they could get to set up the stage for the main event, but that meant The Babys had lots of time to simply hang out and wait.

It's one thing to play at a place like Whisky a Go Go. But playing in the Coliseum? This was where the Oakland Raiders and Oakland Athletics played. Led Zeppelin performed its final two North American concerts at this very arena in 1977.

How'd I end up here?

A hundred snapshots littered my mind, revealing a hundred footprints in the mud and sand and snow of building a musical career. I hadn't won a music competition, but I suddenly found myself in this place I'd spent a decade and a half competing in to get known. Sometimes winning, and sometimes losing big-time.

I stopped skating as I reached an exit and stood in the middle of empty seats. Staring out across the massive stadium, I realized this was a major win. This was the very definition of *big-time*. Yet I wasn't shocked or surprised to be there. I felt I belonged there, that I had paid my dues and continued to pay them show after show.

This would be a start of a routine for me. Along with roller skating to alleviate tension before a gig, I'd also play a particular game. I picked out various locations in an arena, sitting and standing like the fans would be later at night. I imagined them watching the show from different vantage points as they clapped, cheered, and sang along. I put myself in their shoes and asked the same questions that would run through their minds:

Am I going to believe that guy down there on the stage?

Is he going to move me?

Am I going to clap for him?

What about that keyboard player?

I'd sit in all those places in the house, playing this game and imagining. It was a way to prepare myself for stepping onto the stage below.

There's one thing I know: you *have to* be prepared. I've spent my whole career doing just that. So many things can happen—and often will—that are out of your control, so you have to be ready to control as many things as you can. Even this simple act of looking at the fans' perspective was a way to remind myself who would be watching and who I was playing for.

It was March 28, 1980. This was the start of our moment, of opening up for a big-name band. Sitting in the stands, the sound of a guitar wailing across the arena got my attention. I looked down and noticed the headliners coming onstage to rehearse. The foursome named Journey was the real deal, an act that had definitely hit the big time. They had gone platinum and were the reason we had arrived at the Oakland Coliseum. The guy jamming on the guitar was Neal Schon. I didn't know a lot about the other guys, but I did know about Neal. He was already somewhat of a legend in the music industry, one who joined at the age of fifteen.

Neal was a guitar prodigy who ended up playing on Santana's No. 1 album, *Santana III*. After Santana broke up, manager Herbie Herbert helped form a new group called Journey, with Neal and bassist Ross Valory. Their first album, titled *Journey*, was released in 1975 and consisted primarily of instrumental jazz-rock. They began building a small but devoted fan base. The addition of their lead singer changed the direction of the band in 1978, when their fourth album was released.

I remember being on the road with The Babys. We were opening up for AC/DC. It was late at night, and people were coming back to the hotel from a Rolling Stones concert at Soldier Field. All they could talk about was the band that had opened for the Stones.

"This band Journey just kicked butt."

"Journey?" I said. "Really?"

Everybody agreed they were mighty. They didn't just say they were good; their reaction was a little more like, *We just saw a super group!* That got me interested in the group, and it motivated me to buy and enjoy their 1978 album, *Infinity*. Since then, both *Infinity* and *Evolution* hit platinum, and their latest album, *Departure*, was in the Top 10. "Any Way You Want It," their newest single, was a hit on the radio.

Journey's manager, Herbie Herbert, contacted us to see if we'd open up for them on their next tour. Coming off *Departure*, they were planning to record a live album for their label, Columbia Records.

Steve Smith, a drummer they had recruited from Ronnie Montrose's band, was checking his drums, and guitarist Neal Schon was blazing machine-gun riffs into the empty cavernous space. Once Ross Valory arrived and began playing his bass, singer Steve Perry leaped onto the stage in blue jeans and in his old-school white Nikes with the red swoosh. Perry took control of the sound check as his tenor voice soared on several songs before he stopped the band to do *a cappella* vocal rehearsals.

Perry was clearly in charge as he ran the band through the paces, asking for different frequency boosts and cuts on his microphone. As I circled the arena to watch them from various angles, I noticed something special about these guys. They harmonized well and played soulfully together. I hadn't heard Perry's voice live before. Possessing a potent combination of soul, pop, and rock, he phrased deftly and never missed a note.

Steve and Neal had a rock swagger that was different from John Waite's swashbuckler confidence, almost to the point of arrogance. I had been with the club bands, and now The Babys, on the other side of the tracks, dealing with debt and a shifty record company. Meanwhile, Neal and Steve seemed to have built their ship from scratch with Herbie at the helm, a man who had been everything from a roadie to an owner of a sound company. Unlike my band, these guys were making money on the road, and they had Columbia Records behind them.

For a few moments, my surroundings disappeared and I was lost in the music. No longer a musician, but a fan. And yes, I believed that guy down there singing. Yes, I was going to cheer for him. And yes, he moved me more in person than he did when I listened to his first album with Journey.

I became a diehard Steve Perry fan on that day.

It was fun to be opening up for these guys.

A monumental change had already been taking shape in my life. Since the moment in 1978 when one of my closest friends from Chicago introduced me to a young blonde living in his apartment building, I had been crazy about Tané McClure. Alfredo told me she was gorgeous, and he had been right. The daughter of actor Doug McClure from the TV show *The Virginian*, she was an aspiring singer, and she wanted to meet me. Over a period of time, we dated a few times. At first, I admitted to my friend that although she was a nice girl, she wasn't for me. I came to change my mind over the next few months as Alfredo played middleman, delivering love messages from his long-legged blonde neighbor who said she was crazy about the keyboard player in The Babys. Before I went back on the road, our relationship had grown serious.

I had mentioned Tané on the phone to my parents, so they knew about our relationship and wanted to meet the girl I'd been dating, the daughter of a movie star. When I finally showed my mother a photo of Tané, she stared at the black-and-white photo and almost instantly proclaimed she was the one I should marry. I was almost thirty, and it was time to settle down. I admitted I was worried about the two of us being in show business and how there could be conflicts down the road. Amazingly, my parents didn't think there would be any problems. After all, she was the daughter of someone who had been very successful in the industry. They were certain we were in love and should go ahead and get married.

After settling down to life after touring with The Babys and Journey, I had the blessings of Tané's family to marry her. It was ironic that her father eventually turned out to love me more than she would. The first time I met Doug McClure at his home in Pebble Beach, he was returning from a film shoot in England where he had fallen in love with a young English woman on the set. This would have been fine—except that Doug was married to Barbara Luna, an actress, who heard about the affair and moved out of their home at Spyglass. In fact, she cleaned the place out. When Tané and I arrived at Pebble Beach, we learned that Barbara had sold all of the furniture and had Doug's belongings placed in storage.

Doug McClure was a tall, burly, aging surfer with broad shoulders, kind blue eyes, and a square chin. He had recently been struggling with a drinking problem and was slowly sliding down the other side of success. Once the golden boy, he was no longer on the A-list after burning some bridges in Hollywood. He was now fighting animated dinosaurs in B films and hustling to make ends meet. It seemed like his luck with women was as bad as the movies he was now starring in.

I couldn't help being in awe of the guy when I spent time with him. I'd grown up watching him on *The Virginian*. Doug looked and acted like a true movie star, with a charisma and presence that was undeniable. Just as when I watched Nick Papas's tumultuous downfall, I could see the benefits and the perils of being a celebrity from spending time with Tané's father. His drinking and four divorces took a toll on him, but I couldn't help fall in love with this big bear of a man. He was a charming, funny guy who could do an amazing Burt Lancaster imitation. He knew a ton of jokes and liked to trot them out whenever anybody would give him the stage. Whenever Tané and I were out in public with him, he was recognized and hounded for photos and autographs.

In the fall of 1979, Tané and I were married at First Presbyterian Church in Santa Monica, with a reception at the nearby Sheraton. I went into the marriage with my mother and father as the examples I intended to follow. For me, this was a "till death do us part" union, a sacred vow I was making with Tané. Being back in church brought me back in the presence of God, a feeling so profound that I ended up weeping later that night from the magnitude of the day.

It was a small wedding with only 135 people. While most of my family came, I didn't invite any of my bandmates in The Babys. The reception was in a small ballroom, and Tané's family had been extremely generous, giving us almost five thousand dollars. After a series of heartfelt toasts, we danced to "Let's Stay Together," played by a hired DJ. There was an upright piano in the corner, so I played a song I had written for the wedding, "Open Arms." I only had lyrics for the chorus, so I sang them for the family and friends at the reception.

As I finished the closing chords, I felt a slab of wedding cake hit my face and cream frosting burn my eyes. Nick Papas, my crazy advocate and friend, had hit me with my own wedding cake. Blinded by the frosting, I struggled to get up from the piano bench. My father grabbed me by the hand, offered a few choice words to Nick, and led me to the men's room to help me clean up.

With the money we got from the wedding, we decided to take a honeymoon to Puerto Vallarta. Eventually, Tané and I settled into a cozy one-bedroom apartment in Encino. It was small but in a good location, close to Ventura Boulevard and the freeway. Neither one of us had much, so we used the rest of our wedding money to buy furniture for our new love nest. Tané still had her job as a singing waitress at the restaurant, so she was bringing in a few bucks to help pay for things.

Despite their bleak financial situation, The Babys planned to do a new album. After two albums with Ron Nevison as producer, they chose Keith Olsen to oversee the release that would be titled *Union Jacks*. Keith worked out of a studio in the Valley, Sound City Studios, where Fleetwood Mac, Tom Petty, and REO Speedwagon had recorded hugely successful records. It was a complex in an industrial park off the freeway that featured earth-tone decor and vintage audio equipment. Unlike the full-blown pop production Ron Nevison had recorded with female vocalists, brass, and strings, Keith was going for the raw street-band sound the band had morphed into with Ricky and me on their debut album.

During the recording sessions for *Union Jacks*, John Waite wanted me to sing a song I had written in Japan, "Turn Around in Tokyo." Tony Brock came up with a signature rhythm that used a cowbell and a four-on-the-floor kick pattern that had my song up and rockin' in no time. Everybody was patient with my lead vocals, and we had the song finished in an evening. Not only was I writing with John, but I was getting to sing and write my own songs as well. It was something I hadn't dreamed would happen when I joined the band.

We also recorded "Stick to Your Guns," the song John had liked when I played it for my audition. It came out powerful, dark, and moody. Yet when we tried to sequence the record at mastering, it sounded out of place. After listening to the finished song, I shook my head and looked at John Waite sitting next to me.

"Cut it," I told him. "Take it out."

"But it's your song," he said.

"It doesn't belong."

"Turn Around in Tokyo" sounded more like The Babys, more like the album we were doing. It had more of that bubbly, pop rock and roll sound. As much as I wanted my songs to be shared with the world, I knew those secondary dreams and ambitions couldn't distract us from the primary objective of making a great album. And "Stick to your Guns" just didn't fit.

I can't be selfish like that.

The song will always be mine and will always move me. It will be my calling card in a way to this world, even if the world won't ever know about it. It will always remind me of my father's faith in me and his never-ending belief that this was "just a stepping-stone" to something greater.

Union Jacks was one of those stepping-stones. Released in January 1980, it would get the attention of one band in particular—Journey. It turned out the entire band loved the new Babys album, the one that just happened to have the name "Cain" written all over it.

On tour with Journey, I hung around after our set to watch the band play. Then after they were done, I'd stick around instead of going off and chasing girls. I was a married man, so I wasn't interested in finding someone other than Tané. Neal would often want to go somewhere and jam. He seemed to know where the bands were playing, and a few of us joined him from time to time.

When John Waite came with us, Steve Perry played drums and Ricky Phillips was on bass as we played old-school soul jams like "Funky Broadway" and "Mustang Sally." It was during these musical conversations that Neal and I found some synergy and realized we could bring out the best in each other's playing. He complimented me on my ability to solo and my knowledge of chord voicing and harmony. I loved the way he played the guitar so effortlessly, like it was an extension of his body.

Because I frequently stuck around to watch Journey after we played our set, I found myself getting invited to elaborate catered band dinners where a private chef prepared a meal after their show for road manager Pat Morrow, Herbie, and the band. Some nights, Pat had a chef prepare freshly made crepes or sushi, a far cry from the usual tired deli tray we had in The Babys' dressing room. Because Journey commanded the high guarantee by packing the fans in, they could afford perks like these.

There I was, a guy from a band where everything was going wrong, invited to break bread with a band where everything was going right—at least financially, since Journey was a well-oiled, money-making machine. It wasn't a fluke, however. Herbie Herbert had started as Neal's guitar roadie and had studied the business from the very beginning. Early on, he bought a PA company and a lighting company. Herbie learned all the ins and outs of what it took to be a success. When Journey started up, they were driving around in a station wagon, and it slowly grew into what it was now. Herbie had helped them get Steve Perry, even when the rest of the band didn't want him. He essentially told them, "You're *going* to get Perry."

Rolling Stone did a profile on Journey in 1980, with Herbie front and center in the article. I remembered reading a quote from their keyboardist at the time, Gregg Rolie: "Seven years of finding the right personnel and honing their act have made them a seamless hard-rock unit. Schon says they could last another ten years, easy," and then Rolie added, "Things have been running so smooth we're going to be pretty boring to write about."

I soon learned things weren't going quite as smoothly as the band's keyboardist described. I knew this, since I'd be the one to replace him in less than a year.

One day during a crew lunch at the venue, John Waite announced he was going solo and planned on leaving The Babys when the tour ended. Ricky, Tony, Wally, and I sat in disbelief. Neal Schon was there too. John told Neal he was tired of being in debt and didn't think The Babys could ever get into the black as an opening act.

Weeks later, we were in Detroit after a show at Pine Knob. As usual, I stayed for dinner, and afterward, I rode back to the hotel with Neal and Herbie in their stretch. I was in the front, while Herbie fired up a joint next to Neal and Pat in the back. They were all laughing and the radio was turned up, so I barely heard Herbie when he said, "What's it gonna feel like to be the next keyboard player in Journey, Caino?"

My head questioned what my ears clearly heard. I put my face in the barricade and squinted as my eyes burned from the reefer.

"What'd you say?"

Herbie just looked at me and rolled his eyes. "Oh, nothing."

They all kept laughing like schoolboys while I wondered if there was anything to the offhanded comment. In the limo that night was the first time I caught a bit of the whirlwind that was about to change my life.

The limo ride wasn't the only handwriting on the wall that I came to see. A few months later in the summer, as The Babys played a gig at the Oakland Coliseum, all the guys from Journey, including their managers, showed up, hanging out and being chummy. They were calling me Caino and talking and checking us out, and all the while, my bandmates in The Babys were staring at me, wondering what in the world was happening.

Did you know they were coming? were the sort of looks I was getting. *Did you plan this? What's going on?*

In reality, the Journey team was scoping me out. Plans were already in the works to recruit me. At the time, however, joining a band like Journey still felt like a far-off pipe dream—especially since I was struggling financially along with the rest of our band. I had learned at an early age to be responsible with my money, and I became accustomed to saving my earnings when Tommy and I performed at the clubs. The music business showed me that sometimes your financial situation is completely out of your control, as was true for my time with The Babys. Like figuring out the correct keys to write a great song and discovering the precise tools to produce one, I made a promise to myself that I would try to influence any decisions related to financial matters.

One day I want to be the one responsible for them.

The summer of 1980 was quite balmy in sunny Southern California, but money was running out for out for me and Tané. Out of the blue, The Babys' management got a call from the folks at Dr. Pepper to record a radio spot for the soft drink company. They offered to pay us a $35,000 flat-fee buyout. We had already finished work on our next album, *On the Edge*. The title suited our mood at the time. We all needed the money, so we reunited with Keith Olsen at Goodnight L.A. and came up with a punked-out version of their slogan. The money came to us quickly and saved the day for most of us—so did the radio spot that hit rock radio in a hurry. "Be a Pepper—we're all Peppers—drink Dr. Pepper!" John Waite snarled on the electric guitar-driven jingle. It was the last time we set foot in the studio together.

I spent the fall helping Tané with new songs we had written. We found an inexpensive home studio in the Valley to record and lay down the tracks, which were a mix of rock and pop—Blondie meets Benatar. I produced and played keyboards.

Tané's voice got stronger with each pass, and the songs got better as we homed in on a style and sound unique enough to present to a label. I hadn't written songs from a female point of view, so it took a bit of trial and error to capture the correct lyrics and the proper tone with her music.

As the year ended, I found myself at yet another crossroad. So much had happened in the last couple of years, but I was still stuck. All the hard work had helped me grow in my ability to write and play and handle things outside the studio, yet my bank account was still bare.

The leadoff song from *On the Edge* became yet another prophetic song I'd end up helping to write: "Walk away. Gonna build our plans to start again."

This was exactly what would happen with The Babys as 1980 came to an end.

AS I WALK ACROSS THE BROWN SHAG CARPET IN OUR ONE-BEDROOM apartment in Encino, "(Just Like) Starting Over" plays on my boom box. I pause before turning down the volume to make a call. The radio stations have been playing nothing but songs written and sung by John Lennon. This is in tribute to his tragic passing only a week ago.

On December 8, 1980, Mark David Chapman shot Lennon in the back multiple times. As the world mourned the loss of John Lennon, his words and music lifted so many jolted lives. Song titles take on a deeper significance when listening to them in this heartbreaking context. "In My Life." "Grow Old with Me." "Give Peace a Chance." "All You Need Is Love." And, of course, "Imagine."

Only a day after Lennon's sudden and unexpected death, John Waite's boot gets stuck on a large audio snake on stage, and he tears his ACL as The Babys play a concert. We only perform one more show, with Waite on crutches.

I know the ebb and flow of an artist's journey depend on tides outside of his control. Fortune can be found in talents and in the ties that bind, but our fate is determined by how those two things intersect with this thing called timing. The new Babys' album has just come out. With no airplay, no lead singer, and too much debt, The Babys are finished. It's the last time this lineup will ever play together.

After turning off the radio, I walk into the tiny kitchen with the bad linoleum and stained kitchen sink to call my father. I need to tell him the latest. The year is drawing to a close, and those all-too famil-iar questions are back to haunt me. Where will the next check come from? What's going to happen to The Babys and my musical career? What will I do with the songs I've written and still want to write?

When my father's words come once again like warm embers in the dead of winter, they aren't surprising. He's been saying words like these ever since the fire. He's been the adult telling his child to not give up on God or on himself. He's reminded me what John Lennon reminded the world: he might be a dreamer, but he's not the only one.

My father held dreams for me before I could even imagine them. He also knew words can be powerful.

"Things will get better, Jon."

My father encourages me yet again. Like he did after the fire and when I worked at Lou's deli and after we moved to a new neighborhood and as I began to play the accordion.

Time after time.

Affirmation after affirmation.

"But I don't know what I'm going to do," I say.

"Don't stop believin', Jon."

It's another phrase from my father that I write down. A part of me deep down knows that in some way, I'm going to use those three words in a song one day.

I also realize that my father will never stop believin' in me. Never.

FIFTEEN

"LAY IT DOWN"

When the moment came, I showed up armed with ideas, ambition, and enough energy to see them through. I arrived at the Journey camp with more than a decade of experience, and since I already knew the band and had jammed with them, joining them felt natural.

At the end of 1980, I received a life-changing phone call from San Francisco. It was Pat Morrow, the road manager for Journey, informing me that I had been chosen as the new keyboardist for the band. I dropped the phone on the kitchen floor of our small Encino apartment in disbelief.

"When do I audition?" I asked Pat.

"No need to audition. We've watched you enough with The Babys. You never missed a lick. Steve and Neal have been raving about your versatility and how much you know about music." Pat told me that even the departing keyboardist, Gregg Rolie, had given his blessing.

By the time I arrived in Oakland for the first day of rehearsal with the band, I had already told everybody, said my good-byes, and prepared myself as much as possible. An important call had gone out to John Waite to explain that I'd been invited to join Journey. I told him I'd still be there if he needed me. Waite assured me he had already decided to go solo. He hadn't undergone his knee surgery yet, so there wouldn't be any touring for at least a year. He was planning to leave Chrysalis and get another label, probably EMI Records, he explained. The Babys were still nearly a million dollars in debt, and there was no way, short of a miraculous hit album, to get even. Every dollar of revenue we earned from touring and album sales went toward this insurmountable debt. It was like we were in the army, living off our per diems.

Chrysalis Records, our label, seemed indifferent about us as well. "It's all about Blondie, Pat Benatar, and Ian Hunter anyway," John said.

The excessive cash demands The Babys had racked up in their early days had finally caught up with them. I wondered if John could walk away from his obligations there. I had been lucky to have kept my publishing. I knew they had his. John congratulated me on my new gig and wished me luck as we ended our conversation.

The Babys were suddenly just a footnote in rock history. I couldn't help but be relieved. John Waite was a swashbuckling rock star with a tortured poet's heart. He had also been a good friend and bandmate. Excited as I was to start with Journey, I would miss him and the rest of the guys.

I spent the rest of that afternoon calling Tony Brock, Wally Stocker, and Ricky Phillips, who weren't quite as understanding about my departure. Even dropping the bomb that Waite had decided to go solo didn't seem to get through to them. They vowed to find a new vocalist so they could continue as The Babys. Tony seemed to take it the hardest. I could hear the disappointment in his voice as he told me he could keep the band together if I stayed on. I told each of them I had made up my mind. I simply couldn't pass up this opportunity. It was what my father had predicted years before when I was ecstatic about getting the gig with The Babys.

"It's just a stepping-stone . . ."

Herbie Herbert had wanted me to fly up to see the rehearsal place in Oakland and meet with the guys. They had sent for all my gear that was stored at SIR's rehearsal studios and had it set up by the time

I arrived. Having toured with the band, I already knew they were highly organized.

Herbie picked me up at the Oakland airport in his Porsche 928 and took me to the studio. After hugs and handshakes, we jammed for a bit and took off for lunch at Herbie's headquarters. "Nightmare Inc" was a house in Cow Hollow—a neighborhood in San Francisco not far from the Golden Gate. After Herbie and Pat fired up a joint (I'd come to find there was always a lot of marijuana on hand), we discussed the way I would participate as a new member in Journey, along with the way Gregg Rolie would exit the band. They were offering me equal membership—sharing in record royalties, touring, and merchandise.

The offer was incredibly generous. Gregg would get a small, de-escalating percentage of my touring revenue for three years as a severance payment. I would be songwriting with Neal Schon and Steve Perry for the new album. All five band members—along with Herbie, who got a one-sixth share—shared half of the publishing revenue in the entire Journey catalog. I was elated with my deal. I was treated as an equal member, not a sideman. I wanted my lawyer, Chuck Hurewitz, who had kept Chrysalis Records from taking the songs I'd written for The Babys, to represent me and pore over the contract Journey would eventually ask me to sign.

What came as a pleasant surprise was that Pat Moro and Herbie also wanted to know if I had any softball skills, because they had a team—the Rockdogs—that played local radio stations in the Bay Area for charity. I assured them I had game. I'd been playing regularly on Sundays in LA when I came home from the road with rockers from various bands in Sherman Oaks. Who knew that softball would be a prerequisite to joining such a prestigious rock band?

One of the first things I would do with the band was play a soft-ball game. In my first game, I hit two home runs. Herbie couldn't help but laugh with excitement.

"If you can write songs the way you play softball, we're in for a good time here," Herbie told me.

Before I even began to write songs with Neal and Steve for the next album, I knew some fundamental things when it came to Journey. Above all, I knew what a tremendous responsibility had suddenly fallen on me. Being a member of a group like Journey meant you were a music ambassador to the world. And their fans were gold plated.

"You need to write songs about your fans and to your fans, and they have to be from the heart," I said to them.

I didn't know the band's true chemistry, so I was a bit apprehensive when I arrived, unsure of how we would gel. But I carried certain opinions with me after having studied the band. They already had the title of their next album—*Escape*. And I already had some idea of where the heart of the album might be. Coming off writing with John Waite, I had newfound confidence in my craft as a songwriter and wanted to incorporate songs about the working class in this new album.

Watching the shows as a fan while I was on tour with Journey, I noticed that the core Journey fans were blue-collar folks who were eager to rock and had spent hard-earned money to see them in concert. As a Springsteen fan, I felt we could take a page from his songbook and write songs that spoke to the working-class lifestyle, singing about the very issues they were thinking and dreaming about.

Springsteen had given us permission to write about the street life, something that hadn't been done much before. Until the late sixties, there wasn't a lot of depth in rock songs. Think about "For Your Love," which repeats the three-word title more than twenty times. Music had been pretty shallow until groups like The Moody Blues showed up. *I'll sign up for that*, I told myself after discovering them. I loved The Moody Blues and thought they were a great band. I discovered that Steve Perry was also a fan of that type of music.

By the late seventies, artists like Bob Seger and Elton John had arrived on the scene, telling specific stories about specific people— folks trying to get by, falling in love, struggling with fears, and living life with music in the background. Johnny Cougar had been doing it for years and was a couple of years away from his commercial breakthrough, *American Fool*—a rock and roll album full of storytelling and the pursuit of the American Dream. This was the sort of music I envisioned Journey doing. *Let's sing to those dreamers*, I thought. I felt if we were successful in connecting with these folks, we could be like the American version of The Who, the rock band that embraced the everyman's street lyrics and rich melodic anthems.

This was certainly a lofty goal, but it was my secret hope for what we could accomplish with *Escape*. "Keep on Runnin'"—the first song Steve, Neal, and I wrote—captured this concept: "Workin' in the city, this town's got no pity, Bossman owns a heart of stone."

The members of Journey were keen to change and were willing to listen to some new ideas. We were on our way.

Steve Perry was obviously the leader in control of the band. While Steve steered the boat, Neal Schon was the fire that fed the engine. As lead guitarist, Neal was keen to make his singer happy and continue to feed him. There was a creative tension I quickly discovered between Neal and Steve, one that reminded me of what the great producer, Gabriel Mekler, once said about working with Steppenwolf: "Tension within a band can be a great thing." This would be the case as it showed up in beautiful ways on the album we made.

Ross Valory brought more to the band than simply the cello-like bass lines he created. His humor and wit emerged at any given moment, especially since he could see the funny part in pretty much everything. Ross even added physical comedy on the spot, using voices and hysterical faces to ease the pressures of work and stress. He instinctively knew when to cut up to break the tension. It's no surprise that the lyric I wrote, "We all need the clowns to make us smile," was inspired by Valory.

While Steve Smith could joke with Ross, he could also be dead serious about the music. Our drummer brought a sureness and spiritual calm to our circle. His musical prowess as a Berklee College of Music graduate completed the engine that could rocket to any musical place. He brought an orchestral backdrop to our rhythm section that dazzled in dynamics, multiple layers of velocity, and subtle time variations.

In the midst of the band's success, I could easily spot the musical differences in the direction going forward. Steve's ideas tended to be more vocal oriented, leaning toward soul and pop. This was fine with Neal, but he also wanted to explore more progressive rock and classical influences, the sort of thing he had been doing his whole life. Neal had at least six ninety-minute cassettes filled with these ideas. After he played a few for me, I asked if I could borrow them to see what I heard lyrically and melodically. Most of them were powerful signature guitar riffs and chord progressions he had recorded, at home or alone after rehearsal. I felt like we could present Neal's ideas to Steve with some melodic and lyric direction that would broaden our musical repertoire. To my ears, Journey had always been a blend of soul, rock, and pop anyway, so I hoped I could be the glue that bound their styles together on one album.

After logging each of Neal's ideas in a spiral notebook, I put tape counter numbers, descriptions, and tempos for each idea. There were some memorable ones that I loved, but I heard them sometimes in a different order. To see if I was headed in the right direction, I bought another JVC cassette machine and wired them in tandem so I could edit certain chord progressions and riffs to make road maps that would eventually become songs. The title song "Escape" came out of this process; the tune came from four different tapes Neal had made. They were riffs I liked—this bit here and this bit there. Neal wanted progressive rock, but Steve couldn't wrap his head around it, so as we played around with different parts, I hummed Steve a melody. "Mother, Father" was another example—a marriage of Neal's complex chord structures with Steve's melodies and flawless voice.

My common sense as an editor helped turn those songs into sweeping rock anthems.

Poring over Neal Schon's tapes, I was blown away by his grasp of harmony and structure. *This guy is a guitar wizard*, I thought. Neal had a million ideas for the next album, and so did Steve. As I joined them, I hit the ground running, and to be honest, it was pretty easy. It's one thing to have a ton of ideas, but the key is to be able to blend them with other creators.

Steve Perry surprised me in multiple ways. I was impressed by his instincts and had no idea he was such a great technician. I also discovered that Steve enjoyed singing ballads. He loved the space on the slow songs where his high tenor voice could truly soar. While finishing up the song "Mother, Father" at his A-frame home in Corte Madera, he asked if I had brought any love songs. Ready to create, I had packed my Wurlitzer piano into the back of my Mazda, and I dragged it into his living room.

I knew exactly the song I needed to play for Perry: "Open Arms."

The song was one I had partially finished for Tané and played on our wedding day. I had played it to John Waite as a possible Babys' song, but he had passed, saying it was too flowery and sentimental. Years later, in a documentary about Journey, I quoted John as saying that—something he held against me for many years. Yet the interviewers had failed to offer my complete statement on the matter, as I also said that good singers instinctively know what they can and can't sing. The British rocker had known "Open Arms" wasn't his cup of tea.

Steve instantly loved the melody and the title, so he wanted to finish up the verse lyrics that were missing. Two hours later, it was complete, except for the key it'd be in. As a high tenor, Steve sang in a different key from how I wrote it, so I moved it up a perfect fourth—five half steps up the scale. The chorus soared. Both of us were thrilled with the song's innocence and tone and were excited to bring it to rehearsal.

As I drove home, I popped the cassette in my car and blasted "Open Arms." One thought burned inside of me:

Wait till the world hears this.

"Open Arms" fit with another key factor in Journey's music—the persona that Steve Perry had built as a singer. He was the boy next door with a broken heart who never got the girl. Just a guy from Fresno—a simple guy with simple needs. All of his songs portrayed this sort of guy, and I really liked this character—the guy who ended up never getting the girls. There's something endearing and fragile about lyrics like, "What can this poor boy do when he's hopelessly in love with you?" I wanted the songs for *Escape* to have this feel.

Let's keep him with a forlorn heart, I thought while working on the songs. "Open Arms" is the only time the guy gets lucky. Steve's songs were about that guy, and I wanted to keep it that way. His instincts always fit his character.

"Who's Crying Now" was another one of those heartbreak stories, yet we tried to give it a little more complexity. I remember being in my apartment when Steve arrived with an idea he came up with while driving to my place. He had recorded the idea, mostly humming the opening notes—"bam bam bam bam." So I listened and interpreted it on the piano. Once we had the right chords, Steve began to do his scat singing, where he focused and improvised with only syllables and sounds while I listened to his vowels and translated them.

The music room in my apartment had a skylight, and we heard rain pattering on the roof in the background. As I played the notes, Perry sang what sounded like "wooh ooh, wow ooh wow." *Wow oooh wow?*

"Sounds like 'who's crying now,'" I said.

We had landed on something we kept building together. Since I always had a favorite song of the month, I had the Eagles' "Heartache Tonight" in the back of my mind. Not the tune, but the idea about how someone out there was breaking another person's heart. We envisioned our song to be about a couple who couldn't keep things together, how they were caught in a web and couldn't hold on. How something so good could hurt so bad.

Right away, I knew there was something magical about writing songs with Perry. I felt like I was his genie in a bottle.

We can make a song out of anything, I thought. *With that voice and that guitar, we can go anywhere.*

Neal Schon didn't always share our love for ballads like "Open Arms." After we played it to the band, Neal looked dumbfounded.

"What are we supposed to play on that song?" he asked.

Into the awkward silence, Steve Perry said, "We'll find the right arrangement."

Perry was confident we could turn it into a rock anthem and began suggesting ideas for when the bass and drums could come in. I asked Neal to play the opening theme with me. The song started to grow wings and fly. That afternoon, rehearsing it gave me goose bumps as Steve's voice soared along with the band in our secret warehouse minutes from the Oakland ghetto.

Neal still wasn't sold. The validity of the arrangement did come up again in the studio—but maybe because I'd spent so much time poring over his ideas and sewing them into lyrics and melody, he agreed to give "Open Arms" a chance to live on our new Journey album. The song was a departure, I had to admit. But when Steve sang it and Journey played it, something magical happened that day in the warehouse.

This wasn't the only time Neal would make a concession. It's part of the creative process—learning to listen and let go at times. "Stone in Love" was a good example. Neal had given me a new riff, which I immediately liked. I took the cassette to Steve's house, where we agreed it had potential to be a great rock song. The trouble was, every time we got to the chorus Neal had written, we came up empty for a melody and a lyric. We loved what we had and agreed we needed a strong chorus.

Since Steve and I both loved The Hollies when we were younger, I suggested we write a new chorus that had the harmony parts they might have sung. Steve played the bass, and we came up with a new chorus.

"Those summer nights are callin', stone in love," we sang. Our voices had a rich blend, and I used my two machines to stack vocal parts on top of each other. We finished Neal's rock idea in a few hours. To us, it was memorable and unique—it sounded like Journey. Back in Oakland we played our song for Neal.

"What happened to my chorus, man?" he asked.

"We came up a new one," I said. "Don't you love the harmonies?"

"I thought the chorus I had really rocked, that's all," he said.

After a few more listens, he still wasn't sold.

"Look, Neal, this sounds fresh," Steve said. "Trust me. We explored your chorus for a good hour and came up with nothing."

It wasn't the first time I had substituted one of Neal's progressions. We just added a whole new section to what he had given us—to what he thought was complete. I hoped he understood that Steve and I were only out to get the best song we could write.

Steve got Ross Valory's bass and showed Neal the new section. The rest was history, as we all soared again like the Blue Angels up at our studio above the Oakland 880 freeway, jamming to our new and soon to be classic "Stone in Love." That afternoon, when Neal came up with the brilliant, memorable melody on the outro of the song, I knew the chemistry between all of us was headed in the right direction.

As we recorded *Escape*, Herbie Herbert kept the A&R department away from the inner sanctum. As a result, Columbia Records never heard any of the songs we recorded until we turned in the album—a pretty remarkable thing in those days. It was a very confident and powerful statement for a band to make. Herbie made the single choices with the band and knew a great song when it came along. So we eventually sequenced the album ourselves before turning it in.

After rehearsing and recording in Oakland, we loved what we had, but we wanted to shoot for two more songs. Steve asked if I had any lyrics or melodies that might work for the new album. I went home and paged through all my spiral notebooks. On the last page of my notebook, I found three words scribbled:

Don't stop believin'.

I knew Steve would like the title—the words my father had given me on a long-distance phone call one night. I began trying different melodies, poking away at my white Wurlitzer in the music room with the skylight. I knew his vocal range by now, so I picked notes where he could soar. I also knew he hated to sing the "e" vowel, so I wasn't sure he would want to work on it.

I came up with a cool chord progression and started humming the lyric "don't stop—believin'—hold on to that feelin'" over the changes. I didn't know what the other lyrics were yet, but I planned to show the guys the idea anyway. When I played and sang it for the band the next day at rehearsal, everyone was on board to give my idea a try.

Steve liked my chord progression and suggested we use the same chords for the verse, but with the rolling piano feel I'd played for The Babys' albums. I began without the bass notes, using only the right hand, and Neal started playing what would end up to be the bass line. Ross picked a verse melody that led Neal to some chords for the channel, and we looped over and over until it began to take shape.

Steve Smith came up with an upbeat splash and bell cymbal motif, and we had something unique rocking the warehouse once again.

After the first verse, Neal began to play a staccato guitar line that sounded like a train going down the tracks as we headed into another verse with only piano and vocal. When we finished the first B section, I asked Steve if he wanted to insert my chorus. He said, "Not yet, Jon." Instead, we roared into Neal's guitar part, playing unison with the newly minted bass line. When the second B section ended, Neal burst into the melody I had written, playing it as a theme. I was amazed as the band improv led to the final chorus, breathing life into what seemed to be another Journey classic sound.

Excited to finish the lyrics to our new song, I met Steve at his house the next morning. We both loved strong black coffee, so he had a fresh pot brewing when I arrived. Sitting down in a chair with his Fender bass, I played the cassette we had recorded at the Oakland warehouse.

"Neal's guitar in this section sounds like a train heading down the track," I said. "Makes me think of a song I love—'Midnight Train to Georgia.' You too?"

"Gladys Knight & the Pips—a classic for sure," Steve said.

"What if the lyric was 'the midnight train goin' anywhere'?" I said.

Steve liked the lyric, so we built off it, adding a boy and a girl headed out on that midnight train. We loved this idea of two young people dreaming about leaving their town and going somewhere to make a new start. So we began our song with our two characters and put them in motion.

When Steve arrived at "just a city boy, born and raised in—" he came to an abrupt stop.

"How 'bout making him from Detroit?" he asked.

Journey had just recorded the live album *Captured* in the Motor City, and we knew the city loved us.

"They'll go crazy if we mention their city," Steve said.

"Cool, but we need another syllable to fill it out here. How does south Detroit sound?"

Playing his bass, Steve sang the new lyric. "This sings great. Is there even a south Detroit?"

"Heck if I know," I said. "If it sings well, I say let's move on."

I told Steve about the days I lived with my brother in Laurel Canyon and cruised Sunset Boulevard on Friday nights. I recalled the menagerie of people who were there "runnin' down a dream." I told him about the Whisky a Go Go—how The Babys played there on New Year's Eve and my first live gig with them. I described the small, packed venue, the old bar smell, and the sting of smoke in the eyes. Steve had been there. He knew the scene I had been trippin' on.

"A singer in a smoky room, the smell of wine and cheap perfume. For a smile they can share the night. It goes on and on and on and on," we wrote.

The middle section that Neal had come up with was next. With our conversation about Sunset Boulevard still fresh, Steve and I went on to see the movie we were creating in our minds.

"Strangers waiting up and down the boulevard, their shadows searching in the night."

The "boulevard" was Sunset on a Friday night in 1973. Now it was time to add the dreamers who inhabited a magical time in rock and roll history. From the rockers and the wannabes who hung out at the Rainbow Bar & Grill, to the record biz folks who made career deals at the Le Dome restaurant, to the girls in tight skirts who flirted with anyone who would pay attention. These were the "streetlight people, living just to find emotion, hiding somewhere in the night."

Steve Perry and I had played the clubs. We had paid our dues—in different environments—and we had both survived the process of wanting something more for our careers.

"Workin' hard to get my fill. Everybody wants a thrill. Payin' anything to roll the dice just one more time," we wrote.

These lines summed up the two of us, sacrificing it all to gamble on a dream.

That day, the movie played in our heads, one that had been going "on and on and on and on."

We didn't know it yet, but we had just written an anthem that would stand the test of time.

I WIPE THE SWEAT OFF THE BACK OF MY NECK AS I STARE OUT THE SMALL window and look at the city below. I feel like I'm standing on the edge of a sharp cliff, looking down. Some might see a sparkling, picturesque lagoon, but I simply see a dark, bottomless pool that drowns individuals.

It almost drowned me.

I'm returning to Los Angeles to play to more than 83,000 people in the Rose Bowl on July 2, 1982. It's the last date we'll play on our *Escape* tour, one that began nearly a year ago in Osaka, Japan. More than 130 concerts later, this event will be a celebration of our rise to superstardom.

We've already played here, but something about this concert overwhelms me.

I feel nauseous.

I think about those used-up streets and dirty houses. Nothing's changed about Hollywood since I was there eight years ago.

I vowed to never come back.

LA wounded me. Deeply and spiritually. When I left, I was relieved to be away from all the negativity and rejection. San Francisco was the only place that invited me to play *Windy City Breakdown*, and I told everybody I'd love to live there some day.

I prophesied my own destiny.

I feel an apprehension I haven't felt for quite some time. I know it's the shadows of the rejection and frustration that overwhelmed me while living in this city.

I'm afraid my fairy dust is going to rub off. Someone in this place is going to try to steal it from me.

Is this town once again going to suck something out of my soul?
It can't. I won't let it.

All those doubters who snubbed their noses can line up and get a ticket and see me play.

I know I'm victorious as I come back here. I just have to remember the reason.

SIXTEEN

"LIBERTY"

During a break after the first leg of the *Escape* tour in early 1982, I found myself taking a deep breath and reflecting on the last year of my life. We were halfway through the more than 130 concerts we'd play in support of the album, and already the hard work had paid off. *Escape* had become Journey's first No. 1 album, selling more than a million copies in two weeks after its release and eventually surpassing five million later that year. As I played the tape and listened to the songs I had written and recorded years ago in that tiny apartment full of lost dreams in Hollywood, I realized the truth.

You weren't there, dude. You hadn't arrived yet.

After all those years of writing, singing, and performing in clubs, a resentment had begun to grow inside me. I'd always been wired this way. When I was young, I would be frustrated whenever I was told I couldn't do something or when things didn't go as planned. I couldn't figure out how to tumble in gymnastics, for example, simply because I wasn't coordinated—and this infuriated me. The impatience and dogged determination began there in my youth. All my life, I've had to fight those frustrations. Those years in my late twenties were no different, as I tried to figure out how to get beyond the anger I felt toward people who told me I couldn't sing or couldn't do something.

I just hadn't learned that cowriting was on God's agenda for me. At least for the moment.

When I finally decided to let go of the bitterness and embrace what I loved about music, I fell in love with writing songs. I didn't care if they were good or bad. And now, years later, while on my first tour with Journey, I could see that I hadn't been ready. A lot of the rejection had been justified.

I needed those slammed-shut doors to allow me to keep knocking.

I needed that pain that prompted my father to tell me to stick to my guns.

I needed someone like John Waite to show me how to play a perfectly crafted song like "Isn't It Time."

During the early days in LA, I needed to learn more about writing music. Slowly but surely, month after month, session after session, I began to get under the hood of the tunes and discover why they worked. I studied songs and tried to understand what made certain ones great. When an album like *Hotel California* came out, I marveled and realized the masterpiece that had been created.

That's genius, I'd think. Then I'd begin to ask why it worked so well. That Eagles' album had beautifully crafted songs that felt simple and conversational. I needed to learn how to set up that sort of atmosphere in songs, and to do that was going to take some time. Boston came on the scene with its staggering sound, and again I needed to explore how they came up with it. I was a student of those records. Steely Dan and David Bowie and Joe Walsh kept me company and got me through rough times.

I never gave up, however. And even when I couldn't perform or write, I listened and learned.

Every time we stepped onstage, the Journey team gave the crowd every single thing we could. I can blink and still remember those moments when I first performed with the guys.

I harmonize with Perry as I stand and belt out the chords on the song: "They won't take me. They won't break me."

The set list begins with the explosion of "Escape," and none of us hold back. Steve Perry doesn't stand still during the five-minute song, and we don't pause for even a second to catch our breath before "Line of Fire" shows why Neal is a guitar legend. My fingers power up and down the keys of the red Yamaha C7 grand piano I call "The Whale."

The crowd sings along to "Lights" and loves how we segue straight into "Stay Awhile."

Night after night. Taking a break of a day or two between shows, but not many. Week after week. Month after month.

More than 130 shows, starting in 1981 and raging on into 1982.

Steve Perry never wavers in his passion when delivering "Mother, Father." I never slow down on my piano solo that seems to use every note on The Whale. Neal's playing never seems more effortless as he scales the heights at the end of "Who's Crying Now." Steve Smith never stops on "Where Were You" and somehow always follows it up with an intense drum solo that can stand with the greats in this business. Ross Valory never fails to keep this high-octane sports car running, keeping those chords with the grooves he belts out of his bass guitar.

"Here's some new *Escape* music for you," Steve shouts out to the crowd as I play those chords and hear the screams of celebration. The song isn't even a year old, but everybody seems to know and love "Don't Stop Believin'." Every night, Steve alters the lyrics to fit the venue we're in.

"Just a city boy, born and raised *right here in* . . ."

One night it's Toronto; the next, it's Cuyahoga Falls, Ohio. There's Omaha and Cincinnati and Jacksonville and Nashville and Memphis and Mobile and San Diego and Honolulu and Osaka and Calgary and, of course, Detroit.

"Stone in Love" shows why we work so well together. At the end of the song, I'm at the center of the stage alongside Neal and Ross playing guitar, while Steve is behind us playing the keyboard. Journey is beyond a well-oiled machine. One minute the singer shines, the next the guitarist soars—and I'm in the middle for exactly those reasons.

All of us harmonize and sing and jam on "Keep on Runnin'," and Steve keeps gliding and ascending. His voice is unstoppable.

The sweaty, exuberant crowd sings along to "Wheel in the Sky." And of course, every soul in the building shouts out their best "na na na na na na's" during "Lovin', Touchin', Squeezin'."

Steve Perry has the crowd in the palm of his hand with the last song, "Any Way You Want It." All of us do. It seems like we could keep playing all night. From those first bright lights to the moment all of us lock arms around each other and take a bow, we do our best to show ourselves worthy of those incredible fans who applaud us. Night after night after glorious night.

It's easy to feel invincible standing on the stage at night and listening to the approval of thousands, yet daytime always came and reminded us we were mortal. Our bodies would be sore and spent, our emotions drained. The familiar cycle of rolling on after rocking the night happened like clockwork. Sometimes you couldn't help feeling exhausted and even homesick.

After only a month on the road, those feelings caught up with me as I thought about Tané and how much I missed her. Plenty of distractions awaited us at every venue, since the crowds were predominantly female. Ballads like "Open Arms" certainly welcomed in a new flock of women ready to swoon at Steve Perry's heartfelt delivery every night.

Somewhere in the hum and steady rocking on a tour bus heading to Saratoga Springs, I heard a tune in my dreams and thought of lyrics that woke me up. Finding a pen in the dark, I scribbled the words on a napkin, something I'd never done before.

Highway run into the midnight sun.

The next day, I took the napkin and grabbed my thirty-dollar Casio keyboard. The rest of the lyrics flowed out of me, and I wrote them down almost frantically, as though I was struggling to keep up with the sentiments of my soul. The chords and their progression came naturally. I'd never had a song rise so quickly inside me and take its full form in a matter of minutes. It was an anointed, supernatural thing to write it in a full-out thirty minutes.

I wondered if I could write a song that could be like a musical postcard to home, simply saying, "Hey, I miss you, I love you, and I'm here for you." It wasn't just a cool idea, but it was a statement I wanted to make to my wife.

When I played through the whole thing, I knew. When you've played so many of the remarkable songs of others and tried to write so many yourself, you know when one is good.

This is special.

Instead of bringing the song to Steve Perry and asking him to help me finish it, I did the job myself this time. There was just something special about this ballad.

God gives artists gifts like these, and so many people fail to give him credit. It would take me years to begin to give God praise for these gifts.

I'm so thankful that this song is still known and loved, and we continue to perform "Faithfully" every time Journey plays.

During our second leg of the *Escape* tour in 1982, Journey unveiled something new that concertgoers had never witnessed. It was Herbie's brainchild, though it made sense, since he had started out working in sound as a roadie for Santana. Herbie always thought everything through, going above and beyond what most other band managers did. His idea was, instead of making extravagant videos, why not put that money into doing a more elaborate production so fans could see the best show we could make.

To do that, Journey ended up pioneering the use of giant video screens. Herbie's vision was to put Barco projectors in the venue.

For the first time, fans would not only be able to see what was happening up close on stage, but they could even follow the band as we walked from the dressing room through the hallways and up to the stage. All of us in the band believed in Herbie's vision, so we all put seed money into what became Nocturne Productions.

Right now, state-of-the-art technology with big screens and spectacular lighting are standard for live performances, but in 1982, Journey broke new ground by investing in them. The massive screens made their debut at the Day on the Green concert in Oakland. Not long after that, representatives of artists such as U2, Michael Jackson, Def Leppard, and others began showing up at our offices, wanting to find out how to get that same video experience.

Production was very important to Journey, but there was something that always trumped that. As Herbie liked to say, the equipment is never better than the people who operate it. So we employed the best people we could find, whether they were accountants, managers, lighting designers, sound engineers, or technicians. Herbie once said in an interview that no other band or artist ran its business as efficiently as Journey, and starting with *Escape*, I could see that this was true.

As the tour ended, we found ourselves in the studio to start recording *Frontiers*. Herbie had his unrelenting timetable—when we would be recording, when the album would release, and when we'd be touring. The *Escape* tour had been so long, and yet there we were, recording again. None of us wanted to duplicate that album, but rather to build on it. It would be quite a feat to do that.

The six-week recording sessions for my first Journey album had been absolutely mind-boggling. I witnessed Steve and Neal doing amazing things, such as Steve singing the vocals for "Mother, Father" in only two takes. I knew we could build on everything we had done on *Escape*. We now had the freedom to make the album we wanted to make and the success to do whatever we wanted.

People asked me if I'd been nervous to join Journey and what it was like to write one of the bestselling albums of all time—what it felt like to help write *the* most downloaded song of all time. Was I nervous, and did I know how monumental those songs would be?

I wasn't thinking about any of that at the time. I joined Journey and knew I just had to focus. I wasn't going to look back or freak out.

Successes usually take a decade or two to happen. I had been doing things all my life—knocking stuff down and hitting home runs—when people weren't looking. When I became part of Journey, I knew *everybody* was looking, so I simply focused on the task at hand. I knew I'd be judged later, but for now, I had to put my head down and not look around. I had to focus on what needed to be done.

This was a result of my father's belief that you just put your head down and get it done. It was also a result of working hard as a kid, watching successful businessmen like Lou Venetti show me how to do things. It was my tough Midwestern temperament and a persistent streak that wouldn't allow me to fail. It didn't even hit me until we had finished *Escape* that I hadn't played a single gig with Journey yet.

Dad helped put flesh on what I needed to do once I began writing with Steve and Neal:

- Enhance what you can enhance, and stay out of whatever you can stay out of.
- Don't question the circumstances or the situation.
- Remember that you're blessed to be there.

I did all of those things and never forgot to consider every moment as a blessing.

Looking back, I know that God is the one who clears a way for people like me, people who are hungry and show up after working hard to arrive at the moment. I had worked so hard and wondered along the way what it would be like. Starting with the first time I heard my first song on the radio, "Midnight Rendezvous," remembering how I pulled over on the side of the road and listened with a big grin hung over my face like Mr. Moon. Even then, the irony in life was obvious, since I wasn't even playing a keyboard in the song, but rather a Fender Stratocaster.

For *Frontiers*, we wanted to take the next step. We already had one song ready to go. During the *Escape* tour, we discovered we needed an up-tempo rock anthem, something to wake the crowd up. So I wrote a song on a foot-long Casio, and Steve and I wrote the lyrics in the hotel the next day. We were doing it in sound check on the third day. "Separate Ways" was another example of the chemistry Steve and I had and how things were clicking for all of us.

Frontiers was Journey's most complex album. I knew by then that we had a rock and roll orchestra happening with Neal Schon. There weren't many who could soar and play complex music like he could. I became fascinated with Neal's classical talents and how symphonic he was, even though he hadn't had a technical education. When I joined the band, I knew Neal was talented, but I had no idea all the things he knew.

I thought Journey hadn't always fully utilized the talents Neal brought to them. There were pieces that seemed to be left behind. With Steve Smith's ability to build something up and Ross Valory's lyrical talents on the bass, playing almost like a cello player, we had this incredible arsenal we could take full advantage of for *Frontiers*. So we did—and we had a lot of fun with it.

Joe Montana gave me the best advice during the time we were thinking about recording the follow-up to *Escape*. I met him at a luncheon after the San Francisco 49ers won Super Bowl XVI on January 24, 1982. He was a fan of Journey, and we hit it off. He showed me his Super Bowl ring, which prompted me to ask how he planned to win another championship.

"I'm going to put my ring in the drawer and forget about the Super Bowl," Joe said. "I'm not going to look back. I'm going to forget all about it."

Joe was hungry for another championship, and he found it three years later as the 49ers crushed the Miami Dolphins. Montana was the MVP for Super Bowl XIX.

When it came to Journey's next album, I adopted the same mind-set.

We're just a struggling rock band, I forced myself to think. *We have to make a great record.*

Like those great 49ers teams in the eighties, Journey was riding a high. We were on this magical, powerful ride. Living large and knowing life couldn't get any better.

I just couldn't stay comfortable or complacent.

One of my favorite Journey songs came as easily as "Faithfully." It was a result of seeing my ex-girlfriend, Virginia, during our *Escape* tour as we played the Day on the Green event put on by music promoter Bill Graham every year in Oakland. The Day on the Green concerts had become legendary, featuring multiple big-name acts performing at the Oakland Coliseum. All the big names had played at the event: the Rolling Stones, The Who, Pink Floyd, and Aerosmith, to name just a few. Since we were a local band, Journey was invited to play numerous times.

Ginny surprised me at the gig, and we ended up briefly saying hi. I couldn't help thinking how odd it was to see someone who had been such a big part of my life and briefly greeting her. It made me imagine seeing someone who knew Ginny and telling them to "send her my love." This became the song title, and I wrote it from a third-person point of view, imagining someone singing it for a long-lost love. Once again, the inspiration allowed the words and melodies to come quickly.

I was living on Saddle Lane in Novato, where I had a circular 180-degree view of the valley whenever I sat at my grand piano. I called Steve Perry, like I usually did when I had a new tune in hand.

"Come over here," I said. "Now."

"You're a slave driver," Perry said.

"It'll be worth it."

Perry drove over, and we worked on the song in the living room for an hour or so. I knew key parts of the song and sang them to him. "Been so long . . ." "Send her my love, memories remain . . ." Being a forlorn lover, Steve took the words and melody and yet again ran with them. We had a recurring theme about how falling in love can be painful, about how haunting love can be. It flowed from the minute I wrote it, and then it became pretty magical when it all came together.

As the songs for *Frontiers* continued to emerge, I remembered the advice of two iconic musicians I'd met. One was a rooftop encounter with Isaac Hayes in 1971 while I was in Savannah, Georgia, playing a show. I asked him how he had suddenly emerged on the scene with his sound for the movie *Shaft*. Hayes said he'd been making his signature sound for years; the business was finally ready to accept him as a solo artist.

Know who you are, and be faithful and true to your work is the essence of what Hayes was saying. *Don't go chasing the latest and greatest thing.* I began to try to apply this advice right after I heard it, and I still adhere to it today whenever I create and produce my music.

The other piece of advice came from Stevie Wonder. He and I met backstage before a show at Circle Star Theatre in San Carlos. Both of us loved the same synthesizer, the PPG Wave, so we talked briefly about the keyboard. He gave me some important advice as a songwriter: *Don't leave too many songs unfinished because they can easily add clutter to your creative flow and rob you of the confidence you need to make tough decisions.*

Once again, this became a discipline I follow to this day.

Accepting your place. Paying attention. Working hard. Knowing strengths. Staying true to yourself. Finishing what you started. These were all the things I was doing in my career and in our band. I knew we still had a lot more hits to be recorded.

In many ways, Journey had the freedom to go wherever we wanted. We just needed to do what the title song on our new album said: "We put hope in front of fear."

SEVENTEEN

"RUNNING ALONE"

There's the happy, carefree guy I met during the *Departure* era, the singer who walked the walk and talked the talk. The guy with the swagger who was the king and the boss the moment he stepped out under those lights. Someone completely comfortable in his own skin, with an unstoppable voice that could only be topped by his irrepressible spirit.

Then there's the same guy six years later, reserved and cautious during the *Raised on Radio* years, the celebrity carrying the weight of the world in his head and heart. The one who would admit to us and the rest of the world that he was simply "toast." Making his debut in 1977 as Journey's singer, Steve Perry would tell Neal and me he was done with the band almost ten years later.

Despite honest confessions and soul-searching over the years from Steve himself, fans have always wanted to understand why Steve Perry walked away from Journey at the height of such popularity and success.

As is true in any relationship that breaks down, there is never one single reason, but rather a series of complicated factors that build into an ultimate farewell. In this case, so much of it has already been displayed, but not in magazines, papers, or online.

If you want to decipher the reasons, simply study the songs. You can learn things the songwriters didn't even understand at the time. A young man can emerge out of nowhere, standing patiently and letting the lights shine on him, only to find himself a decade later out of control and close to overload.

Songs are footprints in the snow that never melts. Sometimes they foreshadow the climb yet to come; other times they follow you over a mountaintop and watch as you tumble down on the other side.

Steve Perry was already thinking about a solo album when I arrived and began to write with him for *Escape*. I wanted him to see all the potential he had with Journey. After I played "Open Arms" for him, Steve said he wanted it for a solo project, but I dissuaded him right away.

"There's no reason you can't do ballads for Journey," I said. "You can sing whatever you want."

"Open Arms" validated Steve vocally when it came to ballads. Even though the band stood with open mouths after we played it to them, wondering what in the world they were supposed to do with it, Steve never questioned it. He was confident and knew the song was going to be a hit.

On January 5, 1983, Journey released its leadoff single to *Frontiers*: "Separate Ways (Worlds Apart)." Officially starting on February 22, 1983, in Nagoya, Japan, and a month later, on March 28, in Seattle, Washington, the *Frontiers* tour encompassed more than one hundred shows and lasted until September. The tour had some casualties, such as Ross Valory's and Steve Smith's dismissals from the band because Steve wanted to go in a different musical direction. Unfortunately, they wouldn't rejoin until 1998 and 2016 respectively. And I returned from the tour to find my marriage in disarray and ultimately beyond repair.

There's a common cliché in our industry: *The road takes its toll.* I already knew from watching Nick Papas and Doug McClure that you can become a victim of the business you're in. The long separation from Tané and our two different lives led to a painful divorce.

This was the MTV era, so Journey played the game like everybody else. Neal and I were among the first celebrity VJs to host an entire show with Nina Blackwood from a rooftop in San Francisco's Fisherman's Wharf. We also had fans flying with us to our *Escape* concert in Houston, which would be broadcast live worldwide on MTV and simulcast on FM radio, a first for any band to do.

Then there were those legendary videos we made—like the all-time-classic camp video for "Separate Ways." I'm proud to say I might be the only person in history who played an air keytar in a video. We would have to endure two years of Beavis and Butt-Head poking fun at us in that same video!

I'll admit it was total rock and roll camp. The videos we made for our *Frontiers* songs were a three-for-one deal, costing $5,000 to make each one—and it looked like it. We used the same guy who produced a video for Neal Schon's "No More Lies" off his solo album. Along with "Separate Ways," we also filmed videos for "Chain Reaction" and "After the Fall."

I recall that Steve Perry wasn't so sure about doing the videos. And when we showed up for the video of "Separate Ways" in New Orleans, it turned out that his girlfriend, Sherrie Swafford, was equally resistant after seeing the blonde who would star in the video with us. When it was all over, Perry decided that making rock videos wasn't for Journey. We did live performance videos from that point on. Steve felt that the rock videos ruined it for some of our fans, since it involved a director painting a picture for our songs instead of leaving it to the listener's imagination.

One interesting surprise came after *Frontiers* was released. Columbia Records called to tell me that Prince and his manager wanted to do a conference call about a new song he had written. They explained that the outro had the same chord changes as "Faithfully," so they wanted to make sure I was okay with it, since I was the sole composer of the track.

Curious and honored at the same time, I went to the Santa Monica office. The A&R guy, Mike Dilbeck, played the new song and pointed out the parts where Prince was concerned he had taken too much. Prince was already a superstar, with his 1982 album *1999* going on to become the fifth highest-selling album of 1983. The song featured him soloing on his guitar, similar to what Neal Schon would play over the same chords to "Faithfully." Yet there was no melodic resemblance at all.

"Purple Rain" was a fantastic song. And there I was, one of the first outside of Prince's camp to hear it.

After listening to his song, I assured Prince that he was cool as far as I was concerned. I also congratulated him on a great ballad. I was flattered that a big star cared so much about encroaching on someone else's work. It showed a lot of class.

"Good luck with the song," I said before we ended the phone call. "I'm sure it will be a hit."

"Purple Rain" was more than just a hit; it became one of rock's all-time great songs. Prince's album by the same name was released in 1984 and became the most popular and iconic album the talented and prolific artist ever made.

Another person reaching out to the band during that time was the mother of a sixteen-year-old fan from Ohio. The woman had written a heart-wrenching letter to the Make-A-Wish Foundation about her son, Kenny Sykaluk. He had battled cystic fibrosis his entire life, and his one desire was to one day meet the members of Journey. After we set up a hospital visit, all of the band members flew to Cleveland in

November to meet Kenny. None of us knew the reality of his condition, how his body was only hours from giving out on him. As Kenny struggled for air, all five of us felt breathless ourselves, grieving for this poor young soul.

We had brought Kenny an autographed San Francisco 49ers helmet, along with a signed platinum record award from the band. But we had another very special gift for Kenny—a Journey song nobody outside of the group had ever heard. Originally recorded for *Frontiers*, "Only the Young" had been cut at the last minute by a group vote, something that deeply upset me. The song would eventually be featured in the hit movie *Vision Quest*, gaining notoriety for being played in its entirety.

We really didn't know how important it was that we went to see Kenny that day. As we walked into his hospital room, it was clear he was in a lot of pain. "Only the Young" was on a cassette tape and ready to be played on a Walkman. Slipping the headphones over Kenny's ears, we watched as the kid began to listen to our unreleased song. While the tune played, Kenny looked up and his eyes got huge, and then moments later, he looked up again and seemed to realize we were really there.

Each song has its place and purpose, and "Only the Young" was meant to stay off *Frontiers* initially simply because it belonged to Kenny. The lyrics took so long to finally discover, yet when they arrived, they were truly special. Steve Perry expressed it in an interview taped during the week Journey was enshrined in the Rock and Roll Hall of Fame: "The lyrics to 'Only the Young' are powerful lyrics. I really have to give credit to Jonathan Cain for coming up with the concept to write about before we even knew about Kenny, about 'only the young can say they're free to fly away.' Because there's a certain innocence that the youth have . . . That's just a wonderful gift."

The gift was being able to hear Steve's voice and become inspired to create lyrics like that. And then, ultimately, to see the joy and hope Kenny had when listening to them on the last day of his life. All of us in Journey were heartbroken when we received the news of Kenny's passing the day after we met him.

This was one of those moments when the Lord spoke loudly and clearly to me. Meeting Kenny and sharing with him a rough mix of "Only the Young" was divine intervention, and when I realized this, it hit me like a ton of bricks.

God made it possible for me to be part of this young soul's life—this young man who happened to be a Journey fan.

I was destined to see Kenny on the last day of his life and give him the perfect song to send him off with.

Years later, I broke down in the *Behind the Music* documentary and shared how no kid should have to live with that kind of pain. I knew what it looked like for young kids to die or be physically wounded, so meeting Kenny had a huge impact on my life—not because of the pain he was in, but because of the brief joy we brought to him.

Music brought me hope at an early age. Now I was discovering I could help do the same for others.

As the stage darkened and the spotlight followed Neal Schon as he jammed on his guitar solo, I looked to the side of the stage and saw Steve Perry arguing with his girlfriend, Sherrie—the woman he would title a hit song after. It wasn't the first time they had yelled at each other. I didn't know what they were arguing about, but I knew it was none of my business, so I stayed out of it.

Bringing anyone new into our circus-like life, with one show after another, would have been difficult, but when Steve's girlfriend began to tour with us, a strange dynamic was introduced into the band. Steve's personality changed. I could tell he felt awkward at times, which he hadn't shown before. That confident and in-control guy I met during the *Departure* days was now second-guessing himself. Someone he loved was now in his life, so his attention naturally was focused elsewhere.

As the tension in our group grew, along with the miles and the time out on the road, I could tell Steve was under a lot of stress. During this tour, I began to hear Steve's voice start to get rough. I think we were working him too hard, especially Herbie Herbert. I think Herbie always thought Steve could just fly through those songs night after night. The wear and tear began to take its toll, but the stress also seemed to have a negative impact on his voice. I've seen this happen when singers get stressed—how anxiety can affect their voice. I believe it can produce some kind of chemical that puts a strain on the vocal cords. Singing comes from a joyful place, and if doesn't, there must be some kind of impact.

During the *Frontiers* tour, Steve's voice became so tired and worn out that it shut down, which forced us to cancel some shows. The doctor told Steve he had irritated his vocal cords. Steve didn't want to take steroids; he wanted to let it heal naturally.

Once again, putting another puzzle piece into place, I look back and realize that we could have played things a little differently. If you force a horse to jump over fences too long, it'll eventually resist and finally quit. We should have given Steve more time to recover from the *Escape* tour before going right back out on the road. Maybe he wouldn't have burned out like the toast he said he had become.

Yet Herbie and all of us knew the cliché—*strike while the iron is hot.* Back then, whenever a group toured, their records would become hot and sell like crazy. Any show bumped up the sales of an album. So one naturally fed the other, but the expense, of course, was our flesh. Steve wasn't the only one who was toast after all those shows. All of us were. We began to smell like diesel.

Eventually on the *Frontiers* tour, we got to use a plane for a while. The Canadian turboprop resembled the Doobie Brothers' famous album shot in which they float weightlessly in the cabin due to a free-fall dive maneuver. Now instead of smelling like diesel, we all reeked of the strong pot Herbie smoked as we flew.

The band's relationship with Steve had deteriorated so much that he wasn't flying with us but was doing his own thing in a Winnebago. It was kind of crazy. It was near the end of the second leg of that tour, and Perry was renting a Winnebago with Sherrie and staying at KOA campgrounds. It showed dedication to his relationship, even though in the end she broke his heart.

"All my life I wanted to do this," Steve Perry said in the magazine *Song Hits* about making his first solo album in 1984, *Street Talk*. The quote was telling, considering he had achieved a level of stardom and success with Journey that few singers ever found. Working on *Street Talk* was a different venture for Steve.

When he was interviewed on *Good Morning America*, Steve said, "It was a no-pressure situation. I just said, 'I'm gonna have some fun in the studio, more fun than I've ever had so far.'" He also said the album felt like it was his first. The interviewer would go on to say, "If Steve Perry has fun with his art, he also closely controls it, cowriting the songs and coproducing the album and singing all the parts."

When the rest of the guys from Journey were invited to appear at the end of the video for "Foolish Heart," we were caught a bit off guard. We were flattered he wanted us to appear, and it helped create some obvious buzz: *Is Journey over? Will there ever be another album?*

Interestingly enough, when I showed up for Steve's show at The Warfield in San Francisco, I was turned away because my name wasn't on the list. Herbie was supposed to take care of this for me, so I assumed he had forgotten. I did know one thing: I wasn't going to buy a ticket.

Once again, to see the narrative in this story line, all one needed to look at was the songs. On the second-to-last track, Steve Perry said he didn't mind "running alone." Did any part of this consciously or subconsciously refer to Journey?

When I joined Journey, I had been worried about paying the bills and the debt I carried with me from LA. Neal Schon knew I was stressing about it, so one day he gave me a wide grin and some encouraging words: "After this record and tour, you'll never have to worry about paying another bill again."

At the time, I hoped and prayed he was right. Then when I saw my check for $995,000 for the 1981 Journey tour, I almost believed Neal's words. Maybe I wouldn't ever have to worry about financial matters again. The reality is that people have no idea what it takes to hold on to a million dollars. Instead of seeing Neal's proclamation play out in the next few years, I was haunted by words my mother said when I was a teen: "You'll never be good at finances." After the *Escape* tour, I was suddenly a millionaire, but I realized I had no clue how to make that money last or count in my life. I'd never had the opportunity to make any monetary decisions up to that point. I was used to just getting by.

I decided to go with Ross Valory's accountant—a guy full of advice, always pointing out his expertise, but one who couldn't deliver in the clutch. He encouraged Ross and me to invest in an office building in LA. I didn't know real estate, and treasuries were paying 8 percent, so I argued that it would be a safer investment. The accountant persuaded us that this would be a long-term property that would have deductions and income for life, yet the only problem was we paid too much for it, since we bought it directly from the builder and never had it properly evaluated. Unfortunately, Ross and I lost $350,000 collectively after the office building got into financial trouble.

I had to learn this the hard way—especially since Tané's divorce lawyer would never let me forget it. A million dollars couldn't guarantee happiness, nor could it save a marriage that had been sinking for a while.

My life had been unraveling after returning from the *Frontiers* tour and realizing that things with Tané had become so broken. We'd had difficulties in our relationship over the years, but the final straw was discovering she was cheating on me, though I had stayed committed while on the road. The irony of the guy who wrote "Faithfully" discovering his wife had been unfaithful stung bitterly. Especially after buying our first house in Novato, deducting 23 percent in monthly interest rates, and learning what it looked like to own a house—one that happened to be a Victorian house in the prairie on a hill that needed a fence, landscaping, and a gate. All the responsibilities that descended on me boggled this keyboard player's mind.

While I was dealing with what seemed to be an inevitable divorce and what that would mean, Herbie contacted me and told me Steve wasn't sure he wanted to come back to Journey. Steve had told our manager that recording his solo album had been a really satisfying experience, and he felt like he didn't have the same control in Journey.

"Get him to come over to your house like you guys used to do," Herbie said. "Do whatever you can to get him back into the camp."

Freedom and authority weren't the only things pulling at Steve. His album had done exceptionally well, so it made sense for him to consider what he wanted to do next. In an interview years later for *Off the Record*, Perry revealed his mind-set at the time: "When the *Street Talk* record was done, and it sold more than a million copies, honestly, I didn't know what to do. And it wasn't that I was wimping out on my ability to make a decision. I was just confused, because everything had led to that point. The band was a little singed. We were all a little crispy. A new solo career had just opened up. It was enticing."

I knew the only way to lure Perry back into the Journey camp was to do the thing we did best—write songs. Our original connection had been our love for the radio hits, and we liked the same bands and songs. I began to think, *Why can't we try to re-create some of those songs that are so dear to us?*

At that time, I had a pretty good studio in my house in Novato. A variety of artists, such as Gregg Allman and Michael Bolton, recorded in one of the bedrooms there. I listened to and studied *Street Talk* to see where Steve was musically and what he had enjoyed doing. I picked up the soul vibe of the album, the R&B and Motown thing he had going on.

Since I didn't want to drive ninety minutes to Oakland to write, I decided to create tracks on my own. The technology in music was changing, and with the help of my drum machine and sequencer, I wrote some demos that had a good groove. The songs started sounding a bit like what Hall & Oates had been doing. "I'll Be Alright Without You," "Suzanne," "Happy to Give," and "Positive Touch" came as a result of working like this. They had a Motown feel to them—sweet soul with a backbeat. Neal Schon had started creating songs, coming up with "Be Good to Yourself" and others as well.

Armed and ready, I called Steve.

"I've got these tracks," I told him. "They're awesome."

So Steve came over, and in a way that felt as simple as having a conversation about the weather, he was singing naturally and being his brilliant self. Writing tunes that ultimately would go on *Raised on Radio* was really enjoyable. We worked on a 24-track machine that had an interesting story behind it. God has a special way of reminding us of how far we've come, and for me, this was one of those experiences.

I started to look for a machine that Steve and I could make demos on. I stopped at a store called Harbor Sound in Sausalito and bought a Mara Machines MCI 24-Track Recorder, a tape machine found in many recording studios in those days. I paid eighteen grand for the device and then spent another five grand getting it to work again. When I got home and opened it up, I was shocked to discover I had spent time with this machine before.

It was the same track recorder I had made my first single on.

While working with J. C. Phillips at Quantum Recording Studio, we had written "'Til It's Time to Say Goodbye" on this very machine. I knew this for a fact because the engineer from Quantum had signed off on the last time it was aligned in 1976. "'Till It's Time to Say Goodbye" was the single that caught Dick Clark's attention and gave me the opportunity to go on *American Bandstand*.

Almost a decade later, the 24-track found me, traveling from LA to San Francisco to do so. Steve was in heaven, since he could record double and triple vocals and have a ball making the tracks. I eventually called Herbie to tell him things were working.

"I think we'll have a record," I said.

Since Steve's album had been soulful, I wanted to keep him on his ride. *Let's continue the wave with Journey*, I thought. So we focused on those songs we had grown up loving, having fun connecting with our roots, with the things that turned us on as musicians. For example, a song like "Then Came You" by The Spinners helped to inspire "Girl Can't Help It."

While the outlook for a new Journey album looked promising, I ended up being surprised by the situation we created. In an effort to draw Steve back to the band, we had recorded these songs quickly, in just a matter of months. We left the rest of the band out because of the vibe Steve was going for, which meant we didn't rehearse like we normally did. I never stopped to think that Steve Smith and Ross Valory might have a problem doing it this way; in retrospect, I realize we went about it the wrong way. We should have given it some rehearsal time. Things with our longtime bassist and drummer would have turned out better if we had done that.

After getting a taste of producing his solo album, Steve wanted to do the same with *Raised on Radio*. When Steve Smith and Ross finally joined the process, it was unfair to them. They were put on the spot with the songs we had cut. Steve Smith had never made anything using drum machines, and there wouldn't be enough time for him to learn. Both of the guys were under a lot of personal duress at the time. In the end, after Steve didn't like what he was hearing, we decided to go in a different direction and ended up parting ways with Steve Smith and Ross Valory.

I didn't have time to go to the guys and tell them what was happening. I had told Neal, but I should've done the same with the other guys. Steve Perry had been on the fence about coming back and could have become another Peter Gabriel, walking away never to return. Herbie wasn't willing to throw in the towel; neither were Neal and I. So to try to keep Steve in the brotherhood, seeing that he was heading down a specific musical path, we felt we had to pursue the music he wanted to make. I helped our band make the particular type of sound Steve wanted.

But the new songs came at the expense of our two brothers.

As Journey embarked on the *Raised on Radio* tour in 1986 to support the new album, we were now a trio, performing with session artists like Randy Jackson and Michael Baird. Few people knew how broken our lead singer was. His relationship with Sherrie had deteriorated like my marriage with Tané had, but that wasn't the main reason. Nor was it the price of fame, such as death threats on his mother from a couple of crazy people that forced him to get the FBI and local police involved. Steve was feeling crazy pressure and couldn't believe that his fame had brought trouble to his front door. Somehow, while we were recording *Raised on Radio*, his personal life was threatened, making Steve wonder if this was all worth it in the end.

Though Neal and I had watched Steve dealing with his mother's illness as we recorded the new album, seeing him flying out to spend weekends with her, we had no idea how physically and emotionally exhausted he had become. Steve's mother was a huge reason he had decided to continue with Journey, encouraging him to keep going even as her own body was failing. Mary died on December 4, 1985— Steve Perry's mother and also his biggest fan.

I believe a part of Steve Perry was lost when his mother passed away. In the same way I thought I was making music for my father up to the moment he died, I think Steve believed the same thing about his mother. They had a special relationship, and I could see Steve singing those songs to her whenever Mary was there.

Maybe the music reminded Steve too much of his mother. Maybe after the world had taken all it could from the singer, the last bit of strength he had was taken when his mother passed.

Maybe Neal and I should have expected what would happen next, but it still blindsided us. Looking back and connecting the dots, it's easier to understand now.

The lyrics of the songs explained everything. The story unfolded in their words.

Those songs serve to remind me of the remarkable journey I was on and the hand that continued to guide me, even when I didn't realize he was there.

THE WIND STIRS AROUND US AND SEEMS TO KNOW. OUR CARS ARE PARKED behind us as we walk down the path through the grass, the tranquil blue of Richardson Bay directly in front of us. I've only seen a few people around, but nobody is paying attention to the three guys who don't say much as they walk to the beach.

Steve Perry wanted to meet us here, so Neal and I drove separately, not exactly sure of the reason for the meeting or the rationale behind the spot. Blackie's Pasture is in Tiburon, a thirty-minute drive north of San Francisco. It's a little place out by the water with a stony beach and a beautiful view.

"I can't go on," Steve finally says as he looks out onto the bay. "I can't do this."

The words don't make sense. Neal and I are expecting that we'll settle on how many more dates Steve will do for the *Raised on Radio* tour.

"Guys, we've done it. We can't get any bigger. If we keep going, we're going to end up being some classic rock nostalgia band. We'll end up being just a memory—a shadow of what we used to be."

Our latest album just sold platinum. We sold out every show on the tour.

I look at Neal and see his disbelief.

"I need my life back," Steve continues. "I'm toast. I'm just toast."

We've spent a quarter of our lives interlocked with this man, so we know Steve is resolute. There's no convincing him.

"Don't tell anybody we're over. I just can't keep going. I'm done."

Steve eventually walks away toward his car, leaving Neal and me near the shore. As we stare out at the water, I see the city by the bay.

It feels like a stranger.

PART FOUR

"SHADOWS SEARCHING IN THE NIGHT"

EIGHTEEN

"MY OLD MAN"

The white keys looked still and frozen. I sat hunched over my piano, the afternoon sun that spilled into the room doing nothing to dispel the clouds inside me. Music had always been my salvation in times of sadness, but the weeks following my father's death were followed by a choking silence.

Len Friga passed away on December 23, 1987. I could already feel the absence of his love and wisdom. I missed his laugh. I dearly missed the simple but effective way he dealt with the daily problems that came with living life.

What advice would you give me now, Dad? What nugget of wisdom would you tell me over the phone?

I missed my father the way I used to when I was a little boy waiting for him to come home from work.

Loss had been the theme of the last few years, beginning with my return from the *Frontiers* tour to discover that my wife had cheated on me. I had been the "Faithfully" guy, the one writing *that* song, the one not even dreaming that something like that could happen. After I came to know the truth about everything, and after plenty of tears and emotions and bitterness, I was left feeling numb. I simply wanted out.

"You're too good a man for me," Tané once told me—words that didn't make sense. I knew I wasn't perfect.

Eventually, I realized I needed out, knowing I was better than the mess we had made. Knowing I needed to go to a higher place, refusing to live in the squalor I had come back from the tour to reside in. The divorce proceedings lasted two and a half years, kicked me in the butt, and took more than a million dollars from me.

Meanwhile, my parents had moved to Arizona thanks to the efforts of Danny Zelisko, the native Chicagoan I met at my first Journey concert in Phoenix. After I called to ask Danny for help, he lined up property for them to look at and even got my dad a job in Arizona, which he could start right away. My parents moved to Scottsdale and bought a condo at McCormick Ranch.

When my brother Hal found out our parents were moving, he decided to join them, getting a job as an assistant pro at Orange Tree Golf Club. Hal treated Dad to many free rounds of golf. They enjoyed their time together during those years, especially when my brother Tommy and his wife made trips to see them. I made many trips to Arizona as well. Dad was living his dream; they really were the golden years of Lenny Friga's life.

My parents were happy and content in Arizona until my father began to have pain in his back, along with a ringing in his ears. A friend in Miami—my ear, nose, and throat doctor—recommended my father have a CT scan done, but Dad refused. He was stubborn; I think he knew he was dying. After undergoing a quadruple bypass surgery in 1986, Dad never totally recovered, suffering from memory problems and dementia for the rest of his life.

When I did convince Dad to get X-rays at the University of Arizona Cancer Center in September 1987, they found multiple tumors in his lungs and brain. I was irate that the doctor who performed the bypass didn't see the tumors before he operated, yet they explained they didn't have the same X-ray procedure at the time. After two rounds of radiation, the cancer center sent him home. They told us to keep him comfortable and that he had three months to live. This time, their diagnosis was right, and he passed away at home two days before

Christmas, with Mom and me by his side. We had to watch as Dad developed the death rattle, and there was nothing anybody could do for him.

I'm grateful that before Dad passed away, he had a chance to meet Liz, my girlfriend at the time, whom he encouraged me to pursue. After meeting her, Dad prophesied our future, saying, "She'll give you kids, Jon." Just like so many other times, Dad turned out to be right.

I met Liz one evening when I ran into my next-door neighbor in Novato as he was leaving a club I was entering. He turned around and went back inside to introduce me to a young woman he worked with. When I saw her beautiful blue eyes looking at me from a shadowy table at the back of the club, all I could think was, *Whoa, who is this?* We talked for a while, and then I asked her for a slow dance, and before she left that night, I got her phone number. We dated on and off after that, but I was busy with Journey on the *Raised on Radio* tour and wasn't looking for a serious relationship. Dad loved Liz, however, and he was the one who told me, "What about Liz? You need to call her."

During those last difficult months of my father's life, I couldn't help but look back and reflect on growing up with a father who also was my greatest hero. I recalled how he guided me with his hand and showed me what it meant to be a man. My father had been dedicated to his family and had sworn never to let us down. Full of joyful memories amid this heartbreaking storm, I poured my thoughts into a song:

> *Born a saint, under a Southern Cross,*
> *Wandered to the midwest skyline.*
> *For forty years, he gave his life*
> *To his woman and his dreams.*
> *Sure, all my memories*
> *Will all trace back to him.*
> *I'm gonna miss him*
> *Now that he is gone.*

Two days before Dad passed, I whispered "My Old Man" in his ear. "There's no love that could ever take the place of me and my old man," I gently sang to the one who understood the most why I needed to play music and sing songs in the first place.

My father's eyes were open when I discovered he had slipped away. I will never forget the look of wonder on his face. The moment was surreal. Like something I had seen many times before in movies, I closed Dad's eyes. As he was rolled out on the stretcher, I remembered how handsome he looked under the streetlight.

Such a waste of a good man was all I could think.

Mom didn't want a funeral, unable to bear the thought, so Dad was cremated. We spread his ashes under a five-foot-tall stone pine tree on the golf course where we had played many rounds. It was fitting we were on the hole where Dad would always make a bet with Hal and me. And one of us would inevitably hit our ball into the water. On the same crusty JVC boom box on which I had recorded all my demos and rehearsals—the same one I'd recorded "Faithfully" on—we played "My Old Man" while Hal began to spread our father's ashes around the tree. Mom, Tommy, Danny, my girlfriend Liz, and I all stood watching my brother.

Hal began to do a strange tribal dance all of a sudden, shaking the urn up and down. The ashes began to engulf him. Then Hal bent over and dumped the rest of the ashes at the base of the tree, creating another mist. We watched and wondered what he was doing. I wasn't happy with this impromptu, crazy dance. Yet as the ashes and dust hovered around the tree, with my song playing, an orange cloud that resembled a flame about five inches long appeared just above us in the sky. As the ashes died down, the flame faded, and all of us were in tears.

I thought I was the only one who saw the orange streak, but everybody had. We knew it wasn't accidental. Dad wouldn't have wanted us to feel like he wasn't there to tell us good-bye.

With the arrival of a new year, I wondered how I was supposed to move on now that my father was gone. I thought of the family and friends who had offered prayers and support during this time. Steve Perry had called to offer his heartfelt condolences. Steve understood what it was like to lose someone who understood your dreams— someone you created music for.

The music had momentarily left me, however. I sat at my piano and remained still, my hands unable to move except to wipe the tears off my cheeks. I had always been able to unveil my emotions and then pull them out of the piano keys in a new, cathartic tune, yet now I was truly blocked.

A handwritten letter addressed to me was among the pieces of mail I pulled out of the box that afternoon. It was from my aunt in Arkansas, who had seen my father and me at a family reunion. She must have heard about his passing and decided to write me a letter. A single sentence stood out and caused me to stop and reread it multiple times.

"I'm so happy you have harvested His beliefs."

Holding the paper in my hand, I thought about what she meant. I noticed how she had capitalized the word *His*.

Harvested his beliefs? Is she talking about Dad's belief in me? Or does she mean God? Is she talking about Dad's faith?

I realized that my aunt might have been talking about both of these things. I couldn't help thinking of how my dad was always pushing me. About how a man needed to live a life that required respect and that required faith. Dad would always be giving me encouragement and advice, adding that he knew I would make it because I was his son. "You're my son. You're a Friga, and you don't quit."

I could see him kneeling in church and praying.

I could smell Pat's Tavern while I played and he bragged.

I could feel my fingers playing the accordion.

I could hear him urging me on and on and on and on. That I'd make it. That one day I'd be famous and play for thousands.

"Stick to your guns."

"Don't stop believin'."

Thanks to this little letter, I realized I didn't need any more guiding and encouraging from my father. He would always be with me. I had been busy harvesting his beliefs, and I couldn't stop now.

I have more crops to gather, Dad. The fields are still full of them.

NINETEEN

"WORKING CLASS MAN"

There are no secrets in creating songs. Sometimes your father gives you phrases you write down that eventually become titles. Sometimes you're on the road, missing your wife, and you wake up after hearing a ballad in your head. Sometimes they come from jamming with your bandmates and discovering a melody. But sometimes it can happen while playing fetch with your dog. This was how my unlikely partnership with Jimmy Barnes produced an iconic pop song in 1985. Two years later, it dissolved in chaos. This is how it happened.

Nero was already legendary by the time he helped me write the tune that provided the ending to the 2000 Sydney Olympics. I had rescued the German Shepherd from a Santa Monica pound before marrying Tané and before my adventures with Journey began. He was my guy. When people came to my house and we'd record in Madison's room, they fell in love with the dog. Especially Steve Perry.

"There's something about your dog," Steve once told me. "I just feel good when he's around."

While we were working on *Raised on Radio*, I had to bring Nero to every session. He became the studio dog. I don't think he missed a single day of work with Steve. Nero crawled underneath the console, so whenever Steve began to sing, Nero's ears stuck up and he'd watch him with those big, brown eyes. Since Nero shed so much, every night after work I'd have to clean up the mess he had made all over the carpet. Nero became so legendary that he got to go to his own concert—Steve had me bring him to the Cow Palace during our performance there. He was that crazy about the canine.

During the break between *Frontiers* and *Raised on Radio*, I was searching for a song after getting a songwriting job. Jimmy Barnes was the Bruce Springsteen of Australia, having fronted the country's biggest rock band, Cold Chisel, at the end of the seventies and early eighties before going on his own. Coincidentally, Barnes put out his first solo album the same year Steve Perry released his in 1984. He liked what I had done in Journey, so the rocker asked me to write a song for him. Once again, my father gave me inspiration, this time not with something he said but simply in being the man he was. As I thought of Dad, a title that summed him up came quickly: "Working Class Man." It would take me forever to write it, however.

Gary Gersh, Jimmy Barnes's A&R guy for Geffen Records, called me to ask if I had finished that song for Jimmy. I replied that it was almost finished, yet in reality, I had nothing but the title. Instead of banging my head in the studio, however, I wasn't worried, knowing the rest of it would come. One afternoon in Sausalito behind the Record Plant, while rolling a small tennis ball with Nero, I could hear Jimmy's rough and tough voice and married it to the song title and mental images I already carried. As I watched the German Shepherd race across the grass, a melody came out as easily as breathing.

"Oh oh oh oh, he's a working class man," I sang.

Oh, that's it. That's the chorus.

I pictured Lenny Friga when he was my age, spending long hours at the printer to support the family he loved. As Nero brought me the ball, I threw it again and sang the opening verse.

"Working hard to make a living, bringing shelter from the rain."

Feeling the wet slobber on the tennis ball, I repeated the ritual, toss by toss and line by line. The man believed in God and Elvis. He was a simple man with a big heart, loving his little woman and not worried about tomorrow. After a half hour of playing ball with my best friend, I knew we had a song.

"Nero," I said rubbing his soft fur, "we finished it."

When I eventually finished the demo and played it for Jimmy Barnes, he loved it. The day he showed up to do the vocals, he came with a bottle of vodka, an ounce of blow, and his notorious legend still intact. "Let's get busy," he said after downing a quarter of the vodka and snorting a couple of lines. It only took him four takes to nail the song. "No worries," he told me with his mischievous grin and magnificent voice. I called him Jimmy the Pirate.

With Randy Jackson playing bass, Tony Brock from The Babys playing drums, and Dave Amato, who later became REO Speedwagon's guitarist, on guitar, I knew we had an amazing track on hand. Since this was before the internet, I wouldn't know how big the song had become until someone sent me clips in 1987 from the America's Cup race that showed the Australian yacht Kookaburra III using "Working Class Man" as their theme. The tune was a massive hit in Australia, becoming an anthem much like Bruce Springsteen's "Born in the USA." With lyrics about honest and hardworking people who cared and mattered, the song touched a nerve much like the songs I'd written in Journey.

Two years later, as I found myself without a band, I snagged a publishing deal with Warner-Chappell Music to write songs. It was the perfect segue in my quest to see what life would look like after Steve Perry left. One of my first jobs was working with Jimmy Barnes again, both writing and producing songs for his next album to be released in 1987 titled *Freight Train Heart*. The process turned out to be very different from "Working Class Man." We had Neal Schon this time, along with Tony Brock and Randy Jackson.

As we went to work at the Record Plant studio, I tried to force Jimmy to focus and get rid of his bad habits that were beginning to affect his work on the album.

"Listen, Jimmy, when you worked on the last album, you were snorting and drinking vodka. Can you not do that?"

The singer told me "okay, okay" and promised me he wouldn't self-medicate, but after a couple of weeks, he refused to stop, telling me he couldn't do it. Barnes recently opened up about those days, saying he remembered sitting with Michael Hutchence of INXS while they recorded "Good Times," another tune that became a hit the same year we worked together again. "By that stage in 1987," Jimmy said thirty years later, "I was drinking, like, copious amounts and taking drugs and I remember thinking, *I'm staring into the abyss here, and I don't know what to do.*"

Jimmy the Pirate wanted a musician, not an intervention. So the next thing I knew, there was a mutiny against me. One Monday morning, I came to the studio to work on some roughs and discovered the tapes weren't there. They had been taken from the vault and sent to LA. When I called Jimmy, I discovered he had flown to Hawaii that weekend, not bothering to tell me about his trip or about the tapes. I was furious.

When I finally met with Jimmy again, he made it clear he wasn't doing these songs with me. The label told me the deal was off and Jimmy was moving on. All the work I had already put in felt wasted. "Why didn't he just tell me that when we were working on them?" I asked, but I knew the truth. Barnes didn't want to work with me because I refused to let him drink or do drugs while we recorded.

To finish the record, the label chose Mike Stone as the new producer. It wasn't just ironic that the producer of *Escape*, *Frontiers*, and *Raised on Radio* would be brought on board; it turned out to be a blessing from above. Mike contacted me shortly thereafter to tell me how sorry he was that he had replaced me, but to share encouragement as well.

"I love what you've done with this album," Mike said. "I'm not going to touch a thing."

Mike ended up mixing the album, and I know it was a better

album because of it. I had asked Neal Schon, along with Tony Brock and Randy Jackson, to be part of *Freight Train Heart*, and Neal's performance on the album is some of his best playing ever.

God had taken a project that could have been viewed as a failure and had given it to one of my idols to complete and turn into a hit. Once again, I learned that I could be instrumental behind the scenes as I did the things I loved and allowed others to succeed.

There was life after Journey after all.

It took twenty-two years before I heard from Jimmy Barnes again. The talented singer survived those wild days, yet his equally gifted co-singer on "Good Times" tragically did not. In November 1997, Michael Hutchence was found dead in his hotel room—an apparent suicide.

After Barnes called me to say he wanted me to write, I told him to come over.

"It's only been twenty-two years," I said. "What took you so long?"

"IT'S NOT WHAT HAPPENS, BUT IT'S WHAT YOU DO THAT MAKES THE DIFFERENCE."

I stare at the Tony Robbins quote I had jotted in my journal. Purchasing his Personal Power tapes and listening to them has shifted something inside me.

I know now what the next thing needs to be.

I'm moving on from my losses.

I'm getting my act together.

It doesn't matter that my first marriage failed. I know I can start again with Liz.

It doesn't matter that the managers in Hollywood told me my name is a blessing and a curse. How there's the "Journey stigma," how they think that brand is all I'm able to do, how people don't want "that" sound.

They've forgotten that I've done a variety of sounds.

They don't realize a great song is a great song.

Once again, LA has shut the door on Jonathan Cain.

Tony Robbins suggests I need to design what the next five years of my life look like. So I write down my goals in my journal:

- Build a studio.
- Continue songwriting.
- Produce for other artists.
- Release a solo album.

The last item on that list is my greatest fear. Are the LA managers right? Is there a stigma attached to me?

Am I just a footnote on a list of alumni who recorded and toured with the band Journey? Or do I truly have something?

What am I without the band?

I can hear Tony Robbins's voice talking over my thoughts. "A coward dies a thousand deaths, a courageous man only one," he says, paraphrasing the classic Shakespeare line.

I can't let any fear stop me.

I can't allow any shadow of success to hold me back.

I have defined what I want. I also know the skills I bring to the table in helping others get what they want.

I don't need Hollywood.

I'll build my own studio, and then they'll come to me.

TWENTY

"BEST OF WHAT I GOT"

I couldn't sleep. My hotel room was swallowed by middle-of-the-night darkness, yet I couldn't help seeing the vivid movie in my mind. I saw a white Winnebago driving down the highway, slowly veering off the side of the road and plummeting over the side of the cliff. Or I imagined the vehicle swerving into the other lane and ramming head-on into a station wagon with a family in it. All because it was being driven by one of my stoned sound guys on tour with us.

These were the sorts of nightmares I was having while wide awake in the spring of 1990. Bad English was touring with Whitesnake to promote our first self-titled album that came out the previous year, and we didn't even have enough money to get a bus for our crew. Nor did we have enough to pay for a driver of the Winnebago they were traveling in. So night after night, I kept imagining those guys dying in some tragic accident. All because of financial constraints.

Once again, I was in a new band with John Waite, and once again, we were broke.

Steve Perry telling Neal Schon and me good-bye felt like a decade ago. Both of us had moved on. I had found success as both a songwriter and producer, coming on the heels of working on Michael Bolton's breakthrough album, *The Hunger*.

Neal was finishing up work on his first solo album, *Late Night*. While on the road, I ran into John Waite's new manager, Trudy Green, through touring with Heart. One would never have guessed the petite Englishwoman managed bands like Whitesnake and Heart. I told her to give my greetings to John, whom I hadn't spoken with in years. That began a new conversation about doing something else. John and I had unfinished business, especially considering the abrupt ending of The Babys. Soon the idea emerged to create a super band—a super hairband, as the eighties would call it. It was basically an extension of the glam rock bands of the seventies, with lots of heavy guitars and pop hooks, combined with lots of heavy hairspray.

As it turned out, the bassist from The Babys, Ricky Phillips, was looking to do something new, so when we called and shared the idea, he was in. John, Ricky, and I got together and wrote songs in my house in Novato. We didn't have a guitarist or drummer at the start, but that changed after I called Neal Schon, who agreed to come aboard. He brought Deen Castronovo, a talented drummer who eventually joined Journey for more than a decade.

The band name came during a night of playing pool with the guys. We hadn't figured out what to call our group yet. I was trying to show Neal how to put English on a cue ball—how to give it sidespin— yet every time he hit the ball, it went in the opposite direction.

"That's bad English," I said and then commented how that sounded like the name of a rock group. After using it awhile, the name stuck.

We brought in a great producer in Richie Zito and recorded the album in LA. It was a stab at a super band, and while we knew these types of bands weren't going to last long, we wanted to give it a shot. But once again, the finances got away from us and proved to be our undoing.

Not only did we spend extra money on custom wardrobes, but this was the video era, so every single cent we made went into making overproduced videos. After looking back on the Bad English years, I tallied up the profits and realized it cost me $30,000 a year to be in the band. And that was after making a platinum album. When you spend between $300,000 and $400,000 on a music video, you don't have to wonder where any profits might be going.

While on tour where we opened up for Whitesnake, an idea we hoped would bring lots of fans into stadiums, we couldn't even afford a bus for our crew. I was freaking out with anxiety about them getting into an accident. Eventually I said enough was enough.

"Let's get these guys a bus," I said. "Let's take the T-shirt money we've been advanced and spend it on a bus so they don't all die."

And that's exactly what we did. Thankfully, nobody died. Unfortunately, nobody paid the bill either.

Bad English wasn't the only new partnership I had just entered. In February 1989, I ended up marrying the girl who had made the world stand still while slow dancing with me the night we met. We dated on and off again for several years as I waffled about tying the knot. Eventually, when we decided to marry, my mother rejected the whole idea, so we postponed the date, hoping she would come around. But Mom never accepted Liz and refused to come to our wedding.

We had a wonderful ceremony and reception at a country club in San Rafael, California. The priest who married us would also later baptize our children. Neal Schon was there, along with Ricky from Bad English. I got to play golf with my brothers right before the service. It was a beautiful day.

Liz wanted to go to Greece for our honeymoon, but since I would be touring with Bad English soon, we decided on an easier trip and flew to Hawaii. This turned out to be a bad decision, however, since this was where my ex-wife was from. So many things about Hawaii reminded me of Tané, but naturally Liz didn't want to hear about any of them. That was the life I had led before we met, and she wanted nothing to do with it.

This foreshadowed things to come in our relationship. For instance, Liz wanted to move into a new house so we'd have a fresh start to our marriage. Yet since I didn't have enough equity to move, having lost most of my money except for the house after the divorce, I fought to keep the house.

It didn't help matters that the new band I was in was already starting to implode.

I knew the handwriting was on the wall with Bad English right after we completed our first album and John Waite completely trashed it. We were sitting over martinis at Musso & Frank Grill when the singer told me what he really thought.

"I think it's a piece of crap," Waite said.

I felt like I'd been slapped in the face. "How can you say that?" I asked.

The conversation only went downhill.

"I expected more out of you," John told me. So I told him what I really thought of his opinion, and the argument continued, like two brothers who could love and hate each other in the same breath. At this moment, all I wanted to do was punch him in the face.

"I happen to like it a lot," I said. "It's a great album. You should be proud of it."

"It's not Journey."

I laughed. "John, it never was supposed to be Journey."

"Well, where were you then?"

"I'm just following my singer's lead."

How can this guy be this way?

I left John and his mood swings behind, eventually calling Trudy to let her know the situation.

"This guy's a real piece of work," I said. "I don't get why he isn't proud of the record."

When the album Waite dismissed was eventually released, it hit hard. *Bad English* sold like crazy, and everybody loved it. The sound was a big, bombastic, eighties wall of sound. There was only one hitch I saw coming with the album: "When I See You Smile."

After Waite shared the tune written by acclaimed songwriter Diane Warren, I shook my head and grimaced. "Man, I don't know." It was sappy and sweet and didn't fit what we were going for with the group.

"I gotta sing this," the Englishman said. "It's a hit."

Yeah, but at what cost?

After we cut it, I could almost feel those cold lips on my cheek. Yes, the song was a hit, just like Waite said it would be, but it would be the kiss of death for Bad English. We were hard rock and wild and dangerous and sexy and nobody could mess with us. *But when I see you smile . . .*

Suddenly we had become a pop band.

We knew it when people came to our concerts and sang all the words to "When I See You Smile" while looking at us the rest of the set with an expression that said, *I didn't realize you were a rock band!*

One song can put you in a box you'll never get out of again.

When we went on to do a second album, the wall no longer had writing on it; now it was simply bloodred. I knew going in this would be our last album, but I still had no idea what sort of mistake was waiting until Trudy told me her bright idea. She wanted to put Ron Nevison into the mix, who was hot after producing Heart's "These Dreams." They had made it next door at the Record Plant in Studio B while we made *Raised on Radio*. We shared the same hallway. I had heard horror stories about Ron from back in the day with The Babys, having been told he was impossible to work with.

"Trudy, what about his history with The Babys? They ended on a bad note. Why would we work with him?"

Nevison had just had a couple hit records with Heart, with singles like "What About Love?" and "Alone." He had a long list of bands he had worked with, such as Jefferson Starship, Survivor, and Kiss.

"He's hot right now," Trudy said. "We need him."

"We don't need him. Richie was fine," I said.

Richie Zito had done a fine job producing our first album, despite what John Waite thought. I lost that battle, however. Nevison would be the man of the hour. For *literally* an hour.

On the first day of recording, our gear was stolen. The roadies had parked in front of Ricky Phillips's house instead of going directly to the studio, like I told them to, and the truck was stolen. So even before we entered the studio, we had to scramble to find rental gear. When we arrived at Conway Recording Studios on Melrose Avenue, the place was in disarray, consisting of a plasterboard room that hadn't even been finished.

What are we doing here? I thought. *This place isn't even finished. Still raw plasterboard?*

Ron Nevison was sitting behind the controls. I shook his hand before diving in and starting to cut the first song. John went into the vocal booth and began singing, but a few moments into the song, Ron stopped him.

"Can we stop for a minute?" Nevison said. "I don't like this arrangement."

John Waite quickly replied, "The arrangement is fine. Let's keep going."

I suddenly found myself in the middle of a junior high argument that went back and forth and quickly became personal and below the belt. It became so heated that both men talked about taking it outside and fighting. John became so fed up he eventually walked out.

I walked into the control room wearing an incredulous smile.

"Ron, beautiful job. What a great first day. *You ran the singer off.*

I'd heard a lot about you, but I told myself it wasn't true. Now I'm convinced that everything they said about you is 100 percent accurate."

I made a few more honest statements summing up how I felt—the kind that don't need repeating.

"Unbelievably unprofessional," I finished. "So what are we going to do now?"

"We don't need him here. We'll do the music without him."

In our industry, a little success could bring on a whole lot of arrogance. Once again, I was the middleman, hoping to be the glue that could help this project stick. So sure enough, that's what we did for a while, plowing through the songs without Waite there in person. I had all the click tracks and keyboards in the demos. Soon it became impossible to keep going. John wasn't going to sing. Not only that, but in my opinion, Nevison was becoming unbearable. For instance, nobody tells Neal Schon how to play the guitar, but Ron was telling him exactly what to do with the instrument Neal had mastered when he was a teen.

"Trudy, this guy has to go," I eventually said.

Once Nevison was gone, though still being paid for his efforts, the rest of us finished the album on our own. While doing this, John Waite decided he wanted to change the splits of how we got paid so he could get more. I refused to comply with his wishes, so my response was pretty simple—more or less in these words: *This isn't fair.*

"This publishing deal of yours is not my problem, but you're making it mine," I said. "I quit," I stated without any reservations.

Situations like these could almost make me miss those days of playing songs on my keyboard in that apartment in Hollywood. *Almost.*

I couldn't believe that we not only finished the album but released it, especially since as a group we were already over. We even filmed a ridiculous video for "Straight to Your Heart." By then, John wouldn't even talk to Neal or me. He simply came in, taped his parts, and left. It would be the last time I saw or spoke with John Waite for almost fifteen years.

Five years after the Bad English experience, I got a call from someone at a T-shirt company. They were looking for the $250,000 they had advanced to the band on that infamous tour when our crew members were driving themselves around.

"It's on the books," they said. "Where's our money?"

The other guys in Bad English were covered because of deals they had made, so the T-shirt company decided to go after me and file a suit against me. I had to get my lawyer involved, and eventually we agreed to a settlement.

In the end, Bad English seemed to be a fitting title for the whole experience. On top of costing me $30,000 every year I was in the band, I also had to pay a settlement of around $50,000 in a lawsuit with a T-shirt company. Plus, my relationship with John Waite, someone I admired and had learned so much from, had been set ablaze.

With those embers still hot and burning my skin, I knew it was time to do the one thing I feared the most.

I needed to make another album of my own.

TWENTY-ONE

"BACK TO THE INNOCENCE"

Your luck's run out and the time has come, Jonathan. Time to reinvent your world.

This sounded like a song, so I began to write it down.

Instead of getting better, you got older. It's time to take a chance and go against the odds. To make the big wheel spin.

Steve Perry wasn't coming back. And I didn't want John Waite to come back.

Time to start over again.

So that's what I would do in the early nineties.

Life goes on, but we come back around full circle.

This journey had been so long, and yet it was funny that somehow I was back where I had started.

Naturally, that deserved a song, so I wrote it and called it "Full Circle."

The inspiration for taking on the hurdle of recording my solo album came easily. Especially with one track that was a reply to a question never asked.

I tell musicians if you don't like a song, then write the answer to it. This was exactly what I did when I worked on my solo album. I had always been a big-time fan of Don Henley ever since discovering The Eagles years earlier. So when he sang about the failure of "happily ever after" in his 1989 hit song "End of the Innocence," I couldn't help but disagree with the sentiment in the lyrics.

It's never the end of the innocence, Don. You can always return to that innocence.

So my reply was the song "Back to the Innocence," a tune that would also become the title of my album. I recalled the days before the fire, the hope that overflowed inside me. "Through the endless summers, seemed like life was ours to take. Golden years before the fears, I've seen ghosts of days gone by. Telling me dreams don't die."

This track, like all of them on the album, was autobiographical. I wanted to go back and find the guy who had written "Faithfully." I wanted to recapture the spirit of that song and the heart behind it. So having completed my goal of building a new studio at my home in Novato in 1992, I worked on songs like "Back to the Innocence."

I was at an important crossroad in my life. With the shadow of Journey becoming fainter each year, I had found my new footing in both my professional and personal life. Two years after my father died, I married Elizabeth in 1989. A year later, I turned forty and helped front Bad English. With the super band also a distant memory, Liz and I were hoping to start a family. It was the perfect time to pen songs about my life.

The 24-track recording studio occupied a building next to our house. I called it Wildhorse. The studio was a symbol for me of breaking free from the "stigma" of Journey, allowing me to define who Jonathan Cain was as a writer and producer. I knew that if I was to come to a place of excellence as an artist, I needed a space that was exceptional. I knew I couldn't work in a bedroom, especially when we were finally blessed to have a child in the house. I couldn't make that sort of racket anymore. I built the studio to be a fortress of hope for the future. I was also betting on me, and it was quite an expensive bet, since I had to spend money I didn't have.

Jammin' with the master.

"Full Circle."

Liz and me on
our wedding day.

Suddenly
outnumbered.

Loving being a father.

Liza and Weston.

A growing
family.

The piano I played for "Faithfully."

Me at the Wildhorse studio.

At Wrigley Field with the kids and the Cubs.

Weston and me throwing out the first pitch.

Hangin' out with Ross and Neal.

Our new singer, Arnel.

Journey getting a star on the Hollywood Walk of Fame.

Make-A-Wish Foundation.

Backstage with the kids.

Will always love
performing.

Just a small town boy.

The Rock and Roll Hall of Fame.

Bringin' it every night.

Madison and me.

Hangin' out with Liza and Weston.

Blessed to have found Paula.

Proud grandpa.

Loving life with my baby.

Ministering
to others.

Enjoying time
with my brother
and his wife.

I'd like to thank the Cubs for winning the World Series.

Inauguration Day 2017.

Paula the photographer capturing a moment onstage.

All I had left was my God-given talent and hard-earned experience.

With the old Trident console I had bought from the Record Plant, I recorded pieces of me that had been waiting to come out. At that point in my life, I had been blessed to work with four of the finest singers ever placed on this earth: Steve Perry, John Waite, Michael Bolton, and Jimmy Barnes. I had studied those singers and knew their audiences, and I had constructed music from their point of views. Now all I had to do was be honest and sum up the melodies inside me.

"Little River" was a blessing to write, since I was penning it for the daughter God had blessed Liz and me with. We had been trying to have children for years, even going to a fertility specialist, who told us we were fine and shouldn't be having problems. We were overjoyed when it finally happened. Madison was born on October 4, 1993. All I could do was thank God over and over again—and this was quite something, since he hadn't heard from me in quite a while.

Even though God hadn't been an important part of my life in the last couple of decades, I always knew he hadn't left me. It was like we shared a hotel suite. God paid the bills and made sure my room was taken care of. The door between our rooms stayed shut, however, and I never bothered to knock on it and simply thank him for taking care of me. I never opened the door so we could talk, even though it always remained unlocked. Always.

All those years, I knew God was there, yet I never gave him honor, even after he had done *so much*. Maddie's birth broke down that door and allowed me to walk through with her in my arms simply to praise my heavenly Father. As a new father, I recognized that I had to make sure Madison knew about God and had him in her life. And so I returned to church. Our family of three began attending a Lutheran church. Since I wasn't on the road, I could enjoy our newborn and hold her in my arms. This time in our marriage was probably the best it would ever be between Liz and me.

With Madison's baptism looming, I wrote "Little River" and sang it for her in church. I struggled to keep it together as I sang to my precious girl:

> *The morning you were born,*
> *The rain came down.*
> *I felt it wash my fears away,*
> *Showing me a mirror to my soul,*
> *Reflections of a brand-new day*

As I sang, Madison looked up and fixed her eyes on me. This tiny, breathing soul God had created would forever be linked to her mother and father. She was a precious gift, one that almost made me choke up and break down in tears, unable to finish. Thankfully, God gave me the strength to make it through the song.

> *Run, little river, a world waits for you*
> *As you wind through fields of dreams.*
> *My love will see you through.*
> *Born to be a part of me*
> *Where waters flow as one,*
> *Run, little river, run*

I had been searching for the peace I could see in my daughter, and like Madison, I wanted to be baptized again and to see my spirit set free. God had given me yet another gift, one that renewed my walk with him. Three years later, God would bless Liz and me again. And again.

"Jon, man, I need you."

The voice on the other end of the phone sounded wild and wasted.

"It's one o'clock in the morning," I said.

"You gotta come over here to record."

Once again, I found myself working with an out-of-control legend. Gregg Allman was fresh out of rehab, and I had been writing with him for the next Allman Brothers album. I could tell he was still a mess, since he was drinking again. I wasn't about to take off, however; I had a newborn in the house.

"I gotta stay with our baby," I told the rocker.

Gregg was one of the few guys to give me goose bumps listening to him sing. He truly was a black man trapped in a white man's body. We had written half a dozen songs, and Gregg loved working with me in the studio.

"Come on. I need you here," he said.

"I'm so honored you feel that way, but there's no way I'm leaving. I need to be here with my family."

The music industry would never change, with brilliant and talented musicians battling their own demons while delivering tunes to the masses. My life, however, had changed dramatically, and I wasn't about to let anyone interfere with it—rock legend or not.

Only one of the songs we wrote together would end up seeing the light of day, but it was an important one. Yet again, I'd end up writing my own story before it happened, with the bluesy, sexy "Temptation Is a Gun."

This gun would be loaded, and it would prove to be my downfall.

As 1996 began, our family found ourselves waiting on the angels. Making room inside our hearts before being blessed by our twins. Liza and Weston were born on April 18, once again answering our prayers.

Once again, it would be a time to ask questions about life and search my soul. For a brief moment, seeing those two little wonders washed away some of my deepest doubts and fears. It felt like Liza and Weston had always been a part of our lives.

Once again, God was reminding me that he was there. He was inviting me to love and worship him. I couldn't help but think of Dad, and I put those thoughts into the song I dedicated to the twins, "Waiting on the Angels."

> *A time for innocence,*
> *Childhood dreams.*
> *I pray to find the light, my father gave to me,*
> *Waiting on the angels.*

Before the twins came, however, someone else dropped back into my life unexpectedly. A year earlier, in 1995, while I was in Tampa Bay doing an interview for one of my new songs and excited to see my solo career taking off, I got a call that resulted in work that would keep me busy during the birth of our twins. It wasn't just anybody calling me. It wasn't Gregg Allman calling in the early morning hours. It was someone I couldn't say no to.

"Hey, Jon, it's Steve."

I hadn't spoken with Steve Perry in several years. I greeted him with enthusiasm and curiosity.

"I've been thinking that maybe we should talk about getting back together," Steve said. "I'd like to see what you think. Let's get together for coffee when you get back home."

TWENTY-TWO

"TRIAL BY FIRE"

T he last time Steve Perry had performed with Neal Schon and me was on November 3, 1991, at Golden Gate Park in San Francisco. We had been asked to sing at a tribute concert for the famed concert promoter Bill Graham, who died in October of that year. Few things could have reunited the three of us, but this was one of them.

Neal and I were asked to take the songs down a step to match Steve's pitch. He greeted the thousands in the park eagerly waiting to hear him sing again. Steve gave it everything he had, but his voice had indeed dropped a whole step. Seasoned vets that we are, Neal and I played the different notes of several familiar songs without a problem. Even the guitar solo in "Lights" went off without a hitch.

We played three songs together onstage in 1991, and then we didn't see each other until 1995. The year before we reunited, Steve released his second solo album and toured with it. *For the Love of Strange Medicine* wasn't the success his first release had been. We met for coffee to talk about the idea of re-forming Journey, and the conversation was amicable. We decided to meet again with Neal to see what he thought. Steve wanted to do four shows and talked about possibly making an album. Neal definitely thought we should release a new album, saying fans wanted one after all these years.

John Kalodner, the artist relations manager for Sony, proved to be instrumental in this reunion. He convinced Steve to try the band's original member lineup. We showed up for a loose jam at a studio in LA, and John watched the magic take place all over again as we rehearsed a variety of songs. After we finished that night, John's big grin beamed through his long beard.

"You guys just made me a happy Jew," John told us.

I think Steve had forgotten how good we all were together.

That night at dinner, I spoke about fatherhood to Steve Smith and Ross, telling them how happy I was with just one child. The very next day, I got a call from Liz telling me she was pregnant. God sure has a sense of humor.

An album we titled *Trial by Fire* would eventually come, but like *Raised on Radio*, there was a price to pay for the Journey team. While we ended up with the original band back together, including Ross Valory and Steve Smith, Journey's longtime manager and founder was asked to leave. It was the only way Steve Perry would work on a new album. "I'm just not sure I can work with Herbie Herbert," Steve said.

When asked why, he simply said he couldn't. It was an ultimatum we couldn't say no to. I was torn between my loyalty to a man who took me from rags to riches and an iconic singer and bandmate who made my songs famous. I felt trapped in a no-win situation. Steve's statement was difficult for Neal and me to hear. We knew there was tension between Herbie and Steve before he left, but we thought we could all move on together. I realized we would have to go in a different direction with someone else at the helm. Ultimately, I would be the bearer of the bad news in the winter before we started recording when I told Herbie his services were no longer needed.

Heading into the studio in 1996, I still wasn't sure what to expect. It had been so many years. Was the magic still there? What would Steve's voice sound like? Would the chemistry be the same, the one that had produced so many hits?

Steve surprised me by showing up for our first writing session with a Bible in hand. When we had worked on our last album in 1986, Steve wanted my dog Nero to be in the studio; now Steve always had his Bible nearby as we wrote songs. The Scriptures weren't just there for security, but they provided inspiration for the songs we wrote. He talked about passages that spoke to him. This hit me in a powerful way. I couldn't help but be amazed and, frankly, jealous.

Wow, this guy has found his faith.

After all the years, I was still searching. I had been given plenty of opportunities, yet I still wasn't there with God. While working on the songs for the next Journey record, I was moved by Steve's connection to the Scriptures and to God. He had made some major life changes, and he was bearing the fruit. As he showed me passages, I worked hard to figure out how to weave them into the songs.

The process of working on *Trial by Fire* was effortless and a lot of fun. The songs were truly a joy to write. Steve, Neal, and I sat around the piano as the melodies flowed out so naturally. The magic was still there. *We can do this in our sleep,* I remember thinking. It was unbelievable, as if time hadn't passed, as if it was 1980 once again. Few people have ever played a guitar like Neal Schon can, and few have ever sung like Steve Perry. I was the fortunate fella in between who knew the magic the three of us could make. Steve, Neal, and I still had that chemistry.

I couldn't say the same thing about the chemistry between my wife and me at the time. Having our twins was an unexpected blessing, one that neither of us was prepared for. Nobody can ever be fully prepared for having twins. Going from having one child to three certainly can bring any set of parents to their knees. And it didn't help that after spending the weekend in the hospital witnessing the miracle of their births, I needed to go back to the studio.

Naturally, Liz was caught up in the birth and well-being of our twins. Everything else took on less importance, including a Journey reunion. It was chaotic to have twins and then go into the studio on a Monday morning after getting very little sleep on the weekend. I knew I had to do it, but I struggled with leaving our twin babies. I was fascinated to see the chemistry between those two, how close and loving they were toward each other. I loved seeing how Madison was so caring and helpful when they were born. Watching the three of them interact was precious, and it was painful to have to be away while working on a new album. I was grateful for the help that came from Liz's sister and mother during this time.

Once the album was finished, I was back at home, changing diapers and doing the "dad thing." "When You Love a Woman" was recorded by Journey after the birth of our twins. It became a No. 1 hit and earned Journey our first Grammy nomination. With this encouraging buzz building, I assumed we'd head out on the road, but plans unexpectedly changed. While it was surely a blessing since I could spend more time with the kids, it felt debilitating at the time.

I couldn't believe how quickly things changed after the beautiful moments we had shared creating the new Journey record.

The first time I spotted Irving Azoff, he was strolling through the crowd and then disappearing backstage before an Eagles concert during their *Hotel California* tour in 1976. It was at this concert that the singing had been so good I went to search for a recording truck but found none, realizing the power of impeccable vocals sung live. Seeing Azoff that day made me wonder what it felt like to have that kind of power in managing such an elite group.

With Herbie gone, we were fortunate to have Irving become our manager. He stepped into the role as a fan and a believer that big things were yet to come. He's the kind of guy who always looks at the whole picture and has a good sense of the street perception and marketplace for a band. He knows what he has and what the brand can do. With Journey, Irving knew he had an incredible band, and he wanted us to get the best of all deals. He wouldn't allow anything less.

When Irving first met with us in the studio, he brought a brand-new briefcase that had more than thirty million dollars' worth of concert dates for a tour that never happened. He quickly began to cut deals with the promoters while preparing for the launch of *Trial by Fire*. His goal has always been to get the right deals and to make sure nobody is screwing us over, while at the same time not taking any flak from anybody.

When the new album released in October 1996, it went to the top of the charts and showed that fans still loved Journey. There were plans for promotion and touring and all the other things that went along with riding a new release, yet the pause button suddenly got pressed right before the band was set to start rehearsals. One person had pushed it, and the other four of us wondered what in the world was happening.

I knew that Steve Perry had gone to Hawaii and suffered some kind of injury. Then we discovered his hip was acting up and he was in severe pain. Soon it became problematic after we learned he'd need hip replacement surgery to be able to go onstage and perform like he used to.

None of us were young twentysomethings anymore. I was forty-six years old, and Steve was a year older than me. For our lead singer to be diagnosed with a degenerative bone disease wasn't the most unlikely thing that ever happened, yet it still hit the band hard. The surgery to replace the disintegrating hip wasn't an easy decision to make, and for Steve, it was one he refused to accept. I believe it scared him, and his rebellious spirit didn't want to give in to what the doctors, and eventually the band, wanted.

Little by little, I saw the band I dearly loved coming apart at the seams. For example, we had to turn down an opportunity to perform at the American Music Awards because Steve wouldn't sing. I tried to get him to reconsider.

"Maybe you can share your story about your health situation with our fans," I said. "Maybe it'll help others who can identify with you."

We had been nominated for Best Song, and the exposure would have reminded people that Journey was still alive and well, but Steve simply said he couldn't do it.

My confusion quickly turned to exasperation.

Journey had reunited and released *Trial by Fire*, yet we weren't doing interviews or videos or touring. We had our high-octane engine running, but the driver wasn't even near the vehicle. Soon the gas tank was empty, and the car shut down.

All throughout this time, we asked Steve how he was doing and what was happening. His elusive answers provided no relief.

"Some days are good days; some days are bad days," he said. "I gotta accept this. I can't do music. I gotta live my life."

He was avoiding a major operation and clearly felt the band had no say in the matter. So we just waited. 1997 came, and we were still there, still on pause and not going anywhere. Waiting. The days turned into months, all of us still just waiting.

There are two ways to look back on the canvas of your life. You can let the dark mistakes and misfortunes cover the bright moments and miracles, or you can let the colors emerge and brilliantly cover the old. I try to do the latter, especially when it pertains to those to whom I've been closest. Steve Perry is one such person.

There are many "what ifs" and "should've beens" when one looks back on the days in Journey when we waited for word from our lead singer, but there are also the songs we had created. There have always been the songs. Pieces of us put into melodies and threaded together by expressions of love and longing and hurt. So many of these musical pieces have stood the test of time.

When Steve Perry needed a break from Journey after *Raised on Radio*, there was unfinished business between him and me, just as there had been between John Waite and me. Bad English spelled the end with Waite, as *Trial by Fire* did with Steve Perry. At least in some ways.

We wrote "When I Think of You" about the passing of Steve's mother, and I couldn't help but think of my father as we worked on it. I can focus on the fact that even though it's one of my favorite ballads, it was never performed live with Steve. Yet I choose to reflect on the majesty of the song, how it put some hope into the world, as did many of our other tunes. I witnessed this hope firsthand when I performed "When I Think of You" at a funeral for a friend from church. As I sang it, I thought of Steve's wonderful mother.

One of the last songs we wrote for the new album was the title song "Trial by Fire." Perry said he wanted to write a song about the "jars of clay" passage in the Bible, 2 Corinthians 4:6–7: "For God, who said, 'Let light shine out of darkness,' made his light shine in our hearts to give us the light of the knowledge of God's glory displayed in the face of Christ. But we have this treasure in jars of clay to show that this all-surpassing power is from God and not from us."

In so many ways, that was Steve Perry's life story right there. It's his "Where have you been, Steve?" song. I think he had finally come to realize how blessed he truly was, and it wasn't because of his precious mother. He had sung all those songs to her, yet ultimately it was somebody else who wanted his attention and thanks.

This all-surpassing power is from God and not from us.

I understood what Steve Perry was talking about, especially since I had come to realize I had spent my life making music for my father—and he was no longer here.

What about me, Jon?

God was telling us something. It wasn't about our amazing talents or how hard we worked. It was how much Steve and I were blessed, and how Journey had been blessed for many years. Those songs we wrote truly were treasures in jars of clay.

Steve finally got this. It took me a little while before I did too.

While I was wondering what was going on in Steve's mind when he refused to move, I think God was wondering the same thing about me.

Being in the studio once again with Steve Perry, at work to reclaim our magic, I already knew some important facts about life.

You have to be prepared. You have to keep going down the road ready to jump when your time comes. That's what I had done my whole career, from moving to Hollywood to deciding to write songs to listening and studying and pondering and trying this and that and wondering what sound or song might work.

After Steve Perry called with the idea of getting Journey back together, I jumped because I was ready. We were excited to see the songs come effortlessly. It was what we loved to do. Every single song we created was like the ones before—written with the desire to create a classic.

As we talked, Steve said something quite profound, something he said often: "Timeless music takes time."

We both took our craft very seriously. We considered the songs we had written with Neal Schon to be timeless. We never worried about the critics. We wrote to the hearts of those in our audiences who sang our songs with us night after night.

It's one thing to write hits. But what would it be like to write one that could last for years and even decades?

All I knew was that good songs had to have certain qualities. They needed to go somewhere and take the listeners on a voyage. They had to have a sense of hope, even in seemingly hopeless situations. That's why the world loves them.

Steve Perry could take a good song and take people along on a trip. He could take a melody and make it soar. This was the beauty and magic of Journey—to take a tune that meant something to people and make it majestic.

Timeless music does indeed take time.

It's like a father who plants seeds in his children and then waits, watching them take root and then grow. A father waits and hopes, and he never stops believin'.

"WE'RE NOT GOING TO GO BEHIND YOUR BACK," I TELL STEVE PERRY. "SO IF you hear we're auditioning for new singers, it's true."

I don't want to be talking to him now. I don't want to have to make this call. But it's been more than a year of doing nothing. Absolutely nothing.

Neal and I are in a band, and we have jobs to do. Steve is refusing to budge, and he is refusing to accept our ultimatum. We offer to write another album with him if the road is not an option, but he doesn't want to do that either.

The voice speaking to me is the one that sang "Don't Stop Believin'" a thousand times. It's the sound of our band, the soundtrack to an entire generation. It sounds faint and tired, yet it's also defiant.

"Do whatever you guys need to do, but don't call it Journey," Steve says. "Call the band something else. Anything. Don't fracture the stone. I don't think I can come back if you break it."

He pleads with me about not moving on with the band name, about how hard we've worked and how much integrity Journey has.

We've tried to understand his situation, and we've been patient, but at the same time, we don't want to lose the momentum we have going with *Trial by Fire*. Anything we record now would be meaningful. Steve won't do it, however, saying he's eventually going to have the surgery.

"We need to know when," I said. "We have to get back out on the road."

"Do what you have to do. Just lose my phone number."

Just like that, it's over. The lawyers will soon begin figuring out what Steve Perry's departure will look like legally.

I think of the verse that comes nine verses after the "jars of clay" passage, where we are told not to lose heart. The apostle Paul says that even though outwardly we're wasting away, inwardly we're being renewed day by day.

I don't want to lose heart. I want to be renewed every day. I just don't know how.

If we get our band back, I'll be back on my feet again. Hope and renewal will come. But I'm the only one who can do this. Nobody else is going to help me, no matter how hard I ask and wait and wonder.

PART FIVE

"IT GOES ON AND ON AND ON AND ON"

TWENTY-THREE

"TO BE ALIVE AGAIN"

Three men will be instrumental in helping Journey rise from the ashes left after we moved on without Steve Perry: Steve Augeri, Danny Zelisko, and Neal Schon.

Steve Augeri is the man who replaced the legend and voice behind Journey, while Danny Zelisko is the one who bet on the band after the switch. Both of these men believed there was still music for Journey to make and fans who would eagerly receive it.

It was 1998, and the chorus of one of my songs on my solo album filled my thoughts: "It's funny somehow, we're back where we started. Full circle." The four albums Journey had made since I joined them had sold twenty-two million copies. Yet in so many ways, we were starting from scratch.

I had been in this place in my life before. Several times. I knew what needed to be done.

Time to drag the sled back up the hill.

As Neal and I began to look for new singers after finally telling Steve Perry we were moving on, he remembered Steve Augeri. We had heard him sing when we were making a record with Bad English. We were at a restaurant when "Wild on the Run" played in the background. The rocking tune could've fit on a Bad English album. It came from a band that Steve fronted called Tall Stories, and their self-titled album had been released in 1991 by Epic Records. Neal had said if we ever wanted to put Journey back together, we should look up that singer.

When Joe Cefalu, one of Neal's guitar teacher friends and a friend of Steve's, sent Neal a cassette tape of Augeri's music and his phone number, Neal called him because of this coincidental exchange. It turned out that Augeri had more or less given up on singing. He'd been working at The Gap for more than a year. The Brooklyn-based singer didn't believe it was really Neal Schon from Journey who was contacting him out of the blue. He assumed it was one of his friends playing a practical joke. So I called Steve a few minutes later and convinced him we really were interested in having him audition for the band.

After Steve's great audition, we invited him to join the band, but we didn't know exactly when he would start recording with us. When he finally showed up without notice on our studio doorstep and told us he was ready to get to work, the timing couldn't have been better—especially since Neal and I had written a song a week earlier that was ready for him to sing lead vocals on.

Then a couple of days later, another door opened with a phone call. A record executive was wondering if we had a song he could pitch to the producers of a movie he was working on.

John Kalodner was a well-known, well-respected A&R executive, notable for having discovered Foreigner and having worked with many artists, including Aerosmith. He had placed many songs on soundtracks of movies such as *Top Gun* and *Footloose*. In this case, he was looking for songs for a movie called *Armageddon*.

"As a matter of fact, I just finished a song with Neal Schon and a new singer," I said. "It's called 'Remember Me.'"

Kalodner heard the song and pitched it. Soon something happened that I never thought I'd witness again in my lifetime—an engineer in a studio writing JOURNEY on a tape box.

How monumental is this?

John Kalodner was the guy to get Journey back on the label. We found ourselves in a studio in New York with Kevin Shirley, the producer we had worked with on *Trial by Fire*. I was as giddy as I had been back when I was singing for Buddy Killen and backed up by the Muscle Shoals Rhythm Section. Steve Augeri amazed us, getting the vocals finished in just three takes. The song was the second track on *Armageddon: The Album*, right after Aerosmith's "I Don't Want to Miss a Thing."

We were on our way. Journey had managed to crack the door open. Just barely.

The excitement began to fade when the prospects of touring looked bleak. I had reached an impasse and didn't know what to do. I needed help from another one of my champions who had helped me out over the years.

Danny Zelisko's love of music helped him become one of the most successful and beloved promoters in the industry, while his love of Journey and our family helped us emerge from the ashes after we decided to move on without Steve Perry. He was the Chicago guy who moved to Phoenix to run Evening Star Productions, becoming a concert promoter who worked with every important artist out there. He had been a huge supporter of Journey and a friend for years, being instrumental in helping my parents make the transition to Arizona.

If anybody could help solve our band's current dilemma, it was Danny. So I called him to see if he had any ideas.

The good news was that we had found our new lead singer. The bad news was that we needed our old fans to show up to our new shows.

"We're stuck, "I said. "Irving is demanding seventy-five grand a night—guaranteed. There's no way we'll get that without Steve Perry."

Irving Azoff was a shrewd businessman who knew how to manage groups like Journey. My problem was that we couldn't come close to having enough fans turn up for a show, especially since we were in the midst of a backlash caused by hiring a new lead singer.

"I don't know what to do," I said to Danny. "I have four guys who need work."

At that point, thanks to fortunate business decisions over the years, I was the only one in the band who had money. We had found the right singer, but I had already anticipated some of the hate we'd receive. Thank God that social media wasn't around at the time, because some fans were irate at the thought of anybody taking over for Steve Perry. Because of some of the bad buzz, promoters were skeptical and afraid to book shows for us.

Danny had an idea. He offered to put up one million dollars of his own money and then go to all the venues and tell them to book Journey. If the places refused, then we would book them ourselves instead, promote the concert, and take all the profits.

"Jon, let's go out and show the promoters what this new lineup is made of," Danny said. "Go out for a little money. I can make it so you guys break even. The promoters need to see that they can make some money. It will change their perception."

Danny knew without a doubt that Journey wasn't over. This sort of confidence and belief in others was how he had become so powerful in the music industry.

I contacted Irving Azoff to tell him about the plan. At the time, I was reading Stephen Covey's *The 7 Habits of Highly Effective People* and thought of habit #4: "Think win-win."

As I talked to Irving, I mentioned the idea to him. "Right now, we're playing 'I win, you lose.' But why can't we both win? I have guys who need work. And I have a friend who wants to help me. Can I ask you to back off of the big-bucks guarantee?"

Irving agreed, so Journey soon embarked on our break-even tour. Not a comeback tour, but more like a rebirth tour. We were rebuilding.

Now the only thing I needed to worry about was keeping our new lead singer alive.

When word got out that Journey was replacing its lead singer, some people were angry enough to want to boycott our concerts. Most didn't understand what was happening, and quite a few made it clear they didn't want Steve Perry gone. There were a handful, however, who decided to suddenly come against us for continuing to make music instead of waiting and wondering if we'd ever perform again.

This was the first time I ever received messages on the studio phone telling me basically to eat dog poop and die. I didn't know how they got the number, but it freaked me out a bit. People *literally* wanted me gone—and not just me, but our new lead singer too. How could anybody dare to replace Steve Perry?

Don't they remember Journey had singers before him?

The vitriol was felt front and center as we hit the road in late 1998 with our Vacation's Over Tour. As we prepared to play the Beacon Theatre in Manhattan on October 28, New York's famous DJ, Don Imus, decided to join the fray over our new lead singer. Imus essentially told his radio audience that we were ripping off our fans. "This isn't Journey," Imus told his listeners. "If you bought tickets, bring them over to the station, and we'll give you your money back." I couldn't believe the gall of the DJ. I told Irving Azoff about it, and he made the phone call, and it ended. That's the nice thing about having someone with a lot of leverage managing you.

Just as we had been upfront with Steve Perry, we didn't want to hide the fact that we had a new lead singer. We were billing ourselves as "Journey Featuring Steve Augeri," and that's how it was printed on the tickets themselves. It would end up this way for five years. And yet many still refused to accept it. In Hawaii, for instance, a place where we had always been very popular, we were essentially boycotted. Their message: If you come over here without Steve Perry, there will be riots at the radio station.

I couldn't believe it.

People riot over wars being fought overseas—not about bringing in a new lead singer of a rock band.

I was afraid Steve would end up getting shot at one of our concerts. There were no metal detectors at shows in those days, so it would have been all too easy for something like that to happen. I believe it could only have been God who protected us.

People didn't know we had asked Steve Perry to come back. We had practically begged him. We had been patient, and our lives had been put on hold. All of us had families and responsibilities and concerns and bills to pay, like everyone else. To be waiting on something that might never happen—something completely outside of our control—felt debilitating and unfair. We asked Steve to do anything—make an album, do something. But he wouldn't budge, so we had to move on.

As we pushed on, Steve Augeri was outstanding. His voice in the beginning was superb as we did a "greatest hits" setlist for the modest crowds. Slowly but surely, the venues began to fill as word got out that Journey still rocked. Seven thousand seats were filled at Freedom Hall in Lexington. Not bad. Two sold-out nights at the Beacon Theatre in New York. Pretty good. But our start right out of the gate had truly been a game changer, as we had a fifteen-thousand-seat sellout at The Palace.

Some of our fans had gone their separate ways, but sure enough, Detroit had not stopped believin'.

TWENTY-FOUR

"GONE CRAZY"

The German general practitioner marched into my hotel room, holding a black bag in his slender, wrinkled hand. For a second, I wondered if he would speak to me in his native language and pull terrifying instruments of torture out of his case. Thankfully, he spoke fluent English and asked me about my health concern. I told him I was a musician who played a lot of concerts where the noise could get pretty loud. That night, I told him, Journey was playing a concert in the city of Cologne.

"Since touring in Europe, I've been noticing the mix for my in-ear monitors was getting cranked up high," I said to the doctor. "I wondered if I had an ear infection, so I saw a doctor in Spain, who noticed a lot of earwax built up. He gave me softeners for the wax and an antibiotic to kill anything that might have been growing. I've been using the softener, but it doesn't seem to be working. I'm worried since we're flying next to Zurich. I don't want to damage my ears by not getting the wax out."

"Did the doctor use a syringe on your ear?" the German asked.

"He told me he used to do that, but now he recommends against it. He says it's dangerous for your ear—that the sound can be extreme to the middle ear, like a gun going off."

The procedure of syringing out earwax with warm water was known to damage the tympanic membrane, more commonly known as the eardrum. This tiny but tough layer of tissue helps with hearing. The last thing I wanted to do was to mess around with it. The stern face looking at me seemed unconvinced.

"I've done this sort of thing hundreds of times and never had any problems," he said in his thick accent as he removed a syringe from his bag.

I briefly repeated my reluctance, especially since a doctor had given me a reason not to do this very thing.

"If you fly with ear blockage, your eardrums could rupture," the doctor said. "It's a simple process to clean out your ears."

The elderly man didn't seem hesitant in the least, so I gave in and let him flush out the wax. He cleaned out both of my ears, and sure enough, the sound of the water did seem loud and large amounts of wax clogged the passages. Once he finished, my right ear felt strange, yet he assured me that all would be well in no more than a half hour. He examined my ears for any trace of infection.

"I don't see anything suspicious," he said.

During the press interview before our show that evening, I noticed a hum in my left ear, the sort you might get from a turntable not properly grounded. It was pretty loud, enough to distract me from my interview with the German reporter. I was eager to talk about our latest album that had come out in 2005, *Generations,* as well as my excitement about our latest tour co-headlined with Def Leppard. Journey hadn't been to Europe since the eighties, and we were playing in places we'd never been to. My enthusiasm, however, was drowned out by a deep-rooted panic.

Did the doctor screw up my ear? Did I just agree to do something incredibly stupid?

I apologized and excused myself, briefly explaining my ear issues. During the sound check, I noticed the monitor level on my belt pack was blasting in my ears. The monitor mixer told me he hadn't adjusted the mix to make it any louder, so I figured my ears were sensitive to the volume since the cleaning. As I played familiar chords on my keyboard, I tried to remember the last time I had earwax removed. It had to have been at least four years.

Have I been pumping high dB levels in blocked ears for the last year?

The hum wouldn't go away, ringing in my ears all day and night. After describing my symptoms to our monitor mixer, he told me it was probably tinnitus.

"It's a ringing caused by damaged hairs in the cochlea," he said, talking about the tiny organ resting behind the eardrum.

The timing couldn't have been worse, since it coincided with another medical situation in the band. Steve Augeri had been a warrior as we worked on building a new brand since he joined us. There were still haters out there—and always would be— but we had found solid ground, and our numbers were growing. Yet the performances had begun to wear down his voice.

I always knew how incredible it was for Steve Perry to do what he did night after night, but by the *Frontiers* tour, it had started to tear up his voice. The machine had been unrelenting. Steve Augeri was suffering from an acute throat condition and needed vocal rest even before we began the tour. We announced that he wouldn't be touring with us anymore and would be replaced by Jeff Scott Soto. Neal Schon had worked with Jeff in the band Soul SirkUS, so he knew the singer and his abilities. Thankfully, Jeff stepped in and bravely joined the band on our tour.

Just as I had to accept and deal with Steve Augeri's vocal crisis, I had to do the same with my ear condition, especially since I had agreed to let the German doctor use his syringe. Self-doubt plagued me, along with the constant noise. A weird phenomenon about tinnitus is the blocked feeling you get—as though you have to equalize, yet you can't. This happens because your brain is searching for frequencies that are missing. I knew I'd have to get to the source of my problem once I returned home.

My ear, nose, and throat specialist, Dr. Agbayani, confirmed that I had suffered ear trauma. After taking a test, I discovered the hearing in my left ear was reduced substantially. I suspected the frequency was around 300 to 400 cycles, along with a typical loss from rock and roll from 2,000 to 4,000 cycles. My right ear was normal for someone in my profession. Dr. Agbayani said some patients improved with a drug treatment, so he treated me with massive amounts of cortisone twice during the next three months. He also explained I would need a hearing aid and masker to block out the high-pitched whine. Thankfully, after four months, the ringing subsided.

During this time, I scoured the internet for information about the condition, but I found very few personal accounts. I learned that many celebrities suffer from tinnitus, including a who's who in the music business. Grateful for the relief I found after the long and scary ordeal, I wrote an article about my battle and my blessing, which was published in *Pollstar* magazine. I wrote the four-page article as a warning to all musicians to get their ears checked before a tour. I stressed that our ears are incredibly important tools, so we have to get them checked at least yearly, especially those who use in-ear monitors, like I did. Once a person is diagnosed with ear trauma like mine, the effect may be permanent.

While I battled for my hearing, Journey soon found itself in another familiar struggle. After the throat condition took our brother, Steve Augeri, and after deciding Jeff Scott Soto didn't have the legacy sound Journey was going for, our band was suddenly in search for yet another front man. Soto was a good singer who stepped in to help at a crucial time, yet we never considered him to be a permanent member. As we began a search for a new singer, a bigger struggle in my personal life began to pick up speed.

My hearing wasn't the only thing I was afraid of losing.

I started to fear losing my soul.

THE HEADLIGHTS AND ENGINE CUT OFF, BUT THE KEYS REMAIN STUCK INSIDE
my tricked-out Mustang.

25 Saddle Lane has never looked this empty and abandoned.

I pause and breathe in the night air around me.

I'm eight years old again, staring at the fire in front of me and calling out for those closest to me, yet they're nowhere to be found.

I know I'll wake up tomorrow different than I was when I saw the first light this morning.

Climbing out of the car, I'm in no rush to enter the quiet house full of sleeping souls. I'm in the doghouse once again, except this time I deserve it.

The weight that accompanies me is deeper than guilt. It's a certainty that my marriage is over. Our family of five is finished.

The line I swore and believed I would never cross got swept away by the tide of romance and passion. My marriage hasn't been working and I should've admitted it and said it wasn't working, but I've been trying. I've not given up, because I don't give up. I stay in there and fight and work hard to try to get things to continue working.

But maybe love shouldn't be so hard. Maybe a marriage shouldn't be so much work.

I walk through the silent hallway and stop by the living room piano that has delivered so many love songs to the world. The bright and glorious view I usually see is missing. All I can picture through the surrounding windows is darkness. Endless and suffocating.

The stories that came from my heart and were shared in songs are no longer created in this house. They're made next door in the studio called Wildhorse. Stone and concrete separate those songs from this family.

I've become familiar with living two lives, so this is no different.

The road is indeed no place to start a family. That's why so many of us decide to travel down two of them.

I know it's only a matter of time before the two roads intersect, before the truth will come out and I'll be forced to choose between one or the other.

The scary thing is I feel the choice has already been made.

TWENTY-FIVE

"WILDEST DREAMS"

The encore began, and we started to play "Lovin', Touchin', Squeezin'." I had to sit at the piano rather than stand up like I usually did. My stomach cramps were that bad.

Please, God, let us do a short version tonight.

Of course, we ended up doing a long jam for the song, much to the delight of the Jones Beach crowd. I forced myself to make it through the song as my body kept shuddering from the chills, even though the temperature was in the upper 80s. I thought I was just suffering from food poisoning. I staggered over to bow with the guys for the final round of applause and wandered backstage to find the nearest couch to collapse on.

"Are you all right?" Ross Valory asked me just before I passed out.

The next moment, I was on a gurney carried out of the arena by two paramedics. Fans stared at me in my stage clothes.

"What hospital are we going to?" I asked.

"There are two in the area, but one I wouldn't even take my dog to," one of the guys said.

I was relieved to know I was in good hands just as I passed out again. Our road manager, John Toomey, went with me and was by my side when I woke up in the ER. A very kind nurse examined me as I shook in my hospital bed. I was running a fever of 105.

"What side is the pain on?" the nurse asked.

"*Every* side," I said. I had a hard time talking because my entire abdominal area was swollen and sore.

They made me stay overnight so they could do an MRI and a CT scan. I was shivering so much that I could barely stay still for the tests. As we suspected by then, I was having an appendicitis attack.

"Do you always wear such fancy clothes?" one of the nurses said with a smile, commenting on my fitted Roberto Cavalli designer shirt with a lilac print and Cavalli jeans that had gold piping on the sides.

"Only when I decide to head to the ER," I said.

"I was at the Journey show and saw you onstage," she said. "You guys were great."

"Thanks. The others were excellent, but I wasn't quite myself tonight."

"Your appendix hasn't burst, but in a few hours, that might not be the case," she said as she gave me more morphine so I could sleep.

After I woke up, I met a surgeon surrounded by his nurses who told me he would be removing my appendix that morning. Since it was a Monday morning and our next show in Pittsburgh hadn't sold well, we canceled it and decided to stay in New York City until Friday. By then I'd try to play at Atlantic City.

My recovery didn't go the best. The surgeon gave me Mylanta and told me to walk around the city so the gas that had built up inside of me could dissipate. Unfortunately, my stomach thought the Mylanta was barium, so I was on the toilet every twenty minutes. I felt like the runs were never going to stop, and I panicked and called Steve Augeri's brother, who was a gastroenterologist. He suggested I switch to Kaopectate and all would calm down. He was correct, and hours after drinking the gooey pink stuff, the adventure came to an end.

Unbelievably, while all of this was happening, Hurricane Katrina was decimating New Orleans. I prayed for New Orleans on the night of my appendicitis attack. As I worked on my recovery during those days, I was distracted by the news coverage of people in distress, the Coast Guard rescues, and the devastation and death from the floodwaters.

On Thursday morning, I told our management I would make the trip to Atlantic City, even though I still felt weak. Though I was nervous about taking a four-hour bus ride with my stomach still in turmoil, we got there, and I showed up for sound check and played the gig that evening. I was still floating from all the medication when Steve Augeri announced to the audience that I was fresh out of the hospital, and the audience gave me a rousing round of applause.

I survived the appendix attack, but I found myself once again shivering on stage in a leather jacket on a 90-degree evening as we played outside in Virginia Beach. Now I was suffering from an adverse allergic reaction to my first dose of Cipro, which a doctor had given me for my stomach.

I still can't believe I played those concerts after an appendectomy. I had simply toughed out a lousy situation, Chicago style.

Twenty-five years after joining Journey, I could see how staggeringly powerful the songs had turned out to be. They had become the soundtrack of people's lives. The songs were bigger than anybody and everybody in the band. Like perennial flowers, the songs continued to bloom. They reminded me of grapevines that grew stronger year after year.

In 2005, I decided to plant my own vineyard at my Novato house. I wanted to plant grapevines and watch the baby sprouts turn into vines. For two summers, I watched those little guys grow. All you have to do with vines is prune them. Years later, I recognized that this is a great metaphor for my own life—how God is constantly pruning me back, allowing me to bear fruit. Over and over again, he prunes me, having me start over again. I had seen it happen time after time in my life, as if God would come to my door and say, *That's a little too much success. I blessed you with that million, but now I'm going to prune you and take it back.*

Blessings always come from pruning.

So in 2005, I started the vineyard project and had soil samples tested. I discovered that my property was perfect for such a venture. I planted Pinot Noir grapes, one of the toughest variety to grow, but worth all the extra care. The two hundred vines I planted would be watched over with a special, tender love and care.

It took two years before I'd see the first harvest. This would also be the same time the band discovered Arnel Pineda and rewrote Journey's history forever.

I was a Doubting Thomas when we auditioned Arnel Pineda in 2007. His discovery and path to becoming the new lead singer of Journey was well chronicled in the 2013 music documentary *Don't Stop Believin': Everyman's Journey*. After Neal Schon came across YouTube videos of the singer from the Philippines performing a variety of songs by acts like Aerosmith, Toto, Bryan Adams, REO Speedwagon, and Journey, he had to show the rest of us. Naturally, we were skeptical.

"Does the guy even speak English?" I couldn't help but ask the most obvious question.

Arnel's story is a riveting account of persistence and belief in one's dreams. Much like my own journey, he discovered a passion for music at a young age. He joined a band at a young age and then headed to the big city to pursue his musical dreams, only to find emptiness and closed doors. Eventually the all-too-familiar road to excess brought him to what seemed to be a dead end, when a doctor told the twenty-seven-year-old that his voice was gone and his musical dreams were over. Arnel, however, did what my father had urged me to do: he continued to believe and to stay on the journey.

Initially, the thought of Arnel singing with us made me hesitant, wondering what our fans in places like Raleigh, North Carolina, and regions like the middle of Texas might think. I feared the twisted mentality that went, "That's no Steve Perry—he's Asian." The documentary even showed people making what may have been unintentionally racist remarks and not thinking twice about doing so.

Yet there was a flip side to the idea of having Arnel join our team, one that began to spark and eventually turn into a full-fledged bonfire after he had filled the role for more than a year. In a piece on *CBS Sunday Morning* about the thirty-year anniversary of our song "Don't Stop Believin'," Jim Axelrod said this to Arnel Pineda about his connection to the theme of our classic song: "I'm not sure I know a life story to whom this concept applies any more than yours."

The dynamic of this unlikely rags-to-riches story, along with the introduction of an entirely new element into the Journey story—an international flavor—were exciting things to think about. And after Arnel had been in our studio for a few days and had gotten his voice back after all the travel and restless nights, the voice we heard on those YouTube videos showed up. It was pure, and it was mighty.

There was no question this talented man *had* to be our lead singer.

In an article a year later in *GQ* on Arnel's remarkable journey, Alex Pappademas gave the band a backhanded compliment when he stated that "Journey—Journey!—seem like innovators, in touch with the forces shaping the culture." While not exactly stating that as a fact or a compliment in the context of the full article, the message I took away was that even though we could have chosen anybody, we chose Arnel. We weren't afraid of racial lines. So yes, people could say that Journey sucked, but the writer seemed to be saying we were okay now that we had Arnel.

Journey would be better than simply okay now that we had Arnel. I had been sad to see Steve Augeri go, because he had been a brother and had spent eight years of his life pulling the sled up the hill with us. I'll forever be grateful to him for that, and anytime we talk about Journey bios, I always make sure he's in it. There would have been no Arnel if there hadn't been Steve Augeri.

On June 3, 2008, almost a year after Neal found Arnel online, we released Journey's thirteenth album, *Revelation*. The first release with Arnel as our lead singer went platinum before the end of that year. Journey was once again on solid ground.

A whole new surge of Journey fans emerged when the addition of Arnel brought many Filipino folks to our concerts in the states, including many who had never been to a rock concert. Abroad, the news of his rise to fame helped fuel interest in Hong Kong, Korea, Malaysia, and other places where we hadn't played and that had a large Filipino population. I learned that Manila is the English-language-teaching capital of Asia, and many people from China are sent there to learn English.

After my first divorce took two and a half years of my life, along with millions of dollars, I met Liz and honestly had no business getting serious with her. Before my dad died, he said, "Marry Liz, and she'll give you kids." I guess I was trying to make another one of his dreams come true. She was only twenty years old, way too young for involvement with someone who had just emerged from a traumatic relationship. I was broken in a million little pieces when we began to date; as a result, our relationship never had a classic "falling head over heels" sort of romance to it. Eventually, we moved in together and then we married and then we had kids—and this progression seemed logical and normal.

Years down the road, when the hurt and bad habits had built up stone barriers between us, I'd tell Liz I wished I'd had a few years to heal before meeting her. I had been a mess when we first met, and near the end, I would be even messier. What I know now is that when I first married Tané, I really did believe it was going to be forever, that I would be following my parents' example. Yet after that marriage blew up, I came to a bitter conclusion: *Well, I guess good guys don't win after all*. So I decided to live up to the rock and roll cliché of being a bad boy, having no idea of the baggage I was carrying when I married Liz.

After our spoken dreams and unspoken prayers came true by being blessed with three amazing children, a new dynamic came into play. When I was out on the road, I would miss them terribly. I think it was less painful for them to think of me as gone rather than to miss me all those weeks I wasn't there. When I came home, it would always take time to get back to normal.

Our home had become all about the kids. They consumed us and became the most important thing under our roof. The result, I learned far too late, was a problem that many couples have: We forget the fire that forged the two of us together. We have to keep that fire burning to create a strong bond. Like an Olympic torch, we both have to make sure it's always fully lit.

For example, each of our kids had their own rooms, yet when I was on the road, they'd all climb into bed with Mommy. When I got back home, I didn't want them in our bed anymore, so I made them get out. Naturally, that suddenly made me *the deadbeat dad*. I'd look at Liz and ask her what she was doing. The two of us needed to say together, "You kids can't be here in bed with us," yet I was the only one to say it—with not-so-great results.

When we first started dating, Liz knew about Journey, yet she hadn't been one of the rabid fans. She wasn't some kind of groupie, which I was glad to see. She relished our financial condition and seemed to mildly appreciate my work, yet I felt she resented my lifestyle. Once the kids were born, there always seemed to be an "I'm stuck at home, and you're out there" sort of attitude. I'd ask her to come on the road with me and told her we could get a nanny, yet she didn't want to give up "command central" in the Cain household. Liz began to dislike the music business and became annoyed at the politics and the infighting that sometimes happened. When I'd come back home like a soldier from a distant war, I was stunned at how little regard there would be for how hard I had worked for the money we were blessed with.

I coped with these tensions in the same way I had always coped with stress: making music. I wasn't surprised to find that I became a workaholic, producing and writing songs before starting Bad English and then eventually helping Journey get back out there. I built Wildhorse—my studio—and worked on Neal Schon's jazz record and released my own solo album and then more instrumental, New Age albums. I worked and worked—since that's what I knew to do.

Around the same time we discovered Arnel, I unfortunately came to live the lyrics I had written with Greg Allman in "Temptation Is a Gun." I had everything and more with my wife and three kids, yet I felt something was missing. And then, out of the blue, it happened. "He met her at a night club, on the other side of town. Somehow he could not resist her, she's the best he'd ever found."

After a girlfriend from the eighties contacted me out of the blue, we connected and discovered we had similar life stories. Both of us were unhappily married, had children we loved, and shared other familiar circumstances. Suddenly and foolishly, I ended up being that guy from that song. I look at that tune now and curse.

Sometimes you have to watch what you write.

I was literally writing about what was to come. Just as it was when I wrote "Separate Ways" before my divorce with Tané.

Who's crying now? I was the one crying now.

The affair I began with my ex-girlfriend became a powerful antidote to my passionless relationship with my wife. I knew I wasn't going to run away and leave Liz and the children, and this woman wasn't going to leave her husband, since she also had children. So I began to live a double life that I was all too familiar with.

Just like those songs I had written over the years, or like those grapevines planted next to our Novato home, my deeds and decisions would eventually blossom and grow. I would end up reaping the consequences of the choices I made.

It would turn out to be a very brutal sort of pruning for me.

In the documentary that detailed Arnel's story, he said a couple of things that seemed very wise for a man only a year over forty. When asked about his recent success, he said, "I'm not expecting to be really completely happy. There'll be problems. You gain, you lose. That's how life is."

Well spoken, Arnel. Well spoken indeed.

We had gained an incredibly energetic and passionate singer. Journey was becoming more popular and, even more importantly, more relevant than ever. Yet in the same breath, I was losing my marriage and in some ways my family.

Arnel also talked about the temptations we all face: "I tell myself if you do it, make sure you know how to handle the consequences, or you'll have to pay the price."

Haunting words that certainly had a dark cloud of foreshadowing surrounding them.

When I think of everything Arnel brought to Journey, my statement to Jim Axelrod in the interview for *CBS Sunday Morning* sums up my feelings the best: "He's made our camp a better camp. His spirituality. His faith. His belief is strong."

FIFTY YEARS LATER, I'M STILL A SURVIVOR.

I will always be a survivor.

The children and nuns whose names are read out loud in the sanctuary of Holy Family Church did not survive the fire at Our Lady of the Angels School five decades ago. More than a thousand people are packed into the 150-year old Gothic structure on Roosevelt Road to pay their respects at the memorial service. I pay mine as I remember and light a votive candle.

The sting of smoke and the sound of death still seem to hover around those of us who made it out alive.

When I finally walk to the front to sit behind the piano, I force myself to remain strong and get through the lyrics without breaking down.

They asked me to audition the song beforehand, since the guy in charge had been working for a long time on the program, and the program was packed. I understood and allowed others to encourage him to let me sing today. The ceremony isn't about celebrities, but about celebrating life.

Out of all the songs I've written, this is one I wish I would never have had to write.

"The day they became angels, they left us wondering why," I begin to sing, the notes on the piano drifting over the silent audience. "Young souls joined God's departed, leaving no time for good-bye."

Nobody at the school or living near Augusta Boulevard was left without scars from that horrific day. We all still carry them in some way.

"All that's left are memories . . . of innocence and childhood dreams. As survivors . . . we choose to love beyond our pain. While the whole world stopped to watch our tears, with faith we heal through the years, somehow a cloud of sadness still remains."

We all had to keep living after the fire. To just wake up and keep going, sometimes without coping very well or healing very much. There hadn't been any sort of therapy for the kids. We would have to figure out how to heal on our own.

The black and white keys under my fingers were my remedy.

"What happened fifty years ago will never be forgotten in our hearts. As we carry on and live our lives, the reason we all survived gives us purpose to know who we are."

Fifty years later, I still only partially know the answer to that.

I'm a son and I'm a singer and I'm a father—and those things define who I am now at fifty-eight. But I still wonder. I'm still searching. Just like so many of the other scarred souls in this place of mourning, meditation, and remembrance.

TWENTY-SIX

"AFTER ALL THESE YEARS"

The moment I heard the thirteen-year-old girl sing karaoke to Gretchen Wilson's "Redneck Woman," I realized she could have a career singing country. Of course, I was a little biased, since this was my daughter Madison, but I had already been observing her talent for years. This was the same little girl who had learned the entire Alanis Morissette album when she was only five.

After hearing her country voice, I decided to take her to Nashville to write with a buddy I met during the recording of Journey's album *Arrival*. During that time, we wrote and recorded more than thirty songs. The dream and desire in Madison to pursue a music career began during this time. This was also when the rest of the family came out to watch us work. They also began to fall in love with different neighborhoods in the area—and it got Liz and the kids to look at real estate and decide which homes were beautiful.

An exciting energy and revival began to happen over the last few years for Journey. Some of the kids who had grown up listening to music were now wealthy business executives, and they didn't care if the critics had always seemed to hate us or we had to live with that burdensome tag of being "corporate rock." They wanted their band back, so that's exactly what happened. More and more of our concerts filled up with families. Hardworking folks were now bringing their children and introducing them to the songs that generated many memories.

Pop culture also began to embrace Journey, and it really started on June 10, 2007. The finale of the Emmy-winning, massively successful HBO show *The Sopranos* was watched by almost twelve million viewers. Only three days earlier, Steve Perry, Neal Schon, and I were contacted and asked for permission to use "Don't Stop Believin'" in the show. We had always been very careful with the licensing of our songs, but we all agreed to give permission. I didn't know how the song would be used, and I kept it a close secret from everybody, including Liz.

As we watched the finale, I waited and waited—until the very shocking end. You remember it, don't you? (Warning . . . spoilers ahead.)

Tony Soprano watches the door of the diner and slips a quarter into the jukebox on the side of his table as he waits for the rest of his family. As one song in the background ends, another begins. A very familiar tune. A piano starts to play—the piano I played when we recorded the song inspired by my father.

The Soprano family is hoping to live happily ever after. But something is about to happen. Something's definitely about to happen.

The chorus comes in just as the family digs into their order of onion rings.

Just as the daughter is about to enter the diner and the audience is fully enjoying the song, the music stops and the screen goes black. The screen doesn't just fade; it cuts off to nothing but darkness. Steve Perry doesn't even finish the entire phrase, but he simply sings "don't stop" before silence.

Viewers are stunned, perplexed, annoyed, amused, and entranced. All of the above.

The conversation will begin and never stop about that ending.
Suddenly, half the country is reminded of our song, while the
other half is introduced to Journey.

I loved the ending. It was smart writing, leaving the audience wondering what happened. My family was surprised to hear our song, with Liz in disbelief that I hadn't even told her. The title of that last episode was "Made in America." Those three words seemed to sum up our similarly three-word-titled song.

Another entire demographic appeared on May 19, 2009, when the pilot episode of the successful TV show *Glee* used "Don't Stop Believin'" as a centerpiece for the story, later using it in 2015 in their finale as well. A whole new audience of young listeners was curious where the song had come from, which led them to discover this band their parents knew and loved.

A year after *The Sopranos* finale in 2008, Journey released our first album with Arnel as the lead singer. *Revelation* was truly that for fans who heard Arnel's incredible voice. We couldn't believe how he had come in cold from Manila and not only had to sing our greatest hits on tour but also had to learn a brand-new set of songs from Neal and me. Journey's thirteenth album was released in 2008 and went platinum, being sold exclusively through Walmart. "After All These Years" would become a No. 1 single off the album.

By the time we made *Eclipse* three years later, Arnel was fully entrenched as our singer. Our 2011 release was a departure for Journey. Neal wanted to make a guitar-driven thematic record, and since some of the tracks had an Eastern sound, we ended up with the song "Tantra," which focused on the Hindu idea of spirituality, where everything in the universe is woven into one circle of life. We recorded the album at Fantasy Studios, in the same room where we made *Escape* and *Frontiers.* I had quite a few déjà vu moments as I was able to reflect on the good memories and the great songs we had created there.

I found myself reflecting on the memories I had made at my own studio too, after the family decided they wanted to leave our Saddle Lane home and move to Nashville. I hated to leave Novato and our home. It was crushing to leave behind my Wildhorse studio and my vineyard. But Liz desperately wanted to move, and I agreed we had lived in the same place for a long time. For the sake of our family I thought it might be good to start over somewhere else.

I went back by myself to California to pack the rest of my things and to cut the cords in my studio. Since I had kept kitchen and bedding essentials at the house, I stayed for a couple of weeks and cleaned out the twenty-nine years of my life there. I ended up hiring a crew to help me since I had accumulated so much stuff in the studio, including in the attic.

I had been working on the *Eclipse* album with Neal, so I took one last picture of us together, realizing that my good-luck place would soon be a memory. The backyard for our house had been newly designed, and because I'd been on the road a lot, I hardly had any time to enjoy it. So for a couple of weeks, I lived at my home, swimming alone in the pool every afternoon and cooking myself dinner on the new outdoor kitchen Liz had designed, which I'd never been able to enjoy. In the quiet of the evening, I swore I could hear the sounds of Madison, Weston, and Liza echo through the house. Reverberations from all the songs created in my studio bounced around in my memories. Those two weeks were a blessing as I came to closure with the sweet Victorian house on the hill on Saddle Lane.

When I stood at the front door and locked it for the last time, I thanked God for this house and the studio. I was grateful for all the great years when my children had been born and music had flourished. I had been able to live out my dreams in a lovely place. I fought back tears and said a final good-bye to the place that had been so good to me.

As it turned out, Nashville would be welcoming, but not a place where all our dreams would come true. After living there for a while, I discovered that doors didn't suddenly open. I also watched Madison struggle with her own dreams and ambitions.

The kids began attending Franklin Road Academy, a small Christian school that had fewer kids in their classes, less peer pressure, and a much better environment than the school they'd been attending.

Life in the city had started out so promising. Shortly after arriving in Nashville in 2010, I wrote a song with Jimmy Nichols and Sarah Darling for a movie featuring George Strait. *Pure Country 2* was about rodeo life and love, so the producers asked for a ballad written for a girl. I remember waking up in the middle of the night and writing "I Found in You." This was another song, like "Faithfully," that simply flowed out of me. At the time, I was excited and full of confidence.

I'm on a roll . . . I just got here and I'm already on a soundtrack.

Unfortunately, the song failed to make it onto the album. The director loved our song, but after George Strait submitted a song, we got bumped from the film and soundtrack. Ultimately it was probably because Strait's song had more of a country-style sound and ours was a little more Disneyesque.

This was a foreshadowing of things to come—how I would get shut out of the Nashville scene. Sarah Darling felt bad for us. She slotted the song on her solo album and asked me to sing it with her as a duet. It was a real honor, considering it was scored with an eighteen-piece live string section.

On the plus side, our daughter Madison was introduced to many fine people, and we were welcomed into the community. She was given the opportunity to headline the famous Bluebird Café, and I took her to everything I could to give her exposure. Her dream was to become the next Martina McBride.

A big setback came after Maddy's new manager suggested she meet with a music executive in the city. The big idea was to sing in front of the CEO of a record label. Unfortunately, all the guy did when Madison sang in his office was look at his phone and pretty much ignore her. I was angry after Madison came home in tears and told me what happened, and even more when I saw my daughter beginning to lose her confidence. I knew she was stunningly beautiful and had an incredible voice. She has always sounded more like a pop singer, and I believe if she did an Adele-like album, it would be a complete success. With each song, I could hear her getting better and better.

In the end, we just had to learn to accept reality when our music wasn't succeeding.

There was still music to be made—especially after opportunities I'd hoped would come suddenly disappeared. I found myself surprised when another dream appeared and was encouraged by an unlikely source. Despite the emotional distance between Liz and me, she was the one who encouraged me to build a studio in Nashville.

Building the studio came out of a need to put my gear from Wildhorse somewhere. I had driven my stuff cross-country in a Ryder truck. After trying to sell the gear and finding no buyers, it was worth more to me to keep it, given the historical nature of the equipment— especially my Trident TSM console, which had mixed so many great songs. And then add to that my frustration with my studio inside my Nashville home, where nothing seemed to work and I had trouble concentrating. I'd always felt something was off in the home record- ing room—lights turning on and off, equipment breaking down, and other strange things. I knew it would be great to have a space like Wildhorse, where I had been so creative and productive.

As I questioned whether to build a studio, I began to have strange dreams. I kept seeing Buddy Killen in them, smiling and saying, "Build it and inspire others, like I inspired you." Buddy had died the year we moved to Nashville, and I had never gotten to say good-bye because he passed so quickly. I believe his memory encouraged me to fulfill this dream.

One day, I was driving around in the Berry Hill area, where the famous Blackbird Studio is located, and found that the building at 506 E. Iris was for sale. It had been the home of the Tennessee Drug Awareness Council Center, hence the name Addiction Sound Studios—this would be rehab for the creative spirit. With a huge parking lot and large meeting area, the location and building were perfect. When I asked Liz what she thought after giving her a tour, she saw the potential and encouraged me to move forward. She was willing to decorate and provide design ideas—one of the rare times we saw eye to eye.

I always believed that God helped us put aside any differences between us and expedited the purchase of the property and the remodeling of the building.

I met David Kalmusky when he produced a few songs for Madison and worked with Journey on our *Eclipse* album, fully mixing and mastering it.

David grew up in studios as a third-generation musician who played and recorded music. He was only sixteen when he hit the road as an artist, and he worked in studios in every capacity—producing, mixing, engineering, and playing multiple instruments. Along with Journey, David has worked with artists such as Vince Gill, Justin Bieber, Hunter Hayes, and John Oates, just to name a few of the more than one hundred acts.

Since both of us were already working with our own small studios, we decided to combine our resources and build Addiction Sound Studios. The goal wasn't to create a studio as a viable source of revenue, but rather to build an impeccable space for our own projects and for many other artists who were seeking something special.

In a town full of studios, we were crazy to build another one. But I asked myself, *What if this studio is different? What if there's nothing like it in a town that's full of them.* So I looked around and made notes. *We can do better than that,* I'd say after seeing other spaces. I wanted to build something unique and comfortable, something that felt like home. A place where people could relax.

I had heard stories of artists who rented a trailer and put it next to a studio while they were recording, so I thought, *Why can't they simply crash upstairs?* That's why there's an apartment upstairs. There's a porch outside where they can have lunch on the deck. Catered snacks and meals could be brought in, and there's also a kitchen.

But the best part? The recording spaces themselves. We tried to do things that weren't happening anymore in the business, combining old-school with new-school. We worked on the studio design with Chris Huston, who engineered albums for Led Zeppelin, War, The Who, and The Animals.

With an underground echo chamber, intimate mic'ing, a Trident console, my Fazioli grand piano, and even a Hammond C3 organ from 1958, Addiction Sound Studios blended the classic rock with cutting-edge and state-of-the-art production.

Once again, just as it was with Wildhorse in Novato, I wouldn't have to be knocking on others' doors to make music. Now they'd be knocking on mine.

When the time came to sign the contract to buy the place, just as I put my pen on the paper, the electric clock in the building started spinning forward. As soon as I finished signing, the clock stopped. I looked at David and the real estate agent with a big grin and said, "Well, the folks resting in that cemetery behind us are either thrilled or they're very angry with us."

I'M LOST IN SOUTHWEST FLORIDA AND STARING AT A DESERTED STRETCH OF highway lined by tall Norfolk pines when I start to feel light-headed. I pass a billboard that reads, "Know the Signs" and feel a foreboding. After attending a charity event for Emeril Lagasse in Sandestin, my phone took me to the wrong airport. My flight is taking off in less than an hour and my GPS isn't working. I know I'm driving the wrong way.

It's hard to breathe in the thick summer heat. The air conditioner in my rental car doesn't seem to be working, even at full blast. I begin to panic as I slow the car down and look at my cell phone. I still have no service.

In a world full of so many connections and so much limited space, it's strange to find myself off the grid and surrounded by nothing but open country.

I glance at the time on the dashboard. I curse, knowing I'm going to miss my flight. I stop the car and put it in park, thinking there might be a map somewhere in the vehicle.

I'm searching and searching and suddenly can't breathe. Sweat isn't just popping up, but it's soaking my back and thighs and neck and forehead. As my hand reaches for the car door, my arm feels numb.

No, this can't be happening—not here, not like this!

Swallowing air doesn't help. Opening the door and climbing out doesn't either. For a moment, I lean against the rental car and stare up at the sky and wipe the thick sweat off my forehead. I'm dizzy and can't catch my breath. The sun appears to be wobbling and then bursting open.

I close my eyes and picture the winged scarab again—the beetle so familiar on those covers, especially the first and the biggest.

Am I going to be like that beetle now and burst up into heaven?

Is it my time to go?

I clutch my shirt and curl it up in my fist, looking upward.

"Please, God. Please don't let the enemy take me. Please, God, help me."

This is how it's all going to end. In the middle of nowhere. Everything's gonna go black, just like the ending of *The Sopranos.* Boom. It's done.

I'm empty and alone and silent. I continue to call out to God to help me.

All this time he's been there and I've been the silent one. All this time he's been knocking and waiting.

I've not only ignored him, but I've failed as a husband and a father. I've lost control of myself. The women I've been seeing on the side, the deception I've been living with for years.

I need help. I need forgiveness.

"I'm sorry for waiting so long. For not being there. God, I promise to be faithful to you. I promise to let you lead my life."

There is no voice and no light and no dove, yet eventually there is a calm. The pressure on my heart eases and I can almost breathe normally.

Once again, I've dodged the enemy's arrow.

Once again, I've escaped a date with death.

Once again, God is telling me he's not finished with me. That he still has a plan for the Catholic boy from Chicago.

TWENTY-SEVEN

"SHINE"

After we decided to sell the house in Novato and move to Nashville, I didn't want to move out until I was able to see my first harvest from the grapevines I had planted. That was part of the deal. I wanted to simply see the literal fruit of my labor come to life. So when the guy who bought the house moved in, he asked me what I wanted to do with the vineyard I'd planted.

"It's yours now," I told him. "You bought the house."

He didn't know what to do with it, nor did he have any interest in managing the vineyard, so he told me I could keep the fruit. God gave me back my firstfruits, even after I had already sold it. As long as I maintained the vines and tended to them, I could reap the annual rewards. I simply needed to keep pruning them.

God hadn't finished pruning me either.

"Dad, I'm drowning. Everything's turned black."

My son's voice on the other end of the phone sounded frantic and scared.

"What's going on?" I asked.

Three months earlier, Weston had been fine. The last few years had been rough for my son, but I believed his past troubles were exactly that—in the past.

"I can't take this life anymore," he said. "I just wanna die."

Weston was thinking about suicide. I calmed him down and knew I had to take immediate action.

A few years earlier, Weston had been busted at school for selling drugs. The only thing that saved him from going to jail was getting him into rehab. Weston had been battling demons for quite a while. I just didn't realize how they were overtaking him. Perhaps I couldn't see it because I was battling demons of my own. The same spirits haunting Weston were also haunting me.

My initial affair had turned into numerous ones. Failures I had once believed could never happen were now suffocating my soul.

I would learn a vital truth the hard way: the enemy loves to put evil in the things we love.

The first time Weston called me to tell me the DEA was coming to get him, I told him we were going to deal with this right away. We got him into Newport Academy, one of the few teen rehab centers in the country. I had been shocked to discover there weren't many youth centers out there. The moment we took him there and got involved with therapy, I knew the truth of my life.

I realized that healing my son was going to ultimately wreck my marriage. I knew things were about to be blown apart in my relationship with Liz once we got vulnerable in the counseling sessions. The charade I was playing would be over. The double life I had been leading with other women had to come to the surface. The lies that I lived like sores over my body only visible to myself would be uncovered. All those years of telling Liz I wasn't having any affairs would finally be seen as the deception they were. Watching my son bare his soul in therapy meant I needed to bare my own.

Weston was the one who ended up forcing the issue. While in rehab, he threatened me with a letter, telling me I needed to get him out of this place or he'd tell Mom the truth he had learned years earlier while on tour with me. Weston had found out about my marital indis-cretions during a European tour in 2009. He had fallen asleep in a hotel room in Norway. I had left my phone to charge in the room, and Weston woke up and discovered the text messages. I revealed to him that I had women on the road, yet we never went deeper. He returned home to Nashville with my secrets. We never spoke about it again, not until he threatened me with this information.

I still wonder if Weston's discovery in Norway was the beginning of his tailspin into drugs and alcohol. I began to realize he'd always had a fascination for substance abuse, and I gave him an excuse to use. I felt like the enabler.

Well, if Dad's doing all that, what's the harm of me doing this?

"You're going to bust me out of here, or I'm going to tell Mom everything," he wrote.

"This is your old man you're talking about," I told him when we talked. "No deal."

Right away during our next therapy session, I told Liz everything. It was as if I had just detonated a bomb. Suddenly I was the reason for all of this. I told Weston he was staying in rehab because he was an addict. I had my own addictions and sins I needed to address.

I had prayed after our children were born that they would teach me something, and this was what Weston taught me: Truth matters. Truth will find you. It certainly caught up to me as I tried to help save my son.

I wanted to be me again, the man I used to be. I needed to repent. I had turned into a lying pretender. Yet after dealing with my son and realizing my marriage was over, Weston still wasn't out of the woods. Not yet.

The scourge of heroin kept chasing him. Remnants still clung to him, ones that flared up and almost suffocated him. Now he came to admit he was an addict and couldn't go on. He needed to get away from Nashville, and he needed help. I was going to do everything I could to help him.

You need to do the same with your life, Jon.

I knew that. My son was soon on the road to recovery. God had gotten my attention on the side of a road in Florida, and he had forced me to admit my failures in counseling. Weston wasn't the only person completely broken in our family. He would just be the first one to admit it.

"We can fix things. We can keep going to therapy."

I sat across from Liz at the Hyatt near the airport in Newport Beach. She had called me, wanting to talk. After dealing with Weston's rehab and my confession of all my dirty laundry over the years, I knew things were over. Our relationship had been broken for years, but I was finally admitting everything.

"We can't fix this," I said. "I will always be that guy to you now. I've told you everything I've done."

Maya Angelou once said, "When people show you who they are, believe them." I knew Liz had seen the real man I was, and she needed to believe this. The truth was I didn't love her anymore, and nothing could ever rebuild that love and trust between us.

"I haven't behaved like a husband who wants to be in a relationship," I told her. "It's over. Nothing's going to restore this marriage."

The next week, I came to the Brentwood house with my keyboard tech to empty out my closet and load a few other things into a Ryder truck. I moved into the apartment above the Addiction Sound Studios. I used to joke about the apartment to people, telling them, "If Liz ever kicks me out, I'll have a place to crash." People would laugh, but now it wasn't a joke.

I needed help and therapy in my own life, and I needed them when it came to the kids too. I was done pretending with Liz. My children would have to accept their father, flaws and all.

My first divorce had been dreadful, but this was far worse, since it hurt our children. I knew our girls had been struggling through all of it. They had seen their brother fighting his drug addiction and their parents in the process of getting a divorce. I would have to battle to retain my relationship with each of them.

During a therapy session together, Liza was able to explain her anger and disappointment about my indiscretions. After I heard her, I apologized and told her I loved her and hoped she would forgive me in time. Thankfully, she let me know she still wanted a relationship with me, but she said it would take a while because of how devastated she was. This was the painful but necessary first step of healing my relationship with my youngest daughter.

For the older and heartbroken Madison, I knew there was one remedy: we needed to write music together.

"I have an idea for a song," I said to her, but she didn't want to have anything to do with me.

The hurt and resentment had built up inside her, and I knew it had the potential to drive a permanent wedge between us. She already felt rejected by Nashville, and now she had to witness her family imploding. Madison and Liza couldn't believe the things I had done and how I had lived a double life.

"How could you do this, Daddy?" Madison asked me during counseling.

"I know you're mad at me, but I have an idea," I told her. "I want you to meet me at the studio."

Madison was crying, and it was clear she didn't want to be anywhere near me.

"I want to write a song about your brother," I said. "It's called 'Shine.'"

So after our sessions with a therapist, Madison would show up at the studio with red eyes and mascara running down her cheeks.

"Are you ready?" I asked, and sure enough, Madison bravely stuck it out. Sometimes she would break down during our sessions.

"I'm a mess," she said.

"Don't say anything," I said. "Just sing the song."

This was our therapy, just as it had been for me my whole life. Yet again, here was God, giving me grace. In the middle of all the turmoil and drama, the music took over and took main stage. We focused on the song together, and through its creation, she found a path to forgiveness. Through the songwriting, Madison knew I loved her. Music was part of our healing.

The song was a snapshot of what was happening, and it was written as much for Madison as it was for Weston. She sang the words so powerfully, with a voice full of possibility.

> *She's tryin' to make a name for herself,*
> *Pushing past the lines of all that she had left.*
> *Dig deeper, dig deeper, dig down in your*
>   *heart for that next step.*
> *That's what the voice inside her said.*
> *You'll never know what you have left*
> *Till you have nothing left to lose.*

This was the journey Madison was on and the obstacles she was facing. The chorus was for Weston, Liza, Madison, and also me.

> *Don't fear the darkness.*
> *You're a ray of light.*
> *Believe your dream, don't let it die.*
> *Tomorrow will come, whether or not you try.*
> *So shine.*

I had to keep reminding Madison to shine. For herself and for her younger brother and sister. She couldn't give up on her dreams.

"It's going to happen," I said to my beloved daughter.

I knew that sometimes, when the pruning comes, God strips everything away. He takes away the unnecessary and undesirable parts so they can be replaced by something vital and victorious. The pruning hurts, and I knew, because I was going through it too.

I didn't have a marriage anymore, but I would always have these children. All I wanted was for them to be a part of my life, for them to love their father, for them to not stop believing in me.

Through all this, I could hear God's quiet voice in the distance.

Are you ready to listen to me now, Jonathan?

Just as God speaks to me and wants what's best in my life, I want that for Maddy. Whenever she'd get in one of those doubting modes, I had to tell her, "No, don't go there," and then remind her she had too much talent to stay stuck in doubt.

"Your grandfather and father are believers," I said, channeling to Madison my father's own encouragement. "When it seems like it's your darkest hour, it's God lovingly holding you back until you're ready. When your season and timing is right, God will open a door for you. And I have authority as your father to say that."

The healing had just begun for Madison, Weston, and Liza. I wanted them to know one very important thing: I would always be their father, waiting on them in their own time and loving them all the while.

TWENTY-EIGHT

"ASHES TO BEAUTY"

As I sat in the writing room in the upstairs apartment at Addiction Sound Studios, I glanced at the restored violin in the shadow box on the wall. I remembered hearing my grandfather play this fiddle for the first time. It had sparked so much magic and wonder inside me. The instrument looked beautiful and in much different shape than it had been when I rediscovered it in 2012.

While in Little Rock on tour with Journey, a second cousin on my father's side had given me the fiddle. His sister had it before then. The violin was in its original wooden case, with my great-grandfather's brother's name signed inside it. At the next stop of the tour in Tulsa, I brought it into a violin repair shop, which ironically was near Cain's Ballroom, a famous honky-tonk.

I marveled at how they mended this instrument and brought it back to life. The crack in the neck of the Giovan Paolo Maggini violin was repaired. A new bridge and set of strings were added, and a new chin rest was attached.

Seeing the violin was another reminder of my past, of where I had come from. I had been doing a lot of soul-searching after my divorce from Liz, and I had begun to write my own story, looking all the way back to my childhood. To discover Grandpa's fiddle seemed fitting. Something about being able to rebuild it felt important.

This instrument can still make music and play melodies, I thought staring at the violin. *There are still songs left for it to perform.*

Someone just had to restore it to its original beauty.

Ross Valory was the one who initially inspired me to write my memoir. We'd be on the bus between concerts, and I'd tell him stories about my youth. One day, he encouraged me to put it down on paper.

"You gotta write a book," Ross said.

I laughed. "*You* should write the book. You're the historian."

Ross kept after me, so with the thought tumbling around in my head, I decided to read *On Writing* by Stephen King. He said the same thing Ross told me, how everybody has a book in them. I thought, *Okay, if Stephen King says go ahead, why not?* So I embarked on the quest to do a new sort of writing. Studying my family history and my past was really fun for me. It helped me understand who I am.

During this period, my memoir was always in the back of my mind, and I would work on it whenever I could. It was what I was doing on a two-hour-forty-five-minute flight that changed my life forever and added another chapter to my book.

While on tour, Journey was going to travel to San Antonio for two gigs in Texas. Since I had booked a private room for a steak dinner with a vendor who sold my Finale wine, I convinced the rest of the band to brave a trip on Southwest instead of their first-class flight in order to have an amazing dinner on a night off.

After being recognized at the gate and causing a commotion, I took my seat on the plane and waited to see who would occupy the empty seat across from me. I couldn't help but notice the beautiful, well-dressed woman right away, especially with her red high heels. I figured she had to be a businesswoman of some kind, maybe in banking, or perhaps she was a lawyer. She carried a couple of bags, and I grinned as I watched her try to stuff a suitcase as big as her in the overhead bin. It was obvious she was accustomed to traveling.

After we were in the air, the woman took out her computer, notebook, and several books from her briefcase. One of the books dropped to the floor. It was a large paperback that featured a couple on the cover, embracing and holding outstretched hands, as if they were dancing. I did what I would have done for anybody—I picked up the book and handed it to her. I couldn't help but glance at the title.

Calling in "The One": 7 Weeks to Attract the Love of Your Life.

"I think you dropped this," I said.

She thanked me and gave me a warm and polite smile.

I was just dying to know what she did for a living—so I asked her.

"I'm a pastor," she said.

The likelihood of Pastor Paula White being on a Southwest flight was highly improbable, just like Journey. She had needed to get a flight to San Antonio for some time, and a seat just happened to open up on our plane that very day. Somehow, Paula had been in the C boarding section, which never happened since she flew so many times. God had a plan in putting her next to me.

I would be reminded again that God hadn't forgotten about me.

I struggled to believe what the woman told me.

"You're really a pastor?" I asked.

Paula told me later that she almost never tells people on a plane that she is a pastor, since it results in either two hours of counseling or two hours of debate. This time, however, she revealed her profession—her life's calling. She knew we must have been famous, but she didn't recognize any of our names. Like many, Paula simply knew our music. We didn't talk about that, however. Our conversation drifted to the subject of the memoir I was writing, the one fresh in my mind. As I told her about myself, I opened up about growing up in Chicago and about the fire.

She's a pastor, I thought. *I can talk to her about things like God and faith and the fire.*

So I did. I told her how deep I used to feel in my relationship with Jesus, and then how I had always wanted an answer to why the fire happened. Where had God been? I told Paula that I hadn't been to church much for many years, and how hungry I was for my faith to return.

Returning to my roots and writing about my journey had reminded me of times when God had been important and the moments he showed up again. My thoughts of God were compounded by the guilt I had been carrying around for the affair I had in Novato. Even though it had ended after I moved to Nashville, my cheating on Liz hadn't. There were little things I was still doing on the side, little escapades that eventually backfired on me. I felt unworthy as a man, a husband, a father, and, above all, as someone who knew that God loved him.

Paula listened with a true pastor's heart—with empathy and encouragement. She explained that God is forgiving, and as I truly repented, I would be worthy again in his eyes.

"Is it possible that I can go back to how I felt as a little boy? To know the Jesus I knew as a child?"

"The Lord has something for you," Paula said with a surprising certainty.

Before our conversation ended, Paula told me I would finish my memoir. She also said she sensed a weight I had been carrying for a long time, and that God was calling me to return. The faith I had as a child could come back. Paula didn't speak as one preaching from a pulpit. She opened up about her own trials and the brokenness in her own life, including how her father committed suicide when she was four, and how her own disintegrating marriage had wreaked havoc on the successful ministry that God had given her. Paula had told me she was a pastor—but I later discovered she led one of the largest churches in America.

I didn't know any of that, but I do know she had spoken to my spirit on this flight, encouraging me through my own tears and openness to not forget the very thing my father had told me. For Paula, all she wanted was for me to see the same Jesus she knew and had desperately clung to when everything else in her life had come crashing down.

"When everything in my life began to fall apart, and when the dark desperately tried to eclipse the light, I never stopped looking up and praying to Jesus," Paula said. "I never lost my love for the Lord. That childlike faith in God did not waver. It doesn't have to waver for you any longer, Jon."

After separating from Liz and moving into the studio apartment, I was playing in a golf tournament in Pebble Beach. I had emailed Paula to let her know about my pending divorce and Weston's rehab progress. I couldn't help but wonder what it would be like to be together in such a romantic setting with a woman I shared my life story with on the plane years ago. With a woman who shared her own life story freely and gave me hope about my faith being restored. We had kept in touch, but now I jokingly mentioned that I wanted to fly her out to join me.

To my surprise, she accepted my offer. We spent three days in deep conversation about healing, restoration, and commitment. There were walks along the ocean and kisses that lingered and smoldered like I hadn't felt since I was a teen. The chemistry between us was intimate and undeniable.

Paula spoke to the King in me. She accepted me with all my flaws and showed me unconditional affection. She was what I had been waiting for, and I was what she had been asking God for.

From the very start, I told myself I would never get married again. But watch out when you say never, because God surely has a sense of humor.

As I stepped into the cold water of the pool, about to be baptized by Archbishop Nicholas Duncan-Williams, I thought of how unlikely it was to be in the presence of this prayer warrior in London. He was not only the presiding archbishop and general overseer of the Action Chapel International ministry headquartered in Accra, Ghana, but he also was the spiritual father of the woman I was dating. Never did I imagine that asking Pastor Paula White out after my divorce would lead to this.

Paula had encouraged me when I first met her that I could return to the love of Jesus I had known as a child. After that, she blessed and encouraged Weston and me through his struggles. But ever since asking Paula out for the first time, I realized that dating a pastor was not an easy thing. With the smoke still rising from the charred wreckage of my previous marriage, I met resistance to my new relationship from all sides. My daughters were still angry about the divorce, so they didn't want to have anything to do with Paula. But maybe a rocker dating a pastor wouldn't play well with a congregation either.

Paula told me she wanted me to meet Archbishop Duncan-Williams, so when an opportunity came to meet this man who had been such an incredible influence in Paula's life and ministry, I was eager to go. I couldn't help but be anxious, wondering how he would receive a guy like me from the music industry. When we finally spoke, the archbishop could see right through me, revealing things he already knew about me before I told him, including details about the fire and my own personal failures. "You have a lot of work to do," he told me in a loving and reassuring way.

"Sir, with your help I want to become the man I need to become."

The work would have to begin with me as a father to my three children. I had assured them when I left their mother that I wanted to have a relationship with each of them. It would take a huge effort and a lot of battling and being patient with God and my children. I never gave up. All I could do was just love them.

Their acceptance of me would have to begin with my being able to accept myself and understand that God had forgiven my sins. I knew when I met the archbishop that his prayers were powerful. He said that prayer was the only way to override the enemy of this world. "You're dealing with the prince of the power of darkness," he told me. The devil may control this world, but only through prayer can we be given power to combat the ruler over the earthly realm. The archbishop gave me his prayer book and the prayers I needed to pray.

It took some time to process the things he shared with me in London. The archbishop could clearly see that Paula and I were in love. But he also could already see what I couldn't—the light of Jesus starting to shine through.

In the fall of 2014, I traveled to London and experienced a powerful army of people praying over Paula and me, like something out of a movie. I asked for and received the great blessing of being baptized in Archbishop Duncan-Williams's pool by the man himself, something he rarely did. As I came up out of the water, a crystal-clear realization came over me. I knew I needed to make potent changes in my life. I needed to be transparent to everybody, something I had never been, except through my songs.

God can restore my life. But I have to hand it over to him.

Even though I had told Paula that I didn't plan on ever getting married again, having already failed at two marriages, I knew what I needed to do.

The archbishop gave me the courage to believe God could do good things with me—new things—and that I could be a faithful and loving husband to this woman of God who had accepted his calling. There were lots of prayers that haven't stopped. When I first asked whether I was worthy to be Paula White's husband, I discovered none of us are worthy to be God's chosen. Yet he loves us like a father loves his children.

The song I had written when I first came to Nashville, the one that never made it onto the soundtrack but became a beautiful duet with Sarah Darling, was yet another prophetic tune for my future. The words felt like they had been written to Paula, yet I hadn't even met her yet. "You have given me back a reason to believe a dream can come true. All that I'd thought I'd lost, I found in you."

Archbishop Duncan-Williams married us in a small ceremony on Prayer Mountain outside Ghana's capital city of Accra at the end of

2014. We had another wedding ceremony in April 2015, so we could have a service in the United States with friends and family, with another service shortly after that for the congregation of New Destiny Christian Center—the church Paula pastored.

God knew I wasn't just acting the part of being a pastor's husband. He knew I was no longer leading a double life. I now needed to make sure our families and friends and the church knew I was serious about my faith.

My youngest daughter was the last to accept my surprising and unlikely marriage to Paula.

On the day of my twins' twenty-first birthday in 2016, I thought about the first time I had to go on the road with Journey. They were only about two years old when the newly formed Journey with front man Steve Augeri began our new tour. As I sat on the bus as it got ready to head down the road, I wept, knowing how much I would miss my children.

This is what happens, I told myself. *This is the price you have to pay.*

It was a price my children could never fully understand, and that was okay. They didn't have to understand it. I just never wanted them to forget how much I loved them and how hard it was to leave them. So on this particular birthday, I couldn't help but feel the ache inside, knowing how Liza felt about me and Paula.

Paula had helped Weston deal with his struggles with addiction, so he knew her and loved her. But my daughters weren't signing up for my new marriage. Instead, they fought me. I simply had to be patient—knowing and trusting in God's timing. After Madison showed up in Toronto and met Paula for the first time and heard her preach, she eventually apologized to me for her resistance.

"She makes you happy," Madison said. "I can see it. I was wrong."

Madison had witnessed Paula in amazing form on the pulpit,

bringing jars of clay to the front of the church and breaking them as a powerful object lesson for her message. The sermon absolutely wrecked Madison and stirred something in the hearts of both of us.

Liza, however, was my lone holdout.

"I'm not going to see her," Liza would tell me.

Eventually I pleaded with my youngest daughter. "Why are you acting like this? It's been two years."

She simply told me no over and over.

"I can't acknowledge this," Liza said." I don't respect anything about this marriage."

So while we were in New York City on the twins' birthday, I planned to meet them for dinner. Paula was with me shopping in Soho, but we both knew she would be somewhere else later that evening. That's why the text I got from Liza stunned me.

Dad, don't come alone tonight. Bring Paula to dinner.

I showed Paula the text with joy and astonishment. I wept like a baby for the next thirty minutes, with Paula at my side. There I was, once again, brought to tears because of my overwhelming love for my children.

All the prayers and all the months, turning to years. I never gave up. It had all been in God's timing. He put this together for us.

How amazing is God?

Right away, Paula had a great idea. "Let's go shopping for a birthday present."

She picked out a jacket for Liza. That night, when they met, Liza gave her a hug and said it was so nice to meet her.

All I could do was watch in amazement with a thankful, humble heart. I knew parents who had permanently lost their children from previous marriages due to divorce, but God had allowed me to keep my kids.

I had prayed over each one of my children after they were born, asking God to let them teach me something one day. Many years later, I could see the lessons come to fruition in my life.

It had been the very lesson God wanted me to learn from the day I was born.

I will never give up on you.

I wouldn't—I couldn't—give up on my children. I realized that God had been saying this to me time and time again—in the very same but perfect way.

I won't stop loving you, Jon. I won't stop believin' in you.

God had never stopped wanting me to come back to him.

His mercy is beyond anything we can fathom. And his love for his children is perfect and completely dependable.

All I can do is continue to thank God each and every day.

I shared my thanksgiving to God through my 2016 solo album, *What God Wants to Hear.* It was my love letter to God. My hope was that it would let people know they are worthy and that they have a shot at something special and great—not for their own journey in this life, but for God and for all of eternity. Writing and reflecting on my personal journey, I believe that God sometimes gives you exactly what you want to show you it's not at all what you need.

I understand now what Pastor Clay Schmit at Elim Lutheran Church in Petaluma told me about the OLA fire victims. Pastor Schmit baptized our children, and we had several meaningful conversations about the fire. At the time, I kept asking him how to make sense of losing all the kids and the nuns. He said the enemy sent the fire, but the Lord used their deaths to serve as a sacrifice, so a fire like that would never happen again. So God used the evil for good.

I understand now that Jesus cried with the rest of us on that fateful day in 1958. I don't believe he abandoned us during the fire, and I don't believe God leaves us during any tragedy. A recent song I wrote reflected this belief after a horrific shooting took place in our country.

> *Lord, help me make sense of senselessness.*
> *Take this sorrow that still burns within,*
> *Trapped in this fire of hopelessness.*
> *Remove your judgment.*
> *Let your mercy begin*

As I wrote the lyrics and put them into song, I discovered what my heart was trying to say.

> *Lord, take these ashes,*
> *Create something beautiful.*
> *We will rebuild a temple.*
> *Restore your love in our souls.*
> *Lord, take these ashes.*
> *A new place to start again.*
> *A crown of joy in these embers*
> *Where heaven cannot condemn.*
> *Take these ashes.*

"These Ashes" ultimately turns out to be the story of my life. Like my grandfather's fiddle, I was still there, but I needed someone to restore me. I was an eight-year-old kid who emerged from the ashes of Our Lady of the Angels School and tried to escape the tears and grief through songs and through reliance on myself. Ultimately, only Jesus can replace the despair in my heart—and it was the result of his promises and his grace.

Sometimes a great song waits for its chorus to show up near the end. And when it arrives, it's triumphant and it soars. My beautiful chorus came late into my song, but God is continuing to write its chords and lyrics every day.

If you haven't arrived yet at that chorus, it's never too late.

God is there. He's always there. Waiting patiently. Waiting with open arms.

We're all streetlight people. Searching in the night, learning from the street, and praying for the light.

"HOW'RE YOU GONNA MISS ME IF I NEVER GO AWAY?" STEVE PERRY SAYS with a big grin.

We're back together after a long break, writing songs for *Trial by Fire*, and I've been complaining about how long it's been. His light-hearted comment is one of those classic memories of Steve I'll always carry around with me.

It's 1995, and we find ourselves talking about songs. Journey songs, our own tunes we've written, and even the recent resurgence of The Beatles. A new TV special, *The Beatles Anthology*, recaptured the country's fascination with the band. We marvel at all those magnificent songs they wrote together and say how incredible it would be if that happened to us one day.

"Just like you always say, timeless music takes time," I say.

Steve smiles.

"Wouldn't it be cool to write a song for the ages?"

ACKNOWLEDGMENTS

When I first began writing this book, I realized how many memories I held before finding success in the music industry. Like any life, there are too many chapters and tales to tell in their entirety. This book is a reflection on my journey, a story I'm continuing to discover, and there are so many people who have played important and beautiful roles in it. Here are some of those I want to thank.

The life of a professional artist always has many "firsts" in it, those fortunate breaks and open doors that allow our journey to continue.

- Thanks to Rosana Klich, my first piano teacher, and Ralph Dodds, my theory teacher from Chicago Music College.
- To Buddy Killan, my first publisher and producer from Nashville, for giving a nineteen-year-old songwriter the chance of a lifetime in Nashville back in 1969.
- To Everett Slade, for guiding my brother and me with wisdom and love in the early years and for teaching us secrets of entertaining.
- To Dennis Nicklos, for believing in me from the start.
- To J. C. Phillips, my first LA producer; and Don Kelly, my manager who gave me my name.

- To Wolfman Jack for my first big break, and Robby Patton, the songwriter who convinced me to go to the audition for The Babys' keyboardist.

I want to especially thank my musical family. There have been great times and tough times, but through it all, there has been incredible music that we've made. Here are some of talented artists responsible for a soundtrack to new generations:

Special thanks to my Journey brothers—

- The one and only Herbie Herbert, the manager who invited me to the party
- Steve Perry, for the songs and for making them soar
- Neal Schon, for your fiery guitar, melodic themes, and relentless dedication
- Ross Valory, for being our anchor, holding down the bottom and always making us smile
- Steve Smith, for your zen approach to life and bringing your incredible syncopation and sensibility
- Steve Augeri, for taking the spotlight for eight years of fearless touring and recording
- Deen Castronovo, for the years of your "big grooves" and for sharing your faith and your heart for God
- Arnel Pineda, for your courageous commitment and being our voice when we had none; your heart and presence has made us a better band

And hearty thanks to so many others in my musical family—

- Jimmy Benso and Jimmy Arnold, two extremely talented guitarists who stuck it out in bands during the club days with my brother and me; you always made us better
- John Waite, The Babys' lead singer, and Keith Olsen, our producer and sound engineer

- Pat Morrow, Journey's road manager who showed me the ropes and made the phone call in 1980 that changed my life; Mike Stone, producer of *Escape* and *Frontiers*; and Doc Schaffer, our engineer for seventeen years
- Kevin Shirley, producer of *Trial by Fire*, *Revelation*, and *Eclipse*, and Ricky Phillips, for his rockin' bass playing and for being a friend and trusted bandmate with The Babys and Bad English.
- John Kalodner from Sony Records, who would bring us all together again to make the album *Trial by Fire* in 1995
- Everyone at Columbia/Sony Records, the radio DJs, the program directors, and the distributors who made sure our album made it on the shelves
- Danny Zelisko, for being a friend and believing that Journey could come back in 1998
- John Baruck and Irving Azoff, for your friendship and relentless leadership, battling every storm throughout the years
- David Kalmusky and Ethan Barrette from Addiction Sound Studios

All of the music we made couldn't have been created without our fans, so thank you to all of you who have never stopped believin' in Journey through the years.

Thanks to Kent Abraham, who graciously read and helped with early drafts of my coming-of-age memoir. And to Darrell Miller, my lawyer who landed my book deal. Thanks to John Sloan, David Morris, Tom Dean, and the rest of the fine folks at Zondervan for embracing me and my story. Thanks to Travis Thrasher, writer extraordinaire.

Thanks to Louise Krefting for making me a Cubs fan and loving me unconditionally. To Johnny Sigle, for being the true loyal friend from my childhood and for reminding me of the "historical" moments in life. To Alan Rosen, for your friendship and being the "guy who can get the gear." To Pastor Clay Schmit, for being a guiding light back to

Jesus. And to Paul and Annie Brody for your wisdom and love for me and my family.

Thanks to my brothers—to Tommy, who stood by me in steadfast loyalty and kept incredible time during the incredible early years, and to Hal, who held down the fort and who loved and looked after Mom and Dad when we left for the road, always sharing our vision throughout our musical journey.

Thanks to Liz for loving and being the mother you are to our three amazing children. To Madison, thanks for teaching me to be a father and sharing your soaring music and your faithful love. To Weston, thanks for always being a loving son and for allowing me to father you in battle and for showing me my truths. To Liza, thanks for your kindness, love, and patience and for believing in your father.

Thank you, Paula, for opening my eyes to the road that was paved for me and becoming the love of my life. I've come home to the place where I belong.

Thanks to Leonard and Nancy Friga, who never stopped believin.'

Most importantly, I want to thank my heavenly Father. Thank you for always standing by me and waiting, even when I didn't stand by you. I'm forever yours, faithfully.

"THE SONGS YOU LEAVE BEHIND"

JONATHAN CAIN

No one sees the countless hours you spend
Songs that disappoint you in the end
And few have felt rejection
You've endured

No one knows you've had your dreams undone
No one's faced the battles you have won
Where a melody is lost without the words

As you wait on the spotlight
You've come for the big night
Applause you're never sure that you deserve
Can't bear to see your star fading
Always got something new waiting
Failure's just a word you never learned

And when it's time to leave the dance
Be sure to know the signs
You'll be remembered
For the songs you leave behind
It's about the songs you leave behind

DON'T STOP BELIEVIN'

When the music is your mistress
The months, the weeks the days you've missed
Friends and love you lost out on the road

Every victory has a price to pay
Stealing moments of your life away
While you shine there's no other way to go

As you wait on the spotlight
You've come for the big night
Applause you're never sure that you deserve
Can't bear to see your star fading
Always got something new waiting
Failure's just a word you never learned

And when it's time to leave the dance
Be sure to know the signs
You'll be remembered
For the songs you leave behind
It's about the songs you leave behind

No one sees the countless hours you spend
Songs that disappoint you in the end
No one feels rejection
You've endured

No one knows you've had your dreams undone
No one's faced the battles you have won
Where a melody is lost without the words

As you wait on the spotlight
You've come for the big night
Applause you're never sure that you deserve

"THE SONGS YOU LEAVE BEHIND"

Can't bear to see your star fading
Always got something new waiting
Failure's just a word you never learned

And when it's time to leave the dance
Be sure to know the signs
You'll be remembered
For the songs you leave behind
It's about the songs you leave behind

When the music is your mistress
The months, the weeks the days you've missed
Friends and love you lost out on the road

Every victory has a price to pay
Stealing moments of your life away
While you shine there's no other way to go

As you wait on the spotlight
You've come for the big night
Applause you're never sure that you deserve
Can't bear to see your star fading
Keep them all anticipating
Failure's just a word you never learned

And when it's time to leave the dance
Be sure to know the signs
You'll be remembered
For the songs you leave behind
It's about the songs you leave behind